# SARTRE

## THE ORIGINS OF A STYLE

*Fredric Jameson*

COLUMBIA UNIVERSITY PRESS
New York   Guildford Surrey
1984

Columbia University Press   New York
Columbia University Press Morningside Edition    1984

**Library of Congress Cataloging in Publication Data**

Jameson, Fredric.
    Sartre : the origins of a style.

    Reprint. Originally published: New Haven : Yale
University Press. 1961.
    Bibliography: p.
    Includes index.
    1. Sartre, Jean Paul, 1905–      —Style.   I. Title.
PQ2637.A82Z75    1984      848'.91409      84-7624
ISBN 0-231-05890-X (alk. paper)
ISBN 0-231-05891-8 (pbk. : alk. paper)

# Contents

FOREWORD                                                    vii

PART ONE: THE EVENT                                           1

CHAPTER ONE: The Problem of Acts                             3
CHAPTER TWO: The Nature of Events                           19
CHAPTER THREE: The Rhythm of Time                          40


PART TWO: THINGS                                            65

CHAPTER FOUR: The Satisfactions of Objects                 73
CHAPTER FIVE: Transformations                              89


PART THREE: HUMAN REALITY                                 111

CHAPTER SIX: The Anatomy of Thoughts                      118
    1. The Taste of a Situation                           125
    2. Finding a Place for Meanings                       138
    3. Inside the Mind                                    142
    4. Problem-Words                                      147
CHAPTER SEVEN: The Anatomy of Persons                     157

CONCLUSIONS                                                181

AFTERWORD                                                  205

NOTES                                                      235

INDEX                                                      257

## Foreword

It has always seemed to me that a modern style is somehow in itself intelligible, above and beyond the limited meaning of the book written in it, and beyond even those precise meanings which the individual sentences that make it up are designed to convey. Such supplementary attention to style is itself a modern phenomenon: it has nothing to do with the purely rhetorical standards of elegance and epithet-weighing which dominated periods where all writers basically owed allegiance to a single type of style, setting their variants of it down to "temperament." In our time, when there are no longer any self-justifying forms or any commonly recognized literary language, the very importance of a writer's work comes to be dependent on what is new in it and on the sudden appearance or absence of a style radically different from anything at that point in existence. This increased significance of style, of the continuous manner in which the whole is elaborated, sets it slowly in contradiction with the older forms, until new ones are devised to permit us not merely to notice the style but to direct upon it the principle attention of our reading. And at other moments the two, the inherited form and the style that fills it in spite of itself with more modern content, coexist in a work that thus reflects not so much a weakness of the writer's talent but a new and problematic moment in his situation, a moment of crisis in the history of the development of writing itself.

Such a notion of style is closely related to the idea of mannerisms, of the "typical": we begin to be aware of its presence only after the passage of many quite different sentences which nonetheless somehow remain the same. At this stage the stylistic knowledge we possess is simply the means to a practical end, the instrument of a *recognition:* the characteristic harmonies that permit us to identify a composer, the timing with which a sudden bit of elevated language succeeds deliberately colloquial rhythms after the unmistakable habits of such an author, the favorite, obsessive word that marks a certain hand at work. The various mannerisms characteristic of a single writer are all vaguely present to our minds without being related to each other and without our needing to see more than one of them to realize whose product we are faced with, and after the recognition has taken place this knowledge lapses back into an unformulated, more or less "intuitive" state. Yet the game of recognition leaves its traces behind it: it exercises that specialized function of our minds which is directly responsible for such practical activities as the authentication of paintings, for example. And it also strengthens us in our impression that style is in some way a coherent entity in itself, and that the list of the artist's characteristic mannerisms is not simply an accidental set of empirically noted data, but that these in some obscure manner are related to each other at least as organically as the gesture I use in putting out a cigarette is related to the tone of my voice and the way I walk. And yet the organic ensemble that they ought to form is nowhere, since it is not the same as the individual works and not the same as the individual sentences, both of which are only partial and fragmentary manifestations of it.

Words like "relationship" inevitably tend to impose a kind of spatial thinking on us: the different manner-

isms, syntactical, thematic, verbal, begin to "reflect" each
other, and their irregular presence upon the surface of
the work as symptoms imperiously suggests a center
somewhere, behind the limits of our vision, from which
the various details, of unequal importance, are all equally
distant. Spatial thinking of this kind is attractive because
it holds out the promise of possessing the work, as only
a thing can be possessed; it dispels the malaise that we
feel from time to time in the process of reading, as in our
other activities, where the work passes temporally before
our eyes, never wholly present, rapidly lost from sight or
yet to come. Yet just as the reading of a novel is simply
a very highly developed type of relationship between two
people, so this center that it seems to us we ought to be
able to locate and eventually fix turns out to be nothing
more than a human being. The book, looked back at
from this new point, turns out to be simply an act among
many other different kinds of acts in the development of
a human life, and the purely literary style begins to lose
its privileged status and be confounded with the style of
a life, gestures among other gestures, and in this new
framework yielding the same kind of meaning as the
other more daily gestures.

This study is therefore arranged not according to the
suggestions of spatial patterns but in time. In it the pre-
tense is entertained that the various elements upon
which its attention is directed in some way grow out of
each other, imply each other in a kind of logical progression, and that a single element, if questioned in the right
way, will prove to be the basis of another element of a
wholly different appearance, which in its turn gives way
to a phenomenon unlike either, but profoundly related
to both. Such time of course does not exist: it is not the
time of our reading, where these details emerge fitfully
and without apparent dependence on each other; it is

certainly not the time of the author's elaboration of his works; it is simply the temporal appearance which relationships between phenomena take on when they are exposed in language.

Such an arrangement may seem arbitrary in its unpredictable progression, where nothing seems to dictate the introduction of a given phenomenon before it appears; but once the new thing is present, it is bound to give its qualifications for being there, and the progression is itself as it goes along one continual process of self-justification. What is far more arbitrary is the choice of these particular phenomena and not others, the choice of just this many "typical" elements and not many more. Yet this is accidental only from the perspective of a kind of set of changeless categories of style and of an idea of a complete analysis which would exhaust the work by going down the list. But the work generates its own categories, stamps things as important or unimportant according to its own obsessions and reasons for being; and the reality of the work, the concrete experience in relation to which all other approaches to it are merely abstract and on which they depend, is our reading of it itself. Our unwatched reading mind, with its spontaneous attentions and lapses, takes precedence over any categories we might be tempted to impose on it, and provides, in what it notices and what excites it, the material out of which intrinsic categories evolve. When therefore in this study we begin to see some of the peculiarities of the work in terms of a rather symmetrical opposition between things and consciousness, it will be not because all works ought in some way to have something to do with things and something to do with consciousness but because this particular work turns out to depend constantly and insistently on such an opposition.

We could not however begin with such an opposition:

the unjustified starting point, no matter how profoundly relevant, would mark the examination immediately as
wilful and arbitrary. A beginning must be found which
is not yet the presentation of an intelligible phenomenon,
but which is rather simply a special kind of awakened attention on our part. We have called this an attention to
the Event, where the word does not suggest any particular
type of thing happening but merely directs our attention
toward those moments when something essential *is* happening, whether in an old-fashioned kind of scene climax, or the description of a face, a suddenly electric
gesture of a different quality from the gestures with
which the scene is filled, or the nervousness with which
certain sentences differentiate themselves from the more
indifferent prose in which they take place. Such moments, whatever they turn out to be, are simply those
in which the writer is telling or showing those things
which he thinks it most important or exciting to tell,
which rouse him to the making of a new language; and
they therefore lead us directly to the world which his
whole work is an effort to present in time.

Yet although a single event may dominate a writer's
entire production, if he disposes of several different kinds
of narration, it necessarily varies in appearance from
form to form. The play, for example, is not a wholly literary form; the materials of a novel are sentences, those
of a play human beings who express themselves both in
sentences and in gestures. The events of a play are therefore more likely to be restricted to human acts, and it
is within this more restricted category that the writer's
fascinations will continue to operate, sometimes distorting the form to make a place for themselves, sometimes
satisfying themselves more obscurely within conventional
limitations, calling attention to themselves only by some
heightened interest in this act for which the rest was

nothing but a pretext. It is with such acts, not yet wholly verbal events, distinguished neither by the individual content nor the emphasis of the form but rather by something in the very shape of them, that we now begin.

This study, which in its first form was a Ph.D. thesis written at Yale University, would not have been possible without the encouragement and advice at all of its stages of Professor Henri Peyre. It is also important to point out, in a country where for want of translation their books are little known, that the thinking of this book owes a heavy debt to the works of Theodor W. Adorno and of Roland Barthes. For assistance in publication of the book, grateful acknowledgment is extended to Yale University's Fund for Young Scholars.

F. J.

*Cambridge, Massachusetts*
*February 1961*

PART ONE

*The Event*

CHAPTER ONE:

## *The Problem of Acts*

*No Exit* is without what is ordinarily called action: the
characters are no longer able to do anything, they have
done it all before the curtain rises, and they are obliged
to spend the time of the play simply thinking about
what has already been done once and for all, without
being able to add to it. This is why, in a kind of gross
common sense distinction based on an entertainment
aesthetic, such plays have been described as "idea-plays."
Yet the "ideas" of this philosopher's play are wholly
different in quality from the thoughts developed in the
philosophical works. There also acts are analyzed, are
raised to a meaning; but this phenomenological analysis
is expansive, centrifugal: it attempts to enlarge itself
with more and more detail until the act has been shown
to be the mere central complex of a large and intrinsically
intelligible unity, and its isolation to be illusory. The
characters of this play think about their pasts in the other
direction: they want to reduce the things they have
done to mere examples of qualities, to be able to fix
names and adjectives to them; the meanings they are
looking for have a solid and indispensable core of language. The source of these meanings is popular everyday

value judgment: bravery, cowardice, goodness, evil, mutually exclusive alternates; so that a character like Garcin is imprisoned in his very thought about himself and his life. He faces a kind of schoolbook proposition about himself: that he is a coward; and the only choice he seems to have is to affirm it or deny it. The level on which such problems are posed is in appearance much more primitive than the kinds of consciousness registered by earlier modern writers; and the only possible expression of such a dilemma seems to be talk, the posing of the various alternatives or the settling for one or the other of them.

The image around which the play is organized, the notion of a hell or limbo of this kind, suggests another possible relationship to the past at the same time that it eliminates it as a real issue: Garcin is painfully aware that if he had lived, he would have been able to do something different, he would have had at least the possibility of setting an act of a new quality against the repetitive examples of his past weakness. This act would in no sense have changed the facts of his life, would not even have permitted us to "forget" about them. It would have merely rearranged them, organized them in a new way, and the weight of the new act would have gradually swung these older facts out of the pattern of simple cowardice and lent them the value of mere passing errors, accidents, corrected failings. This suggests that the past can be described in two different ways: it is that which can no longer be changed, which has passed out of reach, still felt as ourselves but fixed forever; and yet at the same time it is constantly subject to change and renewal at our hands: its meaning is as fluid as our freedom and every new thing we do threatens to revalue it from top to bottom. The aspect of the past which is changeless is what Sartre calls our "facticity," but it is only one way in which facticity manifests itself, along with the genetic structure of our bodies and the necessity for us to exist at a given moment of history in a given society, although there is no reason why it should be this one rather than that, any more than there is any reason why our unique consciousness should "inhabit" a body of this particular shape and be born of these particular parents. Facticity is that core of being which resists any reduction to thought, to reasons; it is the necessity for every phenomenon, no matter how intelligible it may be, to be at the same time absolutely unique; it is the necessity for us to be always "in situation," without its making any difference what that situation may be, for us to always have a past no matter what its contents are. Garcin recognizes his past as *his* through the anxiety it causes him, but it is not his to alter any more than he can rearrange the bones of his face by thinking about it. We will come to see later just how heavy with consequences such an idea is for the work of art.

Yet although the meaning of these brute irrevocable facts might be somehow altered by a new act, although no failure is enough to definitively rule out the possibility of change but merely pushes it further into the future, there is no future in terms of the situation of the play and Garcin is dead. He is thus reduced to a purely contemplative attitude toward his own life, he is passive before it, he can only think about it; and in some ways the secret theme of the play is a kind of symbolic playing out of the opposition between a philosophy of knowledge and a philosophy of consciousness or action, between an impressionistic and an expressionistic aesthetic. Garcin is left with nothing but "psychological analyses" of himself: he cannot act, he cannot change the facts, the only area of uncertainty accessible to him, where he might find something to help him resolve his problems one way or the other, is that of his "motives":

> ESTELLE: But you ought to remember; you must
> have had reasons for doing what you did.
> GARCIN: Yes.
> ESTELLE: Well?
> GARCIN: Are they the real reasons?
> ESTELLE: *(annoyed)* How complicated you are.
> GARCIN: I wanted to set an example . . . I had given
> it a lot of thought . . . Are those the real reasons?[1]

This importance of the motive is part of a dialectic of
good and bad intentions that goes back at least as far as
medieval Christian thought; but in it the act is so thoroughly separated from its motive (which can be of another quality) that there is no way back from the motive
to the act: the "reason," or all the different possible
ones, come loose from the act, fall into subjectivity while
the act remains resisting and impenetrable. Any of the
motives seems to fit because there is nothing in the act
itself that can stand in a privileged relationship to this
one rather than that. The world of motivations becomes
autonomous, a kind of self-sufficient mirage reflecting
the solid world of facts upside down, and in this unreal
psychological world, against the perspective of a past out
of the reach of change, subjective decisions suddenly
seem to enjoy far more authority than they did in "real
life":

> GARCIN: Estelle, am I a coward?
> ESTELLE: How would I know, my love, I'm not
> in your skin. You have to decide for yourself.
> GARCIN: *(with a gesture of weariness)* That's just
> what I don't manage to do.[2]

This suggestion of the possibility of a fiat, of a purely
intellectual decision settling the problem once and for
all, is an optical illusion brought on by the terms in

which the problem has been posed. Not only is change impossible in the purely contemplative conditions of this limbo, but the very judgments themselves: bravery, cowardice, will not work from the inside. They are in their vary nature the judgments of other people, fixed to the outside of the individual consciousness with the verb to be. They suggest a convenient reduction of consciousness to a set of qualities or attributes, conveniences for the purpose of predicting behavior, parts of the describable nature of these things which are other people for us. But such "qualities" are impossible to feel from the inside because consciousness never "is" anything, but is always action. Only when we gaze back at the feared similarity of all the things we have done with each other does the impression of a kind of "quality" arise; but we do not feel it directly, we deduce its presence just as if we were looking at the acts of someone else. Yet the alienation of these characters is so complete that the judgments have been passionately interiorized, raised to absolutes before which in vain they try to justify themselves. Their lives after death are the most intense image of lives surrendered wholly into other people's hands—the hands of the living; and no single corner of their minds is safe from these autonomous categories of "objective" social values. It is at this point that the possibility of abandoning such worn-out categories suggests itself, that the possibility of a kind of "authenticity" arises; and it is at this point also that most of Sartre's works stop— with the emergence of freedom at the end of *The Flies,* of the social solidarity of *Lucifer and the Lord,* with the promise of a theory of values at the end of *Being and Not-Being.* For here the problem of individual life can no longer be isolated from the society in which it is to be lived, and is suddenly subordinate to history and the problem of social change.

The play consists therefore of a language in a void, of sentences that can never cross the distance that separates them from the acts they attempt to describe, of thinking turning around and around in a sealed past without the oxygen of a real present or future. It certainly has a didactic purpose but in another sense it reflects the condition of a society without a visible future, a society dazzled by the massive permanence of its own institutions in which no change seems possible and the idea of progress is dead. But this distance between people and their own acts is not merely a function of the specialized situation of *No Exit,* where the intolerable conversation never manages to dent the solidity of the finished lives. It is visible also in those moments when, at the other end of time, characters who have not yet acted are about to do so: in a play like *Dirty Hands,* where a drama which is in a sense that of all action is concealed behind a grosser, more melodramatic category that bears the same name (just as the notion of freedom is simplified, "vulgarized," when it makes its appearance in the novels as a special kind of condition rather than as the essence of all human reality). In this play the desire of Hugo to *act* is to be understood not only against the background of his past, that middle-class existence to which he wants to oppose an existence of a wholly different quality, but also in terms of that malaise of continental intellectuals with their own specialized work which prevents it from ever seeming real work, real action; so that in the midst of the clandestine journalism which is just as much an act or an engagement in its own terms, Hugo has the nostalgia of what seems to him to be its opposite: terror, violence, an activity close to death and to which death seems to lend a kind of gravity.

Yet what is essential in this new kind of action that Hugo wishes for himself is not so much its violence but the quality of its time, not a cumulative everyday action which is lived as a routine and which little by little conceals from the actor the fact that he is engaged in a project, but a single moment, something to be reached across a waiting, through a period of preparation and fear, something that happens all at once, something which can be *anticipated,* as in this moment where Hugo sees another terrorist succeed:

> OLGA: He did it. . . .
>
> HUGO: He did it. Before the week is up, the two of you will be here, on a night just like this, and you'll be waiting to hear something; and you'll worry and you'll talk about me, and for once I'll amount to something in your eyes. And you'll ask each other: what's he *doing?* And then there'll be a phone call, or a knock at the door, and you'll be smiling the way you are right now, and you'll say: "He did it."[3]

The future act, the totally new, already exists in an ill-formed manner in the present: parts of it are being slowly born in Hugo's mind, the easiest parts and those most familiar to him. The room he is standing in, the people he is looking at and listening to, are ready-made material which can be turned into future by making only the slightest of changes. But these words through which the act comes to its first still fragmentary existence are more than a momentary awakening of the imagination inside Hugo's head: they are a way of preparing himself, of making himself believe in something of which there are as yet no traces, no hints, in the real world. They help him weigh the unforeseeable future down with a kind of seriousness, so that it does not float with the lightness of a dream but is stiffened with the expectations of others.

This is very different from a purely "intellectual"

awareness that something is going to happen. It is a kind
of belief, a sudden intuition of the impending act which
is so vivid, that absent as it is, the characters are already
able to see its effect on things. This is what happens when
Hugo's wife suddenly *knows* that Hoederer will be
killed. Her drama is a repetition of Hugo's on another
level: the same feeling of counting for nothing in the
midst of a serious, solid world, the survival of a child's
relationship to grown-ups and their things and activities,
the frigidity in terms of which the sexual act becomes a
kind of crude symbol of human action in general. All
of this prevents her from taking Hugo's act any more
seriously than he does himself; so that the moment of
belief, when it happens, has to change the whole world
to make a place for itself:

> JESSICA: You're going to kill a man.
> HUGO: Do I even know myself what I'm going to do?
> JESSICA: Let me see the gun.
> HUGO: What for?
> JESSICA: I want to see how it looks.
> HUGO: You carried it around with you all afternoon.
> JESSICA: Then it was nothing but a toy.
> HUGO: *(handing it to her)* Be careful.
> JESSICA: Yes. *(Examining it)* It's funny.
> HUGO: What is?
> JESSICA: I'm afraid of it now. Take it back. *(Pause)*
> You're going to kill a man.[4]

Nothing is changed: the gun is exactly what it was, her
husband remains a predictable being, with familiar mannerisms, a familiar face, nothing in the room and its
silence has been tampered with; only suddenly a mysterious depth has opened up in all of these things; clear
and easily covered with a glance, each of them suddenly
possesses a "beyond" that escapes her, gives onto a real

change in everything. The cold dead object, the easily handled revolver, has turned without warning into an instrument that will be used, and handling it suddenly becomes a tempting of fate. In a sense this transformation of things into what they will be has been caused: the bomb unsettled the world that Jessica had been playing in, made her see it in a new way before she knew what she was doing. From a purely intellectual point of view it showed her how dead serious the plot on Hoederer's life is:

> It's not my fault. I only believe what I can see. Just this morning I wouldn't have been able to imagine him dying. *(Pause)* I went into the office a little while ago, there was that man bleeding and you were all corpses. Hoederer was a corpse; I saw it on his face! If you don't kill him, they'll send somebody else.[5]

Yet the essential part of this new belief is not a new piece of information that makes her revise her estimate of the situation; it is the concrete, material fact of seeing the future in front of her. Her own imagination is too weak to have any effect on the outside; she lives it as pure fantasy, as that which in the very nature of things will not take place. But here the world itself horribly begins to do the work of her imagining for her. All she has to do is look, the future is inscribed in the things themselves, in these pale astonished faces which are already frozen into waxy masks.

We can understand the need for this complicity on the part of the world itself through the objective relationship of these people to the world they live in. Unproductive, they have never acted on things or changed them, they have grown up surrounded by objects that seemed as unhistorical as trees, immutable parts of a city landscape divorced from human activity and therefore impregnable to it; nothing in their own experience gives them any confidence in the power of their own subjectivity to leave any traces on this massive wall of things: only the things themselves can announce their impending dissolution. Yet this dizziness of the subjectivity before a silent unresponsive world outside of it is in another sense a moment of all action: Goetz feels it, in *Lucifer and the Lord*, as he gazes at the city he is about to destroy and is astounded that he will be able to have any effect at all on the self-sufficient cluster of roofs and routines and traditions that he can see with his own eyes before him and beside the visual evidence of which the future he plans seems to lack all substance, as weak as a mere wish. For consciousness *is* nothing in comparison to the ponderous being of things, and even in the moment in which it turns on them to leave its presence inscribed in their resisting surfaces, it senses its own lack of being and the presumptuousness of the assault it is about to make.

These moments, in which the future act seems to draw near and to pull the present out of shape under the force of its approach, remain "subjective": the world changes in them, without really changing at all. In contrast to the act itself, the gunshot sound, the floor with a body suddenly lying on it, they have to be told and not seen—and even the scenery that the characters see change has to be described because its changes are not visible for us. Only in the moment of the act itself can something be said to happen really: this moment without past or future, a place of silence and of total freedom, in which Hoederer turns his back and Hugo is left alone with a single wholly new gesture to perform, a trigger to squeeze in a vast transparent lucidity with nothing to help him do it and no way to make it happen painlessly and gradually, bit by bit—this is a kind of symbolic representation of the purest execution of an act, that which permits the freedom of the actor to express itself the most painfully and accessibly to him and to those who contemplate his drama. We know that Hugo misses his chance, and that he finally shoots under other circumstances, in a moment so jammed with emotions and suddenness that he is able to do it almost without knowing what he is doing, or why. But in any case the instant of the act, once it is over, rushes wordlessly into the past, separates itself automatically from the subjectivity that accomplished it, and the world of things, altered, closes up again in front of the consciousness that a moment before had come into decisive contact with it.

It is at this point that we rejoin the drama of Garcin, that struggle against something which has already happened, except that Hugo is in the privileged position of being still alive. In his prison he relives the introspective situation of *No Exit*, the perpetual and circular analysis of his motives, and this experience is long enough to make him realize that the only way for him to possess the fact of the now distant past is to add to it a new act that will give it new value. This possibility, which as we have seen Garcin himself was obsessed with even after it was too late, is what Sartre calls the "assumption" of a past, of a facticity. And once more the intrigue of the play provides a kind of imperfect and striking symbol, in the mode of the unique gesture, of something which the philosophical works show to be part of the permanent structure of all human experience. For we can have no direct experience of our own facticity. In a kind of rough parallel to the earlier philosophy of knowledge in which the things-in-themselves are always out of reach, and necessarily apprehended through the organs of perception that transform them immediately into things-for-us, we necessarily humanize, we *assume* everything we come into contact with, and the basic facticity of the things around us and of our own bodies and lives is felt only as a limit, the most stubbornly inhuman becomes human through the fact of our awareness of it. Thus the steepness of the hill we are climbing is an objective fact, but an abstract one; and each of us lives it in a different way and decides when to stop because it is "too hard." So also our facial structures and our bodies are inherited, but they are not simple static facts that we have to cope with, but are constantly assumed and mediated through expression (and repose is of course a human expression like any other): it is the body in movement which is the concrete phenomenon, and except insofar as they are the result of a historical process, its measurements are abstract. This is why it is impossible to give content to the idea of facticity: any approach to it is already an assumption, all "facts" are human, and in attempting to experience facticity directly we immediately draw it into the human world, and the brute, meaningless core of being which the word stands for retreats further out of our grasp. This is why also the past always is assumed: we are not free to have no attitude toward it. It cannot be changed; but we always lend the changeless facts a meaning in terms of the lives we lead and even the forgetting of them, as Freud showed, is a relationship to them.

But in the play, this *perpetual* necessity of ours to assume our facticity takes the form of a single, an exemplary choice. The brute fact is the death of Hoederer, with its any number of motives: jealousy, political expediency, etc. But when Hugo is asked to forget his old name, and the past that went with it, to enter into a relationship with this act of his which will be no more privileged than a stranger's connection with someone else's life, to work for the party again as if it were the "first time," the intrigue of the play suddenly brings an opposite of assumption into existence, and the oblivion which in philosophical terms was merely one mode of assumption among others becomes, in the distorting mirror of the thought-world of the play, a possibility of total renunciation of the past. This renunciation is at first only tentative: "If I renounced my act, he would become an anonymous corpse, just another one of the party's waste products. Killed by accident. Killed for a woman."[6] The language is still more or less innocuous; the colorless verb "become" hardly imposes any materialization on the abstract sentence that describes a possible meaning of the death of Hoederer; and the renunciation remains here a kind of assumption. But this vocabulary tends to develop on its own, once set in motion; and as the possibility of a real renunciation of the act emerges, the assumption of it is transformed into a striking, solitary gesture far different in quality from what assumption was when it named the process of humanization which is our daily life.

What is involved is apparently only a way of talking about things; yet the gesture that will turn the silent fact of Hoederer's death into a meaning will be itself another wordless event: the death of Hugo himself, the closing of the door on his own assassination as the curtain closes. And its very absence from the play indicates that it has to take place somehow first for us in words, just as the first murder began to emerge verbally long before it really happened.

The inadequacy of mere action, of a self-supporting intrigue the dialogue of which has no autonomy, which constitutes mere gestures among gestures of another order, no more privileged than physical movements, can be sensed if we reflect on the "improbability" of the play's story. The atmosphere of the stage sets, of the play's conventions, of its everyday language, invites us to imagine ourselves witnessing something more or less naturalistic: the stylization is not blatant, it is out of sight and detected only at a certain angle, where we least expect it. Something in the play prevents us, while it is going on, from being aware of just how "philosophical," how uncommon and even unlikely is this spectacle of a man getting himself killed for an interpretation of history.

Undoubtedly Hugo's relationship to Hoederer permits us to think of this act in terms of personal devotion. But it is above all the presence of death that transforms the merely abstract quality of the act, that returns against the exemplary decision to confer a new reality on it. Since Hugo *has* given his life, it is the problem of "meaning," of historical value, that is suddenly changed, that suddenly becomes an idea crucial enough to die for. Only the extremest act of assumption is enough to make the assumption "credible" at all: the only realism possible in this situation is its most violent outer limit, and without the "extreme situation" everything dissolves into abstractions and mere discussed problems.

The presence of death is also that which permits the language to reach its most figurative limits without becoming decoration: "I haven't killed Hoederer yet, Olga. Not yet. I'm going to kill him right now, and myself along with him."[7] The possibility of a renunciation has become real at the same time: it is no longer a mere figure of speech to say that Hoederer has not yet been killed—the act, in the past, did not manage to take place completely, it still remains to be done, it can still go unfinished, drift into the past and simply vanish; and if it is the death of Hugo himself that gives him the right to this language, it is at the same time this language, this image of an act which has happened and yet not happened, that makes the death speak, that lets the new fact, taking place outside the dialogue, confirm the solidity of the dialogue that it finally seals.

What does subject matter like this imply for the work of art? The act is always at a distance from the person who commits it, to whom it "belongs"; it is not self-sufficient, has no ready-made meaning of its own, but has to be constantly assumed and reassumed. It never really happens objectively: it has to be anticipated beforehand; when it takes place it immediately alienates itself, and afterwards it has to be made to happen again for it to have happened at all.

This unsubstantial, alienated nature of human action is a category imposed on our attention by plays; and it is the stage itself that is partly responsible for the terms in which we have had to think the problem. For the theater is a kind of mixture of language on the one hand, and the merely seen, sets and gestures, on the other. Things can take place before our eyes, and then be discussed as well and enter a purely verbal mode of existence. It is thus possible for a play to have its area of facticity: the brute visual facts, the moments of pure happening; and its area of assumption: the speeches in which these events are taken up into the language. And once an aesthetic of the theater is established on the basis of this opposition, the events themselves begin to come loose from the play and slide out of it: dialogue establishes itself on the stage before us and the off-stage becomes the place in which things "really" happen. Or in another sense it is in the language that things are really taking place, and the events themselves, off-stage or on, become merely necessary and not sufficient. This seems a curious description of a theater so full of violence, so little "poetic" in the bad sense, as Sartre's; but it is precisely the

violence, the most exaggerated kind of facticity, that en-
sures the meaning of its opposite, and without it the
language would weaken and become gratuitous embroidery, a sterile poetry. So that along with the naturalism
and the melodrama, there is another perspective in which
all these violent events turn out to be illusion and only
the language really happens: the plays are strange examples of an inherited melodramatic form which has
been subverted into literature, into occasions for the
elaboration of a new language.

In prose however the opposition between dialogue and
stage action no longer exists: the gestures and the settings are themselves described, and dialogue is no longer
the only way to show the relationship of characters to the
things they have done. The subject matter is moreover
greatly expanded; the novel is not limited by the nature
of its medium to human beings and the things they do;
as in the movies things and landscapes can become active
participants in the drama, and the larger form, in which
everything is now language, transcends the category of
human acts and opens onto events in general. It is certain that if this structure of acts which we have examined
is the way in which Sartre's world has to express itself in
the play form, it corresponds to something in that world
that will find its way into the novels; but it is certain
also that within the new form it will appear in a wholly
different way.

# CHAPTER TWO

## The Nature of Events

With the breakdown of traditional life patterns, unquestioned ritual that lives developed along, and with the rise of boredom as a possible quality of life, the notion of an event, of an experience, of something really happening, becomes problematical: when not everything is real living, only certain things can be told and can constitute anecdotes or stories. The novel itself, in its beginnings, was just such a new category of the event, appearing at the moment of the breakdown of the feudal world; but in modern times even this form, which reflected through its historical and national variations some of the homogeneity of middle-class society, has itself become questionable—there are no universally recognizable patterns of life that are worth telling; the writer invents for himself out of the isolation of his own life those moments that awaken him to language.

There are more or less primitive ways in which these moments can make their presence felt against the smoother narrative time that prepares them. The physical stiffening and acute attention in the presence of sudden danger is translated here into a suspense, a feeling of something about to happen which is not itself a new detail added to the story line but rather an underlining of

all of it, an italics in which the sentences suddenly begin
to be written; and the indication of the fear, the explicit
remark that "something was about to happen," is not intrinsically interesting but designed to pull all of the
other sentences around it into a continuum, to make
them lose the autonomy that as individual sentences they
also possess and turn them into pieces of a sudden form.
The man immobilized and alert, staring with sharpened
attention at the suspect environment, is at a new distance
from it, is now reflective and separated from it, whereas
before the area around him was merely the place of an
activity that itself completely absorbed him. That kind
of drawing back from a situation which transfigures it
without changing it, that sudden jog in the solid passage
of things before the eye, implies other possibilities, implies for example that the man might not notice until
it was too late, that he might suddenly be awakened to
a finished event and find that the thing had *already* happened:

> Mathieu had approached the vase, with his hands
> behind his back, and nervously swaying back and
> forth had stared at it: it was terrifying to be nothing
> but a little pinch of white dough in the midst of this
> crusty old world, in front of an imperturbable vase
> three thousand years old. He had turned his back on
> it and had begun to make faces and snuffle in the
> mirror, without being able to take his mind off it,
> then all of a sudden he had returned to the table, he
> had lifted up the vase, which was quite heavy, and
> he had thrown it on the floor: he just felt like doing
> it, that's all, and right afterwards he felt as light as
> gossamer. He had looked at the broken pieces of
> porcelain, wonder-struck: something had just hap-
> pened to this three thousand year old vase, between

these walls two generations old, beneath the antique
light of the summer, something terribly irreverent
that resembled a morning.[1]

This passage announces itself as straightforward narration, the description of a stance and of the consciousness
that takes it, new gestures apparently performed in full
awareness by the child. But these new gestures, as they
get rapider and more and more precise, leave consciousness behind. The decision they reflect passes out of the
boy's mind and into the gestures themselves which happen in a vacuum: the body momentarily moves all by
itself with a decisiveness terrifying in contrast to the
slovenly conscious movements of the beginning. Only
afterwards is feeling released again: the weightlessness,
the astonishment at discovering something done; and this
astonishment is ours as well because the sound has been
turned off in this passage—the moment of the event is
absent, the vase never hits the floor, never shatters, and
in a strange kind of censorship or skip in time there is
no passage provided between two serenely existing
things: the vase being lifted and the mute wreckage on
the floor. This event is not witnessed, it has to be deduced
from the traces it has left in things: "something had just
taken place," and yet the something is at once larger and
more intangible than the mere breaking of a vase: it is a
kind of atmosphere located between the points of two
mutually exclusive qualities. The qualities are of course
easily translated into meanings: the irreverence is the
breaking of a taboo, the insult to age and tradition, and
the destruction of an object sacred to the elders, just as
the morning is the age of the boy himself in the maze of
the world of grown-ups. Yet the concrete sentence cannot
be reduced to this mere explanation. These qualities of
such different substance are deliberately juxtaposed and

fail to blend like complementary colors together: they
are separated by what they describe, the "something" that
had happened; their simultaneous presence works against
each other individually for the benefit of the larger entity in which they participate. We can only read the
sentence as the appearance of a kind of glimpsed personification, a Something fleetingly seized at from these two
alternate angles. It is this Something which is the face
of the event that has just happened, distinct from it in
one sense insofar as it is not itself in the present tense, reflecting it, and yet at the same time replacing it, since
the real event is not there at all, becoming itself the
event.

There seem therefore to be two series of realities implied by such a passage: the unsensed, unheard, unseen,
purely material changes going on in the world of things,
and their reflection—the registration of them or ignoring
of them—in consciousness or, what amounts to the same
thing, in language. This way of describing what we have
found however is prejudiced by too many images: reflection, series, the implied split between a world of things
on the one hand and a world of consciousness on the
other, for which the standard of knowledge is accuracy in
a received image of things-in-themselves. The following
long passage from *Nausea* uses wholly different instruments to show an equivalent reality at the same time as
it brings the problem of the event directly in contact with
the problem of narration itself:

> This is what I decided: in order to make an ad-
> venture out of the most banal event, what you have
> to do is *tell* it and that's all you have to do. That's
> what fools people: men are storytellers, they live
> surrounded by their own and other people's stories,
> they see everything that happens to them through

such stories; and they try to live their lives as if
they were telling them.

But you have to make up your mind: either to
live or to tell stories. For instance, in Hamburg,
when I was with this Erna whom I didn't trust and
who was afraid of me, I led a crazy life. But I was
inside of it, I didn't think about it. Then one night,
in a little café in San Pauli, she left me to go to the
bathroom. I was alone, a phonograph was playing
*Blue Sky.* I started running through in my mind all
the things that had happened since I got off the
boat. I said to myself: "The third night, as I was
going into a dance hall called the Blue Grotto, I
noticed a big woman, half-drunk. And I'm waiting
for that very woman right now, listening to *Blue
Sky,* and she's going to come back and sit down beside me and throw her arms around my neck." At
that moment, I had the feeling, violently, that I was
having an adventure. But Erna did come back, she
did sit down beside me and put her arms around my
neck and I hated her without really knowing why.
Now I understand: when she came back, I had to
begin living again and the feeling of adventure had
just vanished.

When you live, nothing happens. The scenery
changes, people go in and out, that's all. There are
never any beginnings. The days pile up without
rhyme or reason, an interminable monotonous accumulation. From time to time you add up part of
it: you say: I've been travelling for three years, I've
been in Bouville for three years. There aren't any
endings either: you never leave a woman or a friend
or a city all at once. And besides, everything looks
like everything else: after a couple weeks Shang-
hai, Moscow, Algiers, all look exactly alike. Once in

a while you take your bearings, you realize that you're stuck with a woman, or that you're mixed up in something shady. Just a flash. Then it begins again, the endless procession, you begin to add up hours and days. Monday, Tuesday, Wednesday. April, May, June. 1924, 1925, 1926.

That's what living is like. But when you tell it, everything is different; only nobody notices the difference: the proof is that people talk about true stories. As if there were such a thing; events take place progressively and we tell them the other way around. You seem to be starting at the beginning: "It was a beautiful evening in the autumn of 1922. I was a clerk in a lawyer's office in Marommes." And in reality you have started at the end. The end is there, invisible and yet present, it is the end that lends these words the pomp and value of a beginning. "I was taking a walk, I was out of the village before I knew it, I was worrying about money." Taken literally, this sentence simply means that the fellow was absorbed, morose, miles away from any adventure, in precisely that kind of mood where you let things happen around you without even seeing them. But the end is there, it transforms everything. For us, this chap is already the story's hero. His gloominess, his money worries are far more precious than our own, they're radiant with the light of passions to come. And the narrative unrolls backwards: the minutes don't pile up haphazardly one after another any more, they're snapped up by the story's end which draws them toward it and makes each of them draw to it in its turn the moment that precedes it: "It was dark, the street was empty." The sentence is dropped carelessly, seems almost superfluous; but it doesn't fool us, we make a note of it:

it's a piece of information whose importance we will appreciate later on. And we have the feeling that the hero lived all the details of this particular night as annunciations, as promises, or even that he lived only those details that were promises, blind and deaf to everything that didn't belong to his adventure. We forget that the future was not yet there; the man took his walk in a night empty of premonitions, a night that offered him its monotonous riches indiscriminately, and he did not choose among them.

I have wanted the moments of my life to succeed each other, to be arranged in order, like the moments of a life you remember. You might just as well try to catch time by the tail.[2]

The literary problem of which this is a statement is that death agony of the old-fashioned story to which we have already referred. It is however not so much an attack on the novel, on all narration, as it is an attack on the anecdote and a standard against which to judge the presentation of real lived time in narrative form. Yet it is characteristic of Sartre's way of dealing with such literary problems that he should tell an anecdote to demonstrate the impossibility of anecdotes, that he should possess the means to make this lived time spring drearily from the page at the same time that he is demonstrating how irreducible it is to language. The modern impossibility of telling anecdotes does not bring him to invent something new, like the enormous four-dimensional anecdotes of Proust. Instead he uses the older unacceptable solutions that are at hand, only exaggerating and deforming them until we become aware how much they distort reality, and are able to come into sudden contact with it by correcting the distortion the form has left in our minds. We hear the story of Erna twice, in two different anecdotes of identical substance—one of which is part of the other like the vanishing boxes within boxes. The first shows us life as it is lived, the other life as it is told: the two anecdotes neutralize each other. The one which is "told" is marked unsatisfactory, so that it turns against the first, so similar to it, and strips off its narrative surface as well, transforms it into an appearance behind which there is the resistance of something real, just as two slightly different photographs suddenly juxtaposed might make us aware of the artificiality, the abstract nature, of all photographs, and let us glimpse a real three-dimensional face beyond them which each tried to approach in a different way like an unattainable limit.

This oblique approach to things is even clearer in the next section, which seems to be an abstract exposition of what real "lived" life is. The abstractions however are constantly mediated: we do not come into direct contact with a thought developing itself; in these sentences we watch Roquentin himself thinking it, we see his attempt to express as much as we see the expression. There is a schematized narrative concealed in this paragraph, an extremely generalized image of the progression of a life through 1924, 1925, 1926, through distant cities and love affairs and work begun and stopped. It is a matter of indifference whether this progression corresponds to the details of Roquentin's own life, although it certainly reflects the quality of it. What we are watching is the process by which Roquentin attempts to communicate the feeling of a life to us, either choosing details from his own, or imagining a few, not too precise, not too hopelessly general and abstract—a tracing which we can recognize, through which we can see some of our own experience. The life involved is not our own; it is in a period style, a dated twenties life. Yet our failure to recognize it is also necessary, for in refusing this life pattern we are at the same time recognizing it as something that belongs to someone else, as something the details of which still preserve some of the warmth of their place of origin. Didactic, generalized, even fictitious, these skimpy facts are still the vain instruments through which Roquentin had tried to give a little of the feeling of living; and past them, in their very failure, through the gaps they leave in this interminable and monotonous series of days, surges his own life and what he means by real "lived" life. Such dates, place names, mere indications, show us nothing in themselves: they are merely the proofs, the evidence in support of the existence of the dreary empty life that stretches behind them that we cannot see. Because we have been told that it cannot be told, we realize what it is, we take possession of it through the very words that seem definitively to forbid us access to it, and the reality rises in the place of absence marked out for it by the futile language.

We will find that this negative projection of reality is the path along which both objects and consciousness accede to language in this work; it is the way in which the reality of the breaking of the vase was preserved—the real temporal change which words only name was simply omitted, and the Something, the assumption of this non-human datum by consciousness, was deliberately labeled as subjectivity and left powerless to distort the facticity behind it. For in the single-voiced reality of the novel there are no solid visual facts to play off against the words: there must be something within the sentences themselves to sustain the break between story telling, subjective assumption, on the one hand, and the naked event, the inexpressible presence of facticity, on the other. It is precisely on account of this that these novels, so highly subjective, never drift into mere impressionism; for against these impressions the events preserve their own solidity; the place where they ought to be and in which we will never be able to find them, is held insistently before our eyes. This narration is therefore not so much an attempt to avoid humanization or assumption, for all language is the taking of a human position. It is an attempt to avoid the alienation of language in an appearance of false objectivity, of placelessness, whether it be through the use of "scientific" vocabulary and syntax, or through the presence of a common sense that puts an end to thought and that projects inherited and unjustified categories unquestioned into the world itself.

Subjectivity seems to have suffered in this description of ours. In the face of a world of things as they are it takes on the appearance of a distortion, a falsification, a mystification, it seems to acquire a kind of direful autonomy and the world breaks in two as in the earlier idealistic philosophies. But we will see later that this impression is the result of the extension of an image rather than the concrete development of a thought: something in the pattern of the philosophy suggests that image of a split world which the philosophy itself rejects. The very term "subjective" which we find ourselves obliged to use has in it a residue of inherited meaning that tends to develop autonomously and contradict the use we are trying to make of it. For if everything is subjective, human, necessarily assumed in some way by consciousness, then in a sense there are no longer *any* merely subjective moments (moments which imply in contrast the possibility of purely "objective" moments): every moment of subjectivity becomes a relationship to the world, every type of consciousness is a consciousness *of* something, no matter how mystified or alienated.

The most privileged moments of this work are in fact

those which recover for us the rights of subjectivity, those
which consist of nothing but what used to be described
as mere impression, where nothing "real" seems to happen and yet where the new language permits us to see a
real event in place of the mere atmosphere of earlier descriptions. In the sensitivity to place, for example, the
movement of the sentences seems completely dependent
on the movement of subjectivity, since the place is static
and has no movement in it for the sentences to imitate:

> I had forgotten this morning that it was Sunday.
> I went out and walked through the streets as usual.
> I had *Eugénie Grandet* with me. And then, sud-
> denly, as I pushed open the gate of the park, I had
> the impression that something was trying to attract
> my attention. The park was deserted and bare. But
> . . . how can I say this? It didn't look the way it or-
> dinarily does, it was smiling at me. For a moment I
> didn't move, leaning against the gate, and then
> abruptly I realized that it was Sunday. There it was,
> on the trees, on the grass, like a faint smile.[3]

The day has not been deduced, the process is not exactly
a logical one: in this winter season the park is likely to
have frequently been empty in the mornings; Roquentin
must have often seen it on other days of the week when
it looked just like this. And probably what he senses as a
difference has less to do with the park than it had with
the empty shuttered streets he had to go through to get
to it. Yet it is somehow from the park that he learns the
day; it springs somehow from the quality of the park's
atmosphere itself. "Objectively" this atmosphere is no
different from what it is on a weekday when no one is
there, just as an object remains the same whether the
camera focuses on it in a close-up or lets it be glimpsed
as part of a background before which something is taking

place. But on weekdays the atmosphere in the empty park is *accidental;* on Sundays it is *constitutive.* This is what Roquentin feels; a kind of autonomy somewhere in this emptiness, an extra depth of the silence, a permanence at the heart of this ordinary solitude. We can think of the streets as moments of this realization: changed things only vaguely perceived that set an unformulated feeling of difference in motion. But the park was the first object to be stared at head-on, it profited from the atmosphere of change, it was the first to be recognized. And in the light of this recognition the attention returns to the empty and remembered streets and reorganizes them into the ensemble of things named Sunday.

But this is a historical, "rationalistic" way of translating the thing that happens here into a set of recognizable contents. In the passage itself the contents are ignored and the experience rises to meet us as a unit whose contents are mysterious, a unit named in different ways until we suddenly realize what it is. This unit, the Something, "was smiling at me": the verb through which the effect of this total experience on the spectator is described permits us to judge the great distance between the experience as a whole and the material parts, the shrubbery, the benches, the colors, none of which can be visualized in any direct relationship to a "smile." In terms of the real seen park, its "smiling" is nothing more than an abstract meaning: there is no direct transfer of energy between the two material terms of the metaphor; it has to pass through the mediation of the mind itself which compares the feeling of the park to the feeling of a smile. Yet in spite of the impossibility of the image, it persists; it even solidifies into the smile-thing itself, less figurative at the same time as it has been set in a new relationship with the experience through the smile's preposition. The

effect of the comparison is not so much to focus one
kind of meaning on the experience as it is to insist on
its wholeness, an autonomy that rises from the individual
things like a smile and prevents them from resolving
again into unrelated objects. And yet by this time the
experience is no longer mysterious: it has content, and
it is not difficult to see where that content comes from.
Between the Something that attracted our attention and
the "faint smile" that seals it as a real, concrete presence,
the phenomenon has finally been named, and the empty
image of the smile is slowly filled in with our own experience of that mixture of desolation and leisure that
distinguishes a Sunday, even for the idle. So that in spite
of the complications of the passage, it reduces itself to
the pronouncing of an ordinary word; and this is why
the first version is followed by a simpler alternative: "It's
impossible to describe, you would have to say just this,
rapidly: 'It's a park, in winter, one Sunday morning.' "[4]
Here the images are abandoned, the weight is thrown
entirely on that habitual experience of which each of
these words are signs and tokens. The rapidity of the
sentence is designed to prevent us from turning it over
in our minds, from feeling how thin and worn it is as an
evocation, how little it does itself in the way of the translation of an experience into language. If it is inconspicuous enough, if it takes us enough by surprise, we lend
it common sense content in passing without asking any
questions. The two versions are distinct in the difficulty
with which they are read; but the most important difference between them is the most obvious one, their length.
The first, a paragraph, is self-sufficient; the second could
not possibly stand up by itself, it cries out for other narrative sentences to follow it and to continue the story
of what happened in this "park, in winter, one Sunday
morning." What does this mean but that the second

formulation, the single sentence, sets the scene for an event, whereas the first one constitutes an event in its own right? And yet the experience both of them stand for is exactly the same.

These are not simply two different "techniques" for setting down a kind of atmosphere the world happens to have: they are two different faces of the world itself, they imply the possibility that every prosaic naked sentence on the order of the "park, in winter" conceals within itself a kind of poetry, a large and autonomous development, and this without there being any objective difference between the self-sufficient "poetic" moment and the mere fact. This transformation of a world of bare objects, facts, and settings into a swarm of tiny independent events reflects the enormous creative power of subjectivity over things, but the events are not gratuitously invented, not mere decoration into which the surfaces of things are organized by the freedom of aesthetic play. The appearance of the "Something happening," which is the sign and instrument of these subjective events, adds nothing to them but only focuses them more intensely, reorganizes the facts without damaging them into a new kind of story for the novel's sentences to tell.

In a sense it might be said of these moments that the author of *Being and Not-Being* has a special sensitivity to events in which "nothing" happens; and this quality of theirs reflects the moment of literary history at which the work came into being. The experimenters of the early twentieth century had discovered new kinds of content: new structures of lived human time which they were obliged to invent a new organization in order to express, new complications of consciousness in which they discovered hidden forces that had to be registered with a new language, even new relationships between human beings appearing against the background of the collapse of apparently permanent social patterns. But the historical moment in which such new content makes its appearance is not inexhaustible; and the "innovations" themselves can be gradually alienated, taking on the solidified appearance of tradition which at the beginning they functioned against. So that in the quieter periods following great experimentation the perpetual change of societies and of generations expresses itself in more oblique innovation in the world of art: the new has to take the old to itself in order to come into being at all and is subversively concealed within traditional frameworks.

This description of a characteristic moment in which something happens without anything really happening takes on its full meaning only in terms of the great thematic originality of Sartre's work; for his themes, almost all of them, rise out of the possibility of just such an event and are themselves examples of it.

The "nausea," for instance, is the moment of feeling acutely that we exist; and yet since we always do exist, it is subjectivity, the historical fact of suddenly becoming aware of our existence, that lifts this uninterrupting existence to the status of a special moment in our lives. Thus a realization which is not dependent on any content of our existence becomes content in its turn, and a feeling of existing that transcends any of the events of our existence becomes itself an event. This transformation is reflected in the nature of nausea itself, an awareness that turns into a solid physical fact. At first this sickness has for us some of the quality of a metaphor; we feel it as merely the reinforcement of something subjective, the forcing of the subjective phenomenon out beyond its ordinary limits, since it happens to most of us to live the sensation of existing in anxiety but rarely in physical distress. The nausea takes on the appearance

of new content added to make a subjective event more
striking and more solid. But in reality this content is
nothing but the intensification of something already
there, for Sartre distinguishes between two modes of
nausea:

> A discreet and insurmountable nausea at all times
> reveals my body to my consciousness: it may happen
> that we seek out pleasurable sensations or physical
> pain in order to rid ourselves of it, but this pain or
> pleasure experienced by consciousness displays in
> its turn facticity and contingency and appears
> against the background of the nausea itself. We
> should take care not to interpret the term "nausea"
> as a metaphor drawn from physiological disturb-
> ances; on the contrary, it is upon the foundation
> of this first nausea that all the concrete and empirical
> nauseas, those tending towards vomiting (disgust
> at rotten meat, fresh blood, excrements, etc.), ac-
> tually take place.[5]

The nausea is therefore a false metaphor: the physical
disgust does not symbolize the discovery of existence
but is itself based on the continuous feeling of existence,
and the process whereby the awareness of existing became an event inside that existing life is repeated all
over again in the image that seemed to "stand for" it.
We will see later on that this structure of the new which
consists in the mere underlining of what was already
there is also that of the other drama of solitude, the
vision of freedom. But besides these events that take
place in the isolation of the individual consciousness,
there are others that transcend it and involve it with
other human beings and these are concentrated in the
drama of the *Look:* this moment in which our first isolation as individuals is destroyed, before all speech and

concrete contact with others, through the sensation of being looked at by them, makes its appearance in *Being and Not-Being* as a kind of myth. Like the struggle between the master and the slave in Hegel's *Phenomenology*, which it resembles in many ways, it constitutes a break in the tissue of abstract reasoning. It is not exactly a historical fact, one that can be localized at a single moment in our lives, but has to take on the form of a historical event to come to full expression. When I am looked at by others, I discover their existence through the alienation of my own: they possess something of mine, my outside, that I recognize as my own in shame or pride, but that I can never have any direct relationship to, that escapes me. But once more, this new dimension of myself that I am made aware of in the "look," my being-for-others, does not bring any new quality of mine to light; it merely doubles everything that was there before, it transforms the contents of my isolation into a skin, an exterior, which was always there latent, since we were potentially visible animals before the event of the look took place. Our freedom is both unimpaired and at the same time converted into a "dead freedom" under the gaze of someone else; our possibilities become "dead possibilities" which others reckon into their estimates of us, without those possibilities diminishing in number. The features of Boris are hardly altered during the overly insistent staring at them of Lola, and yet something does happen: "The left side of his face ached from being looked at so much."[6] Violent figurative events swarm around the drama of the look without becoming any more material: our faces, our world, are *stolen* by the eyes of other people; without the surface of the world changing, it suffers an internal *hemorrhage of being* and we go on existing in an unchanged but now alienated landscape.

We can attempt to recuperate this dimension of ourselves by assuming it and living it in our isolation: not merely suffering passively the seeing of our exterior by other people but constructing the exterior that we want to have them see. This is the meaning of Roquentin's decision, at the end of *Nausea*, to write a novel that will impose his existence on other people and make them think about him: a "salvation" at the same time both real and unattainable since he will never directly experience this attention of the unknown others scattered through the world. It is the meaning of the passion of the actor, in a play like *Kean*, where the consciousness alienated by others chooses its own alienation and pushes it to the extreme, doing nothing which is not destined for other people's eyes, even in their absence. But even here the transformation is dependent on the way subjectivity lives what it does: the content of the act is not immediately transformed; the act is merely performed in a new focus that without changing it, turns it into the *Gesture*, the imaginary. This new drama, which Sartre has analyzed most comprehensively in his book on Jean Genet, involves a destruction of the real world but one which is operated not through the instrumentality of things but by the subjectivity itself. Genet's acts are ways of not acting, of contaminating the concrete acts of others until they become in their turn unreal, of operating precisely that internal hemorrhage of being which a look was enough to provoke. Writing, with its twin faces of concrete activity and dreaming, becomes the ultimate place of this process of "irrealization," but in its beginnings it requires nothing but a look, trained for example on the utilitarian business of a stake being driven into the ground: a look that seizes it and permits it to be described as something *graceful:*

What is it that has happened? Nothing. Nothing;
simply that a practical act, through its precision and
rhythm, and through the memories it evokes, suddenly seemed to be its own reason for being . . .
Whereupon the purpose of this action turns into a
mere pretext. Time is reversed: the blow of the
hammer is no longer struck *in order to build the
merry-go-round,* instead, the fair, the profits the
showman is planning on, the merry-go-round, all
that exists only to provoke the hammer's blow; future and past cooperate to produce the present . . .
The booths, the buildings, the ground, all become
a décor: in an outdoor theater, as soon as the actors
appear, the trees turn into pasteboard, the sky becomes a painted backdrop. In the very instant in
which the act is transformed into a gesture, it drags
along with it into irreality the whole enormous mass
of being itself.[7]

This destruction into which the entire world is drawn,
where nothing is destroyed and nothing happens, seems
to be the most extreme example of a purely subjective
event, something brought by subjectivity to things. Its
implications for the subject matter of narration are obvious, but it is not mere decoration, because the subjectivity involved is not the author's but the "character's":
the author is no longer describing something he is sensitive to in the world, he is showing us a concrete relationship of a human being to *his* world, a new kind of
human meaning which the simple act of seeing something and describing something can come to have. This
meaning, which consists in a new structure of the same
visual contents, is of great human significance because
it does not remain confined to the single episode, it fans

out and infects the whole pattern of a life that chooses an aesthetic, an imaginary relationship to the world; and this new opposition between practical and imaginary activity, between acts and gestures, is perhaps the most important recent development in Sartre's moral thought and is obviously related to the Marxism into which he is trying to integrate the requirements of a philosophy of existence. The "subjective event" here is so far from a mere impression that it is at one with the meaning of the lives people choose. In this single static detail the quality of a whole life is reflected, on the condition that the language is capable of registering that quality in it.

The possibility of the gesture therefore, which was something into which an act changed without really changing, implies a whole series of new acts as well: if the world can be "irrealized," then irrealization can it- self become a motive for acting, and can add episodes different in kind to the novel, episodes which do not however spring from the discovery of a new unexplored area of content. And in a more general parallel to this, it is not only the themes of the work which are elaborated in the framework of the "subjective event" but the mo- tivation of the characters as well. With the notion of freedom and the vision of living as a perpetual unjustifi- able attempt of consciousness to acquire the solidity of some kind of being, in which there are no values that permit an easier or a safer access to that being which re- mains forever out of reach, suddenly every kind of hu- man activity becomes a way of trying to *be,* and every human act becomes self-justifying. The older idea of motivation falls away, being doubled at this point by a new one, and it is no longer necessary to analyze the ac- tivity of a pacifist and of a man with a passion for war, of a glutton and of an ascetic, of a political man and of a non-political man, in terms of their opposites; it suffices to reveal through the presentation of these concrete activities the moment toward which each moves as a fulfillment. It suffices to seize that fleeting instant in which each in a different way feels himself to be *living,* or simply *being,* and the activity is immediately comprehensible in terms of itself. This renovation of the human contents of literature is characteristically oblique: it does not change any of the kinds of activity that had been described before, it merely changes their valence, makes them new at an unexpected point.

These are some of the implications of the "subjective event" for the literary world in which it takes place. The implications are vast because the event is in one sense not a rare, occasional episode, but one which reflects in its very structure all events: the distance between consciousness and things, the necessity for consciousness to assume everything it does and everything it witnesses, the objectively real shaping power subjectivity has over the world. This kind of event is not however a final point beyond which we cannot go; it is itself dependent on a radical split between subjectivity and things which we will shortly examine in its own terms. But as we have seen, these moments, which like the "something happening," the nausea, or the look, reflect perpetual continuing structures of existence, have a tendency once they are focused on to achieve the status of events in their own right, intermittent in the continuity of narration, specialized. Having achieved the right to happen, they can no longer happen all the time; and time, or the illusion of time created by the sequence of the work of art, continues without them, obedient to its own laws. It is to this phenomenon, out of which all acts and events themselves surge, that we now turn our attention.

CHAPTER THREE

## The Rhythm of Time

The writers with the most striking, most nakedly accessible sense of time are those who use long sentences: the exaggeration of the rhythms of normal breathing yields a kind of time whose texture is gross and easily perceived. And among these sentences long enough to let us listen to the beat of time, short sentences, expletives, recover some of their original shock, enjoy new and jarring force. But sentences of more ordinary length can function within some larger unity that controls their cumulative effect: the rhythms Flaubert made his paragraph divisions yield are well-known. Such forms, in which the individual sentences, beaten into solidity, are set together piece by piece into a whole that gives them their meaning, suggest an idea of the work of art as a craft, like handiwork in silver, an idea which hardly survives at all in the universe of mass merchandise contemporary artists inhabit.

The time of Sartre's world is regulated by an instrument in appearance more extrinsic to literature than any of these schemes. Once more, it is a question of the ways sentences are connected together, but it is as if the sentences themselves counted for little in the process, possessed little intrinsic weight or effect upon it, like the bits of valueless material which modern sculptors join together into a form that rises above the cheap or ephemeral nature of its contents. The pace at which this world unfolds is supervised by punctuation.

Of course punctuation has always performed this function. But it has become so standardized that writers who use it as the schools or newspapers direct have no alternatives to choose from at the moments when they are obliged to punctuate. And where there is no possibility of doing something in different ways, there is no possibility of a style. We know this so well as readers that ordinarily we hardly even notice the punctuation at all: we do not have to, the convention is fixed, in a given case a given symbol will make its appearance. Limiting the writer's freedom in this matter even further are more curious restrictions: the colon, for example, is almost never seen in narration; some misfortune, possibly in its appearance, prevents it from ever straying out of the humdrum circle of expository prose.

The freedom with which Sartre uses these inherited symbols recovers for us some of their original freshness; he disposes of at least four different ways of linking sentences together, and this chaos begins to take on some appearance of order if we keep in mind that the marks are in his hands fairly precise symbols of different possible relationships between the complete sentences they separate:

> Daniel filled up with muddy and insipid water: himself; the water of the Seine, insipid and muddy, will fill the basket, they'll tear each other apart with their claws. A strong revulsion came over him, he thought: "It's a gratuitous act." He had stopped, he had set the basket on the ground: "You've got to hurt other people to make yourself feel it. You can never get at yourself directly."[1]

The mingling of thought and objectivity in this passage is characteristic of the third person narration of the later novels, and obviously has something to do with the blinking rapidity with which the punctuation varies and succeeds itself. The rhythm of this paragraph is controlled by three instruments, each one marking a pause longer and more absolute than the others: the comma, the semicolon, and the period. The period comes as a deep silence, a consequential gap; it has something of the force of the past definite tense: after each one new areas are uncovered or new things happen. It is uncertain just how distinct the opaque watery feeling Daniel experiences is from the sudden revulsion which also "fills" him, but in any case the revulsion is the accession of this feeling to a new plane; it has been named, and through the name the vaguer feeling takes on new shape and new intensity. The separation is even more striking after the next period. The sentence which follows it is a skip backward in time; its events, described in the pluperfect, have already happened, but have happened on such a different level from the feelings and thoughts that were going on simultaneously that they have had to be cleanly divided from them, there was no room for them in the earlier sentences. The mind, busy with its unpleasant sensations, did not notice the pause and the setting down of the basket until after it had already taken place.

This silence latent in the period is by no means intrinsic to it through some kind of "nature" that it might possess: its meaning is a function of its use, and the shock, the sudden break it causes, becomes easier to sense when we realize that the normal connection in this special world between straightforward sentences describing concrete actions is not the period at all but the comma. It is because we grow, over pages and pages, accustomed to this privilege of the comma, trained to it, that the period comes to strike us with the force it does. And it is certain that in a consecutive reading, attentive to the continuity of the narration, we have no trouble passing across the distance the period leaves between two sentences, and that the selection of small passages, their isolation and the slower reading they profit from, all exaggerate the effect of this punctuation far beyond what it is in a normal reading. But the magnifying and exaggeration of a phenomenon simply permits us to register more clearly what had to be there in the first place.

When the period is frequently used in a paragraph, the past definite is called into play and the effect is that of a jerky moving forward in time:

> The cats shrieked as if they had been scalded and Daniel felt himself going out of his mind. He set the cage on the ground and gave it a couple of violent kicks. There was a tremendous rumpus within and then the cats were silent. Daniel remained motionless for a moment with a strange electric sensation suddenly shooting through the back of his head. Two workers came out of a warehouse and Daniel began walking again. The place was here.[2]

Each of these sentences is a complete event; the past definite hermetically closes off each of the verbs. We pause at each period and it takes a little effort to leap into the next sentence. And the frequency of "and"s in this passage indicates a will to connect in some way the small units which threaten to fall apart; the "and"s attempt to weaken the divisive period-time, and the pressure of this time is so great that at one point one connective has to be intensified to "and then" in order to hold things together.

This abnormal strength of the period accounts for the very frequent use of the semicolon: it is as if the period were so strong it had to be used with care, reserved for the most significant moments, so as not to wear it out and for fear it prove too powerful for the structure it is supposed to hold together: "It was a bustling square with bars along it; a group of workers and women had gathered around a pushcart. A few women stared at him with surprise."[3] The group around the pushcart is part of the scene described in the first sentence; it develops the description of the square, but it is too leisurely, too contemplative, to warrant the sudden rush of motion which the comma would call up between the scenic framework and the detail. But the two sentences are static, descriptive; neither of them has enough autonomous energy to stand alone, bounded by a period, without falling flat. The semicolon offers a kind of neutral pause, and the real break is saved for the next sentence, so that when the women look at Daniel it will come with the shock of a completely new occurrence.

Let us recall for a moment some of Roquentin's ideas about narration. His criticism struck at the anecdote and only indirectly at the novel. The anecdote is a kind of primitive stage of the novel, distinguished from it above all by its length; the anecdote is short enough so that its beginning and its end can both be held together within the mind without much trouble, whereas the novel (even if it tells a story which can be converted into an anecdote) represents an enormous amount of time that passes in front of the mind and then is lost to view, never wholly existing in the present, always part memory or part anticipation. Roquentin shows how sentences like: "It was dark, the street was empty." are secretly charged with their energy from the impending climax of the story. We know that something is about to happen, and soon, and that these details are only apparently unimportant, that they must have meaning and are to be watched attentively. The end of a novel, much further away, does not exercise this power of gravity over the innumerable sentences that precede it. Only toward the last pages, and at the very beginning, of the novel, is time obviously distorted and stylized in the way Roquentin described; and this distortion can in the hands of a self-conscious artist turn into a bravura piece, a kind of exhibitionistic gesture to show his shaping power over what he narrates before effacing himself. Here (and in the weaker reflections of these moments which are the beginnings and endings of chapters) he can lead us into his story with the most breath-taking details, the most startling perspectives, and break it off at similar points, in the grand manner. For beginnings and ends are artificial, they are not "in nature."

The sentence is not in nature either. Sentences must also begin and end, and as long as our attention is directed to their succession, to the continuity of their subject matter, we are not aware of any violence done to time. But when we examine them more closely, focusing on small areas and attending to the manner in which they are linked together, we find that the time of the novelist, taken for granted, flowing on smoothly before, threatens to fall apart, to leave a ruin of separate moments and separate events, with no way of getting from one to another except by fiat, through a solution by violence.

This possibility of a breakdown in the continuity of sentences is the reflection on an aesthetic level of a technical philosophical problem: that of a theory of time. The conflict between the unity of time, its continuity, and the divisibility and multiplicity of the individual moments, a conflict out of which such things as Zeno's paradoxes arise, does not offer a choice between irreconcilable alternatives but a formulation of two requirements, two simple and incontrovertible facts about time

which the new description will have to take into account.
Sartre unites these opposites in conceiving time as a
"unity which multiplies itself," a relationship within being, and within a being split against itself. Time is therefore not a *thing,* the nature of which we can describe. It
is not somewhere *inside* the world, it is the way we live
the world; we are temporal in the structure of our being
and time is one of the negations that we bring to the pure
simple being of the world by surging in its midst.[4] We
*are* time, are its privileged place of existence.

This has immediate implications for the literary problem we just described. Since we are our time, it is up to
us whether it turns toward us the face of continuity or
that of divisibility. There are no real beginnings, and
yet our time is full of beginnings and endings. We constantly interrupt a time continuity to do something else,
our time sense expands and contracts like an accordion:
fast or slow, continuous, absorbed, or jerky. It is on this
possibility of variations in the quality of time that the
variations we have discovered in Sartre's narration are
founded, and the effect of the period, in particular, is
inconceivable without some possibility of a kind of absolute break in time which it could echo.

This absolute break is the Moment or Instant: but the
break must somehow take place within time, or time
would cease altogether. It cannot take place within the
unity of action, of a project, otherwise it would slip back
into a continuity. The only moments free enough from
a continuity of time already past and from the ceaseless
rush into the future to qualify as Moments, are those
which are in themselves both the end of something and
the beginning of a new thing.[5] The moment is no longer
strongly attached to the dying continuity, and the new
one has not yet taken on enough life to catch the moment
up in its motion. Yet these instants are in their turn

merely the reflection of a more basic reality and happen
on the basis of a more fundamental possibility. These
partial beginnings can happen only because beginnings
are somehow possible, or at least a certain type of beginning is: that of the original choice of our being, the unjustifiable choice that gives meaning to our smallest
attitudes and acts, that accounts for our tastes, our ambitions, our habits. All of these are themes within a
unity, parallel expressions of an underlying reality. The
description of this original choice takes the form of a
kind of myth, as the "look" did: it is the abstract structure which all later choices carry within themselves like
a meaning, and insofar as it is the structure of an act, it
cannot be reduced completely to an abstract idea but
preserves the act's shape. Yet in another sense, since it
precedes our time itself and is itself the basis of the
quality of the time we live, it can never be localized in
a moment of our personal history: we are not born
grown-up, and there is never a full dress moment in which
we can be said to have chosen ourselves, and yet everything happens as though we had. In certain cases, as
with the childhood trauma of Genet,[6] the original choice
can even crystallize into a drama which can be temporally represented, whether in fact it happened all at once
or not. The "myth" of the original choice is therefore an
instrument of analysis that risks perpetuating itself as
a concrete image.

There are nonetheless certain specialized moments of
our personal history that seem to stand in a more privileged relationship to this moment of original choice than
do the ordinary contents of daily living, moments that
have a feeling of beginning about them stronger than
most, that we think of as change, as absolute dates. Such
are those rare moments, in which in our freedom, the
original choice is abandoned for some new choice of

being. There are no "reasons" for such conversions, as Sartre calls them; the idea of a reason for doing something, a motive behind a project, has meaning only *within* a global choice; and very often a will to change completely, the passionate desire to alter from top to bottom that choice which is ourselves, is a kind of rationalization, a struggle against ourselves which is part and parcel of our original choice and not in any sense set against it. Yet these sudden conversions show our freedom at its most absolute, freedom exercising an ultimate power over all reasons and all values, and they have for us therefore a very special fascination, an excitement which the tone of the following passage betrays:

> At every moment I am aware that this initial choice is contingent and unjustifiable . . . Hence my anxiety, my fear of being suddenly exorcized, of suddenly becoming radically other; hence also the frequent coming into being of these conversions which wholly transform my initial project . . . Think for example of the *instant* in which the Philoctetes of Gide suddenly abandons everything, his hatred, his fundamental project, his reason for being and even his being itself; think of the *instant* in which Raskolnikoff decides to give himself up. These extraordinary, marvelous instants, in which the older project collapses into the past in the light of a new project which rises on its ruins and which has hardly even taken full shape yet, these instants in which humiliation, anxiety, joy, hope are all inextricably united, in which we let go of everything in order to seize something new, in which we seize the new in in order to abandon everything, such instants have often seemed to furnish the clearest and most touching image of our freedom. But they are only one manifestation of it among others.[7]

In other words, if we are free at all, we cannot be "more" free at certain moments than at others; freedom is not a quality that we possess degrees of; so that in spite of everything, from the point of view of the idea of freedom, these conversions are not more privileged than any other moments of our lives.

Yet from the point of view of the notion of an original choice, the conversions are in a sense the *only* real moments in our lives, the only real events. This curious difference in perspectives, where an idea suggests more than it really means, suggests something radically different from what it is supposed to mean, is perhaps attributable to the "myth"-like nature of the notion of choice. We will see later on also how certain notions, above and beyond their purely thought content, because their formulations are very close to images, tend to have this double development, in which from their images consequences can be drawn, secretly, implicitly, mistakenly, which range far beyond anything the pure thought of the notion ever intended to convey. In the case of the original choice, in terms of which every detail of a life can be interpreted (an interpretation and a method which Sartre has called "existential psychoanalysis"), the unique individual force of the events of a life seems to fade, the events become mere expressions, simple manifestations of the ever present single choice. So that we approach the strange image of a world in which nothing happens, in which the same thing repeats itself over and over in different forms, in which only one real solid event—the choice itself—has ever taken place and in which only one new event can take place: the conversion, the sudden reversal of values at any time possible. That these extensions and suggestions latent in the notion of choice do not really do justice to Sartre's practice as a novelist is apparent from the impression of a richness of action which his books leave with us. There is little overt effort made to show in some manner an original choice operating behind each of his characters—such an effort would have resulted in a kind of personification, a kind of world of "humors," of character-ideas in action rather than real people. And yet the moment of conversion, so dependent on this whole complex of ideas, occupies a place of great importance in this work. The conversion can seem a waking up, as it does in the consul's office in Indochina, where Mercier urges Roquentin to accept a place in the new expedition:

> I was staring at a little Khmer statuette, on a green cover, next to the telephone. I felt as if I were filled with lymph or with tepid milk. Mercier was saying, with angelic patience that concealed some irritation: "As you are well aware, I have to receive an official appointment. I know that sooner or later you will say yes: it would be better to do so at once."
>
> He had a reddish black beard, highly scented. Every time he moved his head I got a whiff of the perfume. And then, all of a sudden, I woke up out of a sleep six years long.
>
> The statue looked disagreeable and stupid and I realized that I was profoundly bored. I couldn't manage to understand why I was in Indochina at all. What was I doing there? Why was I talking with these people? What was I dressed so oddly for? My passion was dead. I had been submerged in it, swept along by it, for years; now I felt empty.[8]

Here is a moment in which freedom suddenly stirs convulsively, shatters the crust of habits that had seemed to be forming around it, emerges without any connections at all, without any obligations, into a world which had gradually forgotten it was there. And yet the astonishing thing is that this sudden self-assertion of freedom is presented in terms of its opposite: it is something that happens to Roquentin, he himself does nothing, seems hardly responsible for it. He seems merely the passive locus of a wholly impersonal event, like a sudden bodily reaction. He merely "wakes up," and wakes up after it is all over. His passion does not die, he realizes that it is dead. The moment, the leap in time from one world-choice to another, is so sudden and so radical that it apparently eludes the instruments which were supposed to register it. It is deduced after the fact, from its consequences. For this moment is in the beginning wholly negative: the new passions, new interests, new thoughts, which will gradually fill this void have not yet appeared; the astonished mind is alone for the time being with the trophies of its former enthusiasm. That is why the image of death is the privileged expression of this change: the image of the loss of everything familiar, everything to which we are passionately attached, of the pain of the organism acceding to a new condition—so that the emptiness, the abandonment of the consciousness is its first sensation.

The most shocking, polemic statement of this event is the death of love: such moments take on their significance when opposed to the heavy burden of works composed from the very beginnings of literature to glorify love as a divine, irresistible, irrational force—one which begins with the inevitability of a chemical process, mastering the soul and setting it under very real slavery. It is not the reality of these feelings which is denied; but the test of a literature of freedom is the presentation of just such a passion—showing it as it is, with all the passivity it involves, the feeling that it seizes us without our consent, and showing at the same time that it is freely assumed, and that we somehow put ourselves into a passional state, that we make ourselves passive to be "enslaved" by our own freely chosen passions. Yet the direct description of the passion is somehow insufficient. Love, like the passions of Roquentin, is a value, and each value tends toward self-sufficiency, toward absorbing the whole world into itself at the exclusion of everything else. It denies its existence as "a" value and insists on being Value pure and simple. The value is moreover a kind of absence: it is that which consciousness lacks, that path by which consciousness hopes eventually to arrive at its own special form of being: a lack which propels consciousness forward in time, and which all of the acts of consciousness are designed to fill. So that very often the value itself escapes detection, and people even deny they have any: only their acts, often performed under motives which their doers attempt to conceal from themselves, show secretly the ever present influence of this absent center of gravity. Yet in the moment of the death of a value, the eye manages to register it directly; suddenly it becomes aware of what was there now that it is gone; and in the place where the value used to be it seizes it as the outline of an absence.

Thus the real meaning of love as freely chosen, a meaning obscured during its existence by the passive nature of the feeling which is lived as being submitted to, suddenly emerges when love dies. Like the other moments, the death of love happens abruptly and without transition: the person merely wakes up into a world from which his love is gone, he remembers the former gestures inspired by it without any longer understanding them. This sudden absence is not *caused,* is wholly gratuitous. Yet it can happen against the background of a world so unexpectedly and radically altered that the older value, persisting a moment in its new surroundings, becomes incomprehensible, and then vanishes altogether. This is what happens in *Dead without Burial,*[9] after Lucie has been tortured and her world sealed off by the

imminence of death, when her love for Jean, a kind of
peace time love nourished by the idea of a continuing
future, suddenly proves to be at cross-purposes with the
passion in which she wants to live her coming extinction.
Love has nothing to offer her in such a world; it is a toy
she drops without regret.

Yet we should not make any mistake about the tone
of these sequences. They have no trace of any sadness
at the evanescence of human passions or emotions; they
are painful, "humiliation, anxiety, joy, hope" all mingled
together, but they have no built-in effect. The very same
moment, which in *Dead without Burial* had some of the
somberness of approaching death, becomes in *Kean* pure
comedy, in the astonishing scene in which the passion
shared by Kean and Elena suddenly gives way beneath
them and drops them from Alexandre Dumas into a play
of a different nature altogether.[10] If there is any dominant tone in such moments at all, it is more likely to be
excitement, which does not have to be wholly free from
anxiety: a kind of relief of the consciousness at finding
itself once more naked and without any ties, left with
absolutely nothing. There is in it some of the exhilara-
tion of all negativity, all destruction.

It is the ever present possibility of such moments of
radical change, the constant threat that time will collapse into one of these moments and then reissue wholly
altered, that lends the world of Sartre that jerkiness we
have discovered behind the use of the period. It is as if
time might suddenly begin to divide itself into infinitesimal separate units and as if this process, like a chain
reaction, once begun could never be arrested. And
against this threat a host of smaller mannerisms stand
guard: verbs of unusual violence, especially in the philosophic works where milder ones might have been used,
keep things moving explosively forward: such verbs as

"die," "surge," "seize," "invade," and so on. But such
verbs have ambiguous effects: they do keep things going
but at the same time they separate the new thing bursting into being somewhat irrevocably from all that has
preceded it, as if it had been separated by the enormous
gap of one of those instants. And the constant series of
"and"s and "then"s and "afterward"s push the minute
separate events forward, both linking and dividing them.
On every page we find adverbs of violence attempting to
bring new events to birth: "suddenly," "brusquely," "all
at once"—all these lend a kind of abruptness to this
world which occasionally looks like the jerky, over-rapid
and sectional movement of the early movies: "She pours
without replying; all of a sudden nimbly he withdraws
his finger from his nose and spreads both hands out on
the table. He has his head tossed back and his eyes are
shining. Coldly he says: 'Poor girl.' "[11] The new gesture
is so rapid that it will not all fit into the sentence which
was supposed to circumscribe it and leaves some trailing,
static now that the gesture is over, into the next ("He has
his head tossed back"). There are long waits, unexpected
things suddenly happen, time slows again and stops and
then moves.

That jerkiness does not become intolerable because
it is not the only kind of movement in this prose. In the
silences of the period, time shows its possibility of being
discontinuous, fragmented; the requirements of a sentence seemed to image faithfully this starting and stopping of time. Time's continuity is in some ways harder
to fix. The basis for it could not be in the sentences
themselves unless they were highly unusual like Faulkner's, but in the continuity of our reading, which provides the solidity with which the impression is filled out.

Sometimes the continuity is illusory: such is the movement which the colon provokes, a mere flash which

quickly abolishes itself: "Daniel filled up with muddy
and insipid water: himself." The colon here is a little
pause, a slight catching of the breath before the last
word is uttered which permits the sentence to fall, finished. It signifies equivalence between the two parts, an
identity so great that the two sections seem to be held
apart artificially and by force only. Once the colon is
bridged, once the mirror-sentence on the other side of
it has joined its predecessor, the two seem to merge into
one like a rubber band stretched and snapping back, and
they glide as a single unit into the past. The separation
can be as slight as the distance between looking and seeing, between seeing and identification: "Limp little mon-
sters crawl on the ground alongside and stare at the joyous troop through the empty sockets of their eyes: gas-
masks."[12] The colon permits not an abstract description
of the process of seeing something and then realizing
what it is, a description that would use weak and faded
words like "realize" and "it occurred to him suddenly,"
but a concrete presentation of the event in which we
participate ourselves. We are suddenly lifted out of the
realistic world of the rest of the novel, lifted higher and
higher into fantasy the length of the whole sentence, until suddenly the single withheld word is released and the
world immediately settles back to normal again. The sentence no longer displays a merely static meaning; it imitates with its own small drama the drama of its subject
matter. And yet the drama caused by the colon is partly
an artificial one: the colon assures us that there is no
difference at all between the one and the other sentences
it separates and yet it separates them. The colon unity
throws up beyond itself the presence of the thing as it
really is, the unified thing of which the two sentences
are merely aspects, and then against this, the sentence
which attempts to seize the solidly settled object through

motion, through the illusory, snapping motion of the two temporarily separated parts rejoining. The sentence, the subjectivity, creates an illusion of separation, a mirage of dynamism and of happening, in order to convey a basically static reality. The colon here is therefore a kind of symbol of the events in which "nothing" really happened that we have described in the previous chapter; it is also, as we will see later on, a privileged form through which certain objects in this world find their expression.

Such use of the colon permits a characteristic solution to one of the most serious problems in modern narration, that of the "thought." There is no "natural" solution to this problem. The interior monologue of Joyce is not less artificial than indirect discourse; it has merely the virtue of a conquest, of the new. The problem exists because of the relationship between thoughts and words. If thoughts were immediately equivalent to, immediately assimilable to words, there would be merely the ordinary problem of finding the exact words, there would be no question but that words were the perfect and privileged manifestation of thoughts. But the words pronounced inside the mind can be in direct contradiction to the mind's secret awareness, they can be an attempt of the mind to fool itself. Or the real thinking can be done through acts. We can sometimes think directly with the things we handle and use, so that the full dress "thought" is only a much later entity, a kind of reflection of an immediate reality. So unless a little violence is done to the traditional methods of presenting thoughts, the old worn-out notions of personalities and of the nature of thinking and of action will perpetuate themselves.

Sartre's renovation of this state of affairs is along the line of least effort, hardly perceptible: he preserves everything, the equivalence between thought and sentence, even to the quotation marks that give us the impression that the thought-sentence has been lifted bodily from someone's mind and set unchanged upon the paper. But this traditional arrangement is secretly subverted: the colon in itself would not be enough to install any real novelty into this form; its use in direct quotation before a sentence in quotation marks is in fact one of the rare applications of this symbol which is not rejected from French narrative prose; but the colon is the locus of this subtle change: "A strong revulsion came over him, he thought: 'It's a gratuitous act.'" The effect of this "thought" has been prepared by its context, by the kind of sentence that precedes it. The comma separating the two narrative sentences lends the second, carrying within itself the burden of the thought, the same weight as the first, more linear one. This forced equation of two unequal lengths would of course be present even with different kinds of separating punctuation: "He drank. He thought: 'She's pregnant. It's funny: I can't believe it.'"[13] Even here, where the "thought" section is far more complicated than the two words it is dependent on, it has nonetheless been reduced to the status of a mere clause by the influence and the parallel of the preceding small sentence. What the period does here however is to alter the quality of the movement: in the first passage the length of the beginning sentence and the rush ahead caused by the comma help to complete the "he thought" effortlessly with the substance of the thought. In the second group there is an abrupt stopping short that causes the thought to tumble forward under the acquired momentum in a kind of stumbling over its own feet; but in both cases the "thought" has been solidified, turned into an entity, by the parallel with the preceding sentence. What stands between the quotation marks is now no longer language of the same quality as the sentences outside them: it is unitary, and when it happens, it has to be at least as tangible an event as the drink the man takes or the sudden wave of revulsion that comes over him. The shortness of the "he thought:" is essential in lending the vague subjective event the value of a precise gesture, and after it the colon comes as relief, it points forward, indicating an empty space which the thought quickly flows into and fills up; it holds the door open at the end of an incomplete sentence and the completion arrives almost instantaneously. Thus the thought, when it happens to the incomplete announcement preceding it, has now all the force of an act, and the quotation marks, which were supposed to indicate naively that we think in words, are forced to assist in conveying the impression of a gesture of consciousness just as real and as solid as a gesture of the hand. The "words" of the thought are now a kind of illusion: the thought-sentences indicate the sudden decisive seizing of consciousness on things; they are not any longer supposed to give faithfully "word for word" what the consciousness "thought." The words of these sentences no longer stand for the words of the thoughts in question; they stand directly for the thoughts themselves, just as ordinary narrative sentences "stand for" the wordless realities they describe.

The movement which the colon generated was ephemeral and immediately abolished itself, a mere illusion of movement created to be as quickly laid to rest: an instant only, since it could bind only two sentences, could represent nothing more substantial than an exchange of energy between two points alone. The comma, on the other hand, has the seeds of perpetual motion within it: it connects complete sentences, lets them pile up one after another, and suggests no superior structure which would cause a period to happen at any given point, which would of itself set an end to the fissioning development.

But although the sentences it links are grammatically complete, the comma insists on their secret incompleteness, it urges us forward, assures us that everything has not yet been said: "He had stopped, he had set the basket on the ground: 'You've got to hurt other people to make yourself feel it.'" The center of gravity in this unit is in the thought, the other sentences slide down the incline toward it although they in no way duplicate it. The comma is precisely this slant at which complete sentences are leaned and which robs them of their autonomy. But the incompleteness is not a precise one, to be filled and satisfied by a single detail, a single subsequent sentence: it spreads out on all sides and the period that finally puts an end to it is arbitrary and dependent on the angle of vision, like a window frame that shuts off the view at an accidental point. For the comma generates a movement which whirls loose wider and wider. The colon was bounded, centripetal, moving in upon itself to vanish at a given moment; the comma has no natural term; the form which it governs is open, full of loose ends. In a sense the master image of this special kind of movement is the entire novel *The Reprieve,* in some ways nothing but a vast whirl of things linked by commas and which at its most concentrated moments shrinks to precisely the form we are describing:

> Red and pink and mauve fabrics, mauve dresses, white dresses, uncovered bosoms, beautiful breasts beneath handkerchiefs, pools of sunlight on tables, hands, sticky and golden liquids, more hands, thighs bursting out of shorts, gay voices, red and pink and white dresses, gay voices spinning in the open air, thighs, the *Merry Widow* waltz, the smell of pine-trees, of warm sand, the vanilla odor of the open sea, all the islands in the world invisible and present in

the sunlight, the Leeward Islands, Easter Island, the Sandwich Islands, the luxury shops along the seashore, the lady's raincoat at three thousand francs, the costume jewelry, red and pink and white flowers, hands, thighs, "this is where the music is coming from," gay voices whirling in the air, what about your diet, Suzanne? Oh, just this once. Sails on the sea and the skiers leaping, their arms stretched forward, from wave to wave, the smell of the pines in whiffs, peace. Peace at Juan-les-Pins.[14]

This cascade of sensations is pure of any individual minds; the people leave their separate identities along with their jobs and their winter clothing and merge into a common set of feelings, into a common world. The holiday world directs them, not the other way around: it proposes a series of well-traveled paths which they follow through their summer. For a time at least this collective world is the only living entity, the only reality. Yet take this resort as the widest frame of reference, expand its hints and fragments, let the bodies which are attached to the hands and thighs begin to appear, and let the situations attached to the disembodied voices little by little be guessed at, and the form of *The Reprieve* is unmistakably present before you. This form, which attempts to convey both the minute position we occupy in a world filled with history and the fragmentary nature of our awareness of that world, is supposed to be full of loose ends, open, fragmentary, in order to avoid the god's-eye view of the world which some novels that do not remain within a single point of view suggest.

Yet in spite of its difference from the colon form, the comma also suggests a single central reality which the sentences do violence to; but this central reality, instead of being somehow separated in two only to be immediately reunited again, is infinitely divided, infinitely divisible. Time, in order to move forward, must change from moment to moment, but it must also, to be continuous, remain somehow the same. The most striking changes turn out to be grammatical fictions and necessities, the apparently separate events imperceptibly fade into what preceded them and into what will follow. Like the thoughts, the revulsion, the setting down of the basket, they are all distinct because they happen on different levels and have to be separated in their presentation, and yet somehow they are all simultaneous, form part of a single large reality which we sense after we have read all of them.

This movement forward which is also a kind of repetition is a form of generosity: a fear that the event, the reality, has not been sufficiently presented, a turning around it to strike it again and again from new sides and at new angles, so that no single formulation which might have caught your mind more immediately than others, will go unsaid. This sort of repetition is familiar to readers of Sartre's philosophic works; and since these are practical expository works, it is there unashamed and unconcealed. But in narration any real repetition is generally checked by the real movement forward of time, the necessity that very shortly things be in some real sense different from what has preceded them. Nonetheless sometimes this flow forward is slowed down as much as it can be, sometimes time marks time, and little pools of repetition gather:

> But he would have had to say something: Boris felt himself unable to speak. Lola was beside him, tired and all warm and Boris couldn't tear the slightest word loose, his voice was dead. I would be like this if I were a mute. It was voluptuous, his voice

floated deep down in his throat, soft as cotton and it couldn't get out, it was dead.[15]

This repetition, the describing in different ways of the same phenomenon, is not exactly circular: with each phrasing it rises to a new level, and the image of the "dead" voice, colorless and figurative at first, becomes real by the end of the passage. The mere abstract feeling of not being able (not wanting) to talk has become the awareness of a part of his body, an organ, actually gone lifeless. Such a sudden unfolding of development, the quick rushing into being of variations on a single motif, is the characteristic form of a kind of Sartrean poetry. The passages begin from a single central datum or conceit: in this case the voice not working, the idea of the voice as a thing which operates like an organ of the body; and then this central "inspiration" is systematically exploited, used in as many different ways possible, developed as exhaustively as possible, until a kind of feeling of completion is reached, the thing is there before us, and the continuous movement of narration sets in again.

In its most characteristic use, therefore, the comma ceases to be simply the rhythm at which events unfold, and turns into a kind of momentary departure from the narration, a form that develops above the line of the narration like a pause. There is a point here beyond which our analysis cannot pass: the coming into being of the "idea", the central image, the motif itself, the "inspiration"; this surges out of nothingness, the *Einfall* is a kind of irreducible. And yet there is a quality about all of this Sartrean rhetoric, or poetry, which can be formulated: we feel a kind of contortionism in it, a straining which nonetheless remains graceful, lands back on its feet. The motif surges in a kind of receptive tension in the author's mind; at points in the steady continuity he strains his imagination for a certain kind of perception and suddenly, out of nowhere, the right thing comes. But this pressure of the imagination does not exist in a void: it is not content it seeks, but a special way of treating content which is already given in the story line. It is as if the things of the narration were constantly being stared at to yield up a kind of poetry, as if the things were being constantly forced to take the shape of a subjectivity, to take on some of the grace and the autonomous movement of a kind of thought. But what it is that happens to these things, what can happen to them, what this specialized attention directed on them means, we will only find out by leaving behind us the forms into which this content organizes itself, and interrogating the content itself directly.

PART TWO

*Things*

In a sense, *Being and Not-Being* is one enormous theme and variations on the order of the comma form: almost everything in it can be reduced to a single idea, which coming into contact with problems of ever different kinds reveals more and more of its possible riches; and this idea is the simple opposition, expressed in the title, between consciousness and things. This is the only certain fact, this radical difference in being, against which to check all of our ideas, and more than that—since a book of philosophy is also a language experiment—against which to check all of our formulations. In philosophy as in literature the distinction between something expressed and the means or form through which it is expressed is archaic: there is no incorrect formulation of a true idea; the search for the proper expression is the same as the search for the wholly adequate notion.

The use of the word "not-being" to describe human reality is, for example, an attempt to avoid suggesting that consciousness "is," in the way that things "are," to avoid suggesting that consciousness can, even for an instant, lean back and enjoy its being. Because consciousness is temporal, it never wholly "is" in any single moment of time, it is always leaving part of itself behind in the past, and is fretted at and distracted by the empty future which exercises on it a most constant pull like the moon over tides. And besides, there is nothing for it to "be": no essential rock bottom reality it can finally end up with after it gets done thinking its thoughts and experiencing its perceptions, nothing there at all when you take away all the objects seen through its transparency—consciousness is always consciousness *of* something. In this roundabout way consciousness arrives back at the things which it is not but without which it could not exist at all: it is a kind of radiance playing over the solid being of things which would vanish utterly if they were no longer there to support it.

That is at least an image for the relationship. Almost all ideas seem capable at certain moments, at times of fatigue or when the pressure to use them as counters without thinking them through a second time is too great, of sinking to the level of images. These images can be visual schemes of the content of the ideas; but they can also surge directly from the shape of the idea itself. Thus the other half of this opposition which seems to constitute the universe is just as susceptible to a subtle kind of deformation through the words we use to describe it as consciousness is. The words "things" and "Being" describe this same central reality, and yet the idea responds, expands and contracts, at the application of these two very different names. "Being" is unitary, empty, without qualities; "things" on the other hand suggests through the sudden scattering effect of its plural some of the variety and the number of objects among which being is infinitely parceled out.

And "things" is not only an alternate name: it is an expression, a sign which permits us to tell certain writers from others, to distinguish the presence of a very special kind of theme, of interest. For a writer will constantly talk of "things" only in a world where the non-human is set off against us as a block, where the lifeless is felt to intrude, to constitute a foreign body, in drama which ideally should be nothing but inter-personal. These "things" are mute and troubling specimens of another race:

> Tom was alone too, but not in the same way. He was seated astride the bench and he had started to look at it with a kind of smile, he seemed astonished. He put his hand out and cautiously touched the wood

as if he were afraid to break something, then he drew his hand back hastily and shuddered. I wouldn't have gone through all that bench-touching if I had been Tom; it was just more Irish comedy, but it seemed to me too that there was something strange about these objects: they seemed fainter, less dense, than they ordinarily did. All I had to do was look at the bench, the lamp, the heap of coal dust, and I knew that I was about to die. Of course I couldn't think my own death clearly but I saw it everywhere, on things, in the way things had moved back, were keeping their distance, discreetly, like people talking beside a deathbed. What Tom had just touched on the bench was *his own* death.[1]

"Object" is a more sterilized word, a word which in its odor of specialization is less likely to release that indiscriminate naming of being which the other word commands; but the fainter word is useful to fill in until the proper moment for the appearance of the reality in its strongest form. The great distinction that marks the word "things" off from its equivalent "Being," is the distance it maintains between the unit and the individual concrete exemplifications of it. The catalogue of individual things in this passage does not distract from the general category. These few samples live as real and unique manifestations of "things" and they prove that the abstraction is not empty like the abstractions of the older philosophers who when pressed for examples would betray the disembodied quality of their logical systems in proposing their writing table as the only thing that occurred to them. There is a kind of cooperation between the category "things" and the individual things; the reality of each seems to be intensified by the reality of the other.

The meaning does not officially change when we begin to use the word "being," but the catalogues fade, all the unique and individual things continue to be represented by the word but they struggle against each other in such a chaos of sizes, shapes, and functions that it becomes difficult for us to think them in a singular unit unless we draw far enough away for the outlines to blur. Suddenly this new image suggested by the language drags other images with it out of the shadowy place of its origin: the world refuses to be reduced to the colorless extension of that single unit, another character is necessary somewhere, the image has to be balanced, it is incomplete. The idea of being demands the presence within its undifferentiated mass of a kind of not-being stirring, a kind of infinitesimal point, a flickering tiny flame in the midst of the emptiness, something without any dimensions, with a position alone: all images of consciousness. And suddenly, across the gap between these complementary images, whole systems and patterns spring to life:

> This is not your home, intruder; you are in the world as the splinter is in the flesh, as the poacher is in his lord's forest: for the world is good; I created it in harmony with my will, and I am the Good. But you have sinned, and things accuse you with their petrified voices: the Good is everywhere, it is the pith of the elder tree, the coolness of the spring, the chip of the flint, the weight of the stone; it extends even to the nature of fire, of light, your own body betrays you, for it obeys my regulations. The Good is within you and outside of you: it enters you like a scythe, crushes you like a mountain, bears you and sweeps you forward like a sea; it is that which permitted the success of your evil undertaking, for it was the brightness of the candles, the

hardness of your sword, the strength of your arm. And this Evil of which you are so proud, which you claim to have invented, is nothing but a reflection of being, a hoax, a mirage whose very existence is maintained by the Good. Take thought, Orestes: the universe itself cries your fault, and you are a mite in the universe.[2]

All the hollow magnificence of this enormous voice, the decoration of its rhetorical periods, the solemn level at which it develops, are dependent on the opposition between being and not-being, which little by little takes on the character of a primordial dualism, reinforced by all the other oppositions, all the other possible names, good against evil, reality against imagination, space against time. And at this point in the development, the individual things, the catalogues, reappear, but with a wholly different emphasis. They are no longer almost personified, autonomous units; they are now merely the most obscure corners and facets, the most forgotten recesses, of a single undulating organism, Being itself. This shapeless and all-encompassing element gains in force as the individual particles are named, but there is no reciprocity, the objects become mere ephemeral manifestations, forms that appear for a moment and then unform to become kneaded into new shapes.

Thus the mere changing of a name results in a whole new system of images, a kind of dualistic mythology, that leaves its traces everywhere throughout the work. It is designed to interrupt the lived unity of everyday life, to suspend our constant involvement in things, in our projects and our bodies, our lack of distance from the world, and to make us see ourselves suddenly as separate, alien, threading our way among what we are not. Yet this mythology is strengthened by the existence of occasional moments in which that unity is not present, moments which can function not as a symbol of the dualism but as the concrete lived experience of it, moments when, in a kind of lull, our minds slip out of their extrications, and consciousness, idle and dream-like, stares across this new distance at an object which is not itself. The object fills the depths of the eyes as if it were Being itself, we are in a state of *fascination,* and in fascination

> the knower is nothing but pure negation, he can locate himself, recover himself nowhere, *he is not;* the only qualification which he can support is precisely that he *is not* the object of the fascination in question. In fascination there is nothing but a giant object in a vacant world. And yet the fascinated intuition is in no way *fusion* with the object. For the prerequisite of fascination is that the object appear in absolute relief against emptiness, in other words that I be the immediate negation of the object and nothing but that.[3]

But in this purest, most intense confrontation between consciousness and being, the relationship is so primordial as to be almost impossible to formulate: a pure negation, consciousness connected with being in that it is not being. Language, the very element of consciousness, is almost silenced by this thorough disconnection between consciousness and its objects. And yet in another sense language is the privileged agency for passing across the barrier, it is the ensemble of names that consciousness gives the things it is not. How then do the individual things, here and there penetrating the fabric of the work of art, manage to shed this radical otherness with which they are inflicted and become one with the substance of the language?

# CHAPTER FOUR

## The Satisfactions of Objects

What we ordinarily try to do to things is to own them; we domesticate a little part of the absolutely foreign world into which we happen by taking pieces of it and trying to turn them against the rest, trying to tame them and make them form a wall around us to protect us from their more terrifying counterparts in the world outside. We wear these possessions like clothing; they form a kind of intermediate substance between ourselves and that which is radically alien to us.

This relationship is not directly dependent on the economic organization from which the terminology is drawn; it is a reflection of our relationship with the world, with what we are not, and as such it can express our distance from the world, our place in it, without the literal sense of ownership:

> As for me, I already knew when I was seven years old that I was an exile; I let the smells and sounds, the noise of rain on the roofs, the rippling of light, all slip along my body and fall unused around me; I knew that they belonged to other people, and that I could never make *my* memories out of them.[1]

And yet this spiritualized kind of ownership is nonetheless strangely self-contradictory, for it has been turned against precisely those things which are never literally "owned," so that the notion of ownership here exercises a kind of autocriticism, removes from itself by the nature of the things it aims at that part of its meaning which is inappropriate. A kind of metaphor, it rises away from the economic structure from which it took its point of departure and cuts itself loose from that to which it had been compared, carrying off the name alone. The possessive adjective seems to slip in through the idea of memory, for our memories are "ours" somewhat as our possessions are. And yet this image of a possession through memory is the adornment of something even more basic; this is how Orestes would have "owned" the great palace door to which he is now a stranger:

> There I would have lived. . . . Ten thousand times by now I would have gone in and out of that door. As a child I would have played with its wings, I would have rammed myself against them, they would have groaned without yielding, my arms would have learned their resistance. Later on I would have pushed them open surreptitiously, at night, to go and look for girls. And even later, on the day I came of age, slaves would have thrown the door open wide and I would have crossed its sill on horseback. My old wooden door. I would be able to locate your lock with my eyes closed. I'm the one who would have made that scratch, down there, I might have done it by accident the day I got my first lance. *(He steps back)* It's sub-Dorian, isn't it? And what do you think of the incrustations of gold? I've seen things like this in Dodona: very fine workmanship. All right, this is what you wanted: it isn't

*my* palace, it isn't *my* door. And we don't belong here at all.[2]

Thus in so many different ways the door sheds its physical substance, its stubborn solidity, and entering the mind, becomes assimilated to the new element. Quantity seems to play a significant part in this process: the more different memories of the door Orestes accumulates, the more sure his possession of it will be; but this quantity is in reality subordinate to variety. Orestes approaches ownership of the door through the number of different uses to which he will have put it. And use is in fact the approach to and the very meaning of real possession: the wear caused by constant use is the threadbare patch rubbed onto the shiny new object as it gradually settles into the routine of our lives. The brand-new thing is still too anonymous, too mass-produced, for us to feel any familiarity with it; it is not until we have handled it, until we have broken it in in a kind of domestication ritual, that we feel it as ours.[3]

This is the truth of Orestes' speech, but there is also in it a kind of fiction. When Orestes does manage to make his mark upon the city and win a place in it through his crime, he does not stay, he refuses to enjoy the home he has made for himself; that which drove him to commit the crime seems in the doing of it to have abolished itself. But in a more subtle way he had no real advantages to reject. His speech on the door was the expression of a lack, and we are always most highly sensitive to the things which we are not or which we do not have; to them we respond with our whole being which lacks them: this is the basis of the myth of the artist as a social outcast. But it does not follow that when the lack has been abolished, there will be a corresponding kind of satisfaction: there may simply be no feeling at all, no trace of any kind, no scar where the painful incompleteness once was, and a new and unrelated need may surge in the midst of this void. Thus the whole feeling of possession is a curiously evanescent one, a kind of oblique secondary feeling that fades into thin air when we try to stare at it head-on:

> In one sense, I am enjoying my property when I transcend it in use, but if I want to contemplate it, the bond of possession vanishes, I can't even understand what it means to possess something. The pipe is on the table, independent, indifferent. I take it in my hands, I feel it, I contemplate it *in order to* realize this appropriation; but precisely because these gestures are designed to permit me to *enjoy* this appropriation, they fail, I have nothing but an inert piece of wood between my fingers. Only when I transcend my objects towards a use, when I utilize them, do I enjoy their possession.[4]

So the attempt to approach things through ownership gives way to a new assault on them through using them.

This development parallels very closely a kind of literary necessity. Even the most abstract sentences have to move in time, have to constitute an exchange of energy, no matter how weak, for the only absolutely static kind of language is the mere *naming* of something, the saying that it is and no more. Thus for a thing to be *described,* there has to be somewhere, latent in the thing itself, a kind of movement which the movement of the sentence can parallel and register. In the hands of clumsy or insensitive writers this movement inherent in the thing may remain wholly conventional; verbs of movement, faded almost to the point of colorlessness, exist in order to simplify matters: "The house *stands* behind the

trees, *is surrounded* by a hedge," etc. But even here the
fiction of movement must be maintained in order for
the sentence to come into being at all. Thus in literature,
as in physics, things have ceased to be mere static substances occupying some absolute position in space to become fields of energy, a locus of relationships. It is on this
that Sartre bases a kind of recipe for the reality, the solidity of books and the things in them:

> We have to plunge things into action: their density
> of being will vary directly for the reader with the
> multiplicity of practical relations they entertain
> with the characters of the book. Have your mountain
> climbed by the smuggler, by the customs man, by
> the partisan, have it flown over by the aviator, and
> the mountain will suddenly surge at the junction of
> these different actions, will leap out of your book
> like a jack-in-the-box.[5]

What is interesting in this piece of literary advice is
that it suggests a kind of planning of effects in which
the novel as a whole would be a construct or a machine
for causing certain reactions in the readers, as was the
well-made play and the novel of the nineteenth century;
and the little plot he proposes is equally suggestive of a
novel whose form would strike us as old-fashioned. And
yet it is certain that Sartre's novels are dense with the
texture of many solid things, and what is even more astonishing, that his plays are swarming and alive, not so
much with images and brilliant decoration, which are
not rare in the modern theater, but with real things,
dirty, everyday things with the sweat of use or the rust
of neglect on them. Only an uncommon relationship
with things could account for this sudden reality of the
mutely used stage props on the one hand, and for the

breaking through by objects of the trammel of purely inter-personal conversation on the other.

The philosophical language solves the problem of things by a solution through violence. Since the static thing proposes itself to us as an imperative, as the blue-print for a gesture or itself a kind of latent, frozen ges-ture, we simply include the gesture along with the name of the thing and link them with hyphens. Thus the word "pen" is a feeble and inadequate way of referring to the instrument lying before me; and its color, make, age, which would seem to describe it fairly thoroughly in the old sense of description, do not suffice to define it either. The special thing about this pen is that I rarely use it except to sign my name to letters written with some other instrument; this pen is therefore a pen-to-sign-my-name-with, just as this book, which has a name, special con-tents, and so forth, and which I rarely use, is most adequately circumscribed as a book-to-weigh-down-papers-with, rather than as a dictionary of synonyms. Thus little by little the world begins to lose its official, abstract face, where objects are defined by their intrinsic natures, and starts to order itself around me along the routes of my actions, approximating more and more the concrete world I live.

But it is obvious that this solution will not do for nar-ration: the philosophy described a world which we then recognized or did not recognize as our own, we stood out-side the book looking in at it. In narration, even first person narration, the human being is present inside the book along with things; it would not often be necessary to add the potential use, or gesture, to the thing itself: all the character would have to do would be to use it, before our eyes. So that the fullness of being of the objects is no longer dependent on special effects of language, but on the series of actions which the language narrates; and a cumulative building up of different uses of a single object, such as Sartre suggests in his formula, would hardly be a linguistic effect at all. Such things as the three-master which all day long slowly moves into the harbor in *Ulysses,* seen from different places at different times by different characters, are the result of an elaborate planification, not of some specialized capacity of the language itself.

And yet here and there in Sartre's work we find practical applications of the principle of a multiplicity of uses: in Orestes' speech on the door, for example. Suddenly, in the space of a few seconds, this papier-mâché stage prop struggles up through all the stages of being to emerge solid and tangible in front of us. In a speeding up process something like the movie sequences that permit us to watch a shoot breaking out of the ground and jerkily swelling to become a full plant, Orestes manages, without touching it, to make the door go through as many different kinds of uses as he can. But this is very different from the progression of effects which the formula foresaw: it is as if, out of the novel which his life might have been, Orestes had selected all the moments having to do with the door and had set them side by side so that we could take them all in at a glance. The formula is treated impatiently: if an accumulation of different uses is necessary, why not do it all at once and get it over with, profit immediately from the effect without building it as the old novelists would have done? The different uses of the door seem concrete enough, yet they begin to take on the quality of examples: each is made as individual, as striking and irreducible as possible, and yet they are mere exploitations of the abstract notion of use. The passage is therefore a kind of exercise in the comma form: the formula functions as a kind of center or "idea," and the actual speech becomes its development. Sartre's recipe, which seemed a holdover from forms now archaic, has been secretly modernized.

Yet these are isolated moments in the work; its objects can rarely be thus exhausted, and ordinarily they will merely suffer one use at a time, as the action dictates: a use which is more likely to be pure content than to depend on a specialized moment of language. We enjoy however other more static relationships to things than their simple use: we can merely perceive them, apprehend their qualities, and at this point language again becomes essential to formulate these perceptions, to underline those qualities which seem to us characteristic of the object, at the expense of others that we ignore. For just as a thing is not a stable substance, but a meeting place of different uses, so it is not the locus of permanent fixed qualities either. Every consciousness has a sensitivity to certain types of qualities, whether we experience them in disgust or in fascination. What someone else might be unaware of on an object is for us vivid and alive; our eyes are caught and linger at different points along the surface of the room, it turns into a pattern of high lights and zones of indifference which is uniquely ours. Such qualities that we perceive to the exclusion of others remain real properties of things; we do not project them on to the things, but we pay for our perception of those qualities which are most intense to us with the totality of ourselves, our tastes, our original choice of being. We are compromised by the qualities we perceive; they tell something both about the thing itself and about us. It is on the basis of this that Sartre's existential psychoanalysis develops its instruments. Enough information about the qualities to which people are sensitive gives us a kind of short-cut to the choice of being which can account for the way they conduct their lives. But in a literary work such information is dependent on those special moments in which a character is alone with things, stares at them, participates in a drama in which he is the only human partner:

> Madame Darbédat held a Turkish delight between her fingers. She lifted it with great care toward her lips and held her breath for fear that the fine powdered sugar with which it had been sprinkled would be scattered by her breathing. "It's rose-flavored," she thought. Brusquely she bit into the glazed tissue and a stagnant flavor filled her mouth. "It's curious how illness sharpens one's sensations." She began to think about mosques, about obsequious orientals (she had been in Algiers during her honeymoon) and a faint smile stirred on her pale lips: the Turkish delight was obsequious also.[6]

The subject of this story ("The Room") is the flight into illness of two of the characters in order to shelter themselves from the aggressiveness or insistence of their sexual partners. Pierre hides himself behind a world he has constructed and which he pretends to believe in, and society recognizes the distinctly anti-social nature of this conduct by applying the name and notion of psychosis to it. Mme. Darbédat on the other hand, who because of her sex has been able to occupy a non-productive position in society, is permitted a more socially acceptable issue: that of extreme hypochondria, pathological laziness, and asthenia. As her mind wanders along its languid course in this paragraph, the apparently accidental reference to the honeymoon functions as a reminder of the hidden dread at the center of her life; but nothing else in the passage has any direct connection with this drama. Delicately extracting the final savors from her sensations, she seems wholly absorbed in the object she holds in her hand. The activity is almost a poetic one, the final fixing by a single word of the secret essence of the object. This essence, the fragility of the thing (its powdered sugar menaced by a breath), the almost archaic debility of its tissue, the cloying and dusty, surreptitious quality of its taste, are qualities in the object itself; they circumscribe it exactly, you would not be able to project them into some other kind of sweet, into something strawberry, for example. But the small lifeless object is also the woman's chosen partner at that moment; its qualities are lovingly fondled and savored, it throws back a kind of reflection of her world, of the secret of her illness. Harmless, infinitely sensitive to her whims, the opposite of crude or overbearing, a mere burst of delicate sweetness, the object *is* obsequious: it caters without resistance to her secret gluttony, it is servile, overly satisfying, and without danger: in all these things a fit nature to replace her husband who is exactly the opposite. The object in this passage is being used; but its use is a special one, precisely that zone where use and awareness of qualities overlap, for its use is to be savored, tasted, its use *is* the perception of its qualities.

Human constructs are made to be used in certain ways; but the awareness of their qualities does not always coincide with the use:

> And Lucien was playing too, but after a while he couldn't remember what he was playing at. Pretending to be an orphan? Or to be Lucien? He looked at the decanter. There was a little red light dancing inside the water, and you would have sworn that papa's hand was in the decanter, enormous, luminous, with little black hairs on the fingers. Lucien suddenly had the impression that the decanter was playing also, pretending to be a decanter.[7]

The constructed thing is not only use, it is pure matter and its being overflows its simple purpose. This is what the surrealists exposed when they built ordinary looking household objects that seemed to insert themselves inconspicuously into the habits and the transparency of everyday life, and that then suddenly, weighing five times what we expected, tore through the comfortable daily pattern and affirmed themselves scandalously as pure matter (which we can think of as a kind of symbol of pure being). But even on trustworthy objects, the human purposes are not always visible: to someone outside the routines of normal society, to someone, for example, for whom a closed door has lost its ordinary function and becomes a barrier to be cracked open with tools, ordinarily comprehensible objects are merely stared at blankly, and Genet wonders "whether it is true that you drink out of a glass."[8] Thus all conventional objects have their masks, which can fall away, masks of familiarity, habit and conventional use: in this sense they "play at" being what they are. Here qualities and use become opposites.

But again the real qualities of the object are the sources of perception, and this passage is a kind of psychoanalysis of glass. Not any constructed object would be able to give Lucien the same feeling, although the staring at the decanter is also a moment of the staring at, the interest in, "things" in general. Glass is not easily labeled like other materials: under certain lightings we seem to be seeing its surface directly, and with a slight shift in perspective we lose the glass again, we find ourselves looking through it. But cut-glass or curved glass subverts the reality on the other side, magnifies it into grotesque and swollen shapes. It has a family likeness to mirrors and to water, it is a clearly visible medium and yet it is also difficult to fix in and for itself. What Lucien notices is how the glass decanter wavers between having an existence of its own and fading into the things around it, maliciously distorting them as it does so. The decanter seems uncertain just how real it is, just how opaque it ought to be, it suffers from the same lack of reality that bothers Lucien himself; and glass is a kind of figure for consciousness in that it cannot exist by itself but must show its surroundings through itself, just as consciousness is always consciousness *of* something. Yet the symbolic value of the glass is even more profound than this, for the development of the story shows us how Lucien moves from one image of himself to another, trying on each one as it is offered to him by the people of the outside world, attempting to fade into his background until he finally fits into the uniform designed for him by his class.

In such moments as this we glimpse a strange parallel, a kind of pre-established harmony between the two wholly separated realms of being. The qualities, the meanings of things are not exactly projected into them by human beings: this would result in the degraded and paper thin images it is customary to describe by the word "symbol," itself degraded and without much concrete relationship to the realities of works of art. These qualities, perceived by the characters, are also the real qualities of things: the things through this perception preserve all their solidity, their resistance. But as if by some kind of miracle, such things, radically other, whose very being is that which we are not, are human enough to reflect the human beings perceiving them: language, designed for human reality, adapts itself perfectly to those alien substances.

Only sometimes it does not:

> He went and sat down at the foot of the chestnut tree. He said "chestnut!" and he waited. But noth-

ing happened . . . "Chestnut tree!" It was shocking:
When Lucien said to his mother: "My own pretty
mother" she smiled, and when he called Germaine:
blunderbuss, Germaine had cried and complained
to mother. But when you said: chestnut, nothing
happened at all. He muttered with clenched teeth:
"lousy tree" and was uneasy, but as the tree did not
move, he repeated louder: "Lousy tree, lousy chestnut tree! You wait, just wait!" and he kicked it.
But the tree remained calm, calm—just as if it were
made of wood.[9]

The tree is very different from these bits of matter that
have been trained and shaped to fit into the practical
patterns of human life. By accident it does fit into them;
it is also an element of the landscape gardening which
completes houses, or it can lend its image to a painting
or be cut down and used for firewood or turned into
paper. But this use can be seen only in terms of the unity
of which it is a part. When the tree is stared at for itself
alone, it seems to have left behind it all traces of any
connection with human life except for one, the one
through which Lucien tries to reach it: its name. In the
continuing stillness of the tree Lucien thinks he sees a
stubbornness that irritates him; but this silence newly
charged with meaning is merely the result of Lucien's
naming, of his calling the tree, so that in a sense he has
been able to make the tree answer him—for silence is also
an answer, and the existence of the question immediately
changes things, gives everything, positive and negative,
satisfactory and frustrating, the sense of reply. The un-
translatable final pun shows the quality of this discovery
of Lucien's: *"en bois"* can describe an annoying wooden
impassiveness or inertia that characterizes some human
beings as it seems to characterize the tree's empty response. But the tree is also literally made of wood, the

"discovery" is short-circuited, a kind of shaggy dog story, a tautology. The silliness of the pun is a parody of the subjective event itself, where "something" happens even when nothing has changed, where the subjectivity (in this case the situation created by Lucien's questioning) permits something to happen even when "objectively" things are exactly as they were before.

It is at this moment of the progressive interest in things and their qualities that we approach an absolute situation: things have become more and more impoverished, they reply less and less to the subjectivities staring at them; at the end only the mere name remains as a link between human consciousness and the absolutely non-human. But Lucien is never able to experience the non-human directly; even the total silence, the radical otherness, of the non-human *becomes* human by the simple fact of the attention of human beings: the silence is humanized, somehow cannot preserve its discontinuity from human beings under the pressure of the human question. This experience is that of the impossibility of becoming aware of facticity directly: we sense the presence of facticity at the center of this silence, but just as in the older philosophy our perceptions circling like spotlights in pitch-darkness always came between us and things-in-themselves, so here the facticity is constantly mediated, assumed no matter how rapidly we turn our heads to catch a glimpse of it as it is. And the name is the last pitiful shred of language clinging to the thing, the last assumption of the totally non-human after the other kinds of assumptions, use, and the perception of qualities, fail.

Thus things only *seem* to stand in a perfect one-to-one reflection of subjectivity, and these passages, in which a thing is perceived, are only apparently more static, more subjective, than the moments of use. In use, there seemed to be two moments: that of the static object, which gave the impression of self-sufficiency, of merely persevering in being what it was, a kind of image of facticity; and the second moment in which this facticity was assumed through using the thing, and which, returning on the first moment, showed that even the static thing had been a thing-to-be-used, a frozen human act potentially dynamic. Now that we have arrived at a kind of zero point of perception, in which the thing resists and refuses even that last thread-like attachment to language of the word that attempted to name it, it becomes apparent that perception has within itself a facticity far more profound and stubborn than the act of using instruments already shaped to fit into the use we make of them. It is in the moment of staring at the decanter, rather than pouring from it, that we begin to be troubled by a zone of being in it that escapes us. The reflection of subjectivity on the thing, the manner in which a subjectivity betrays its secrets through an apparently objective perceiving of a thing outside it, is possible because this facticity can never be directly apprehended, because it must be *assumed* by consciousness and thus immediately compromises the viewer and reflects him back. In such passages it is the language expressing the perception and its discoveries which is the mode of assumption of the object; here the object is also used, but by the sentences that circle around it and construct it for us; and the movement is not so much in the act of perception, the static sitting in front of the object, but in the language itself which formulates the slow revealing of the qualities of the mute thing.

Yet if all language is a way of "using" things, of assuming their facticity, then what we have said about it does not seem to stand in any privileged relationship to Sartre's practice as a novelist, in spite of his awareness of the split between consciousness and things, and his development of the notion of facticity and assumption. But just as earlier the awareness of the general law about presenting objects through as many different uses as possible was transformed into a personal solution, so here the result of this power of language to assume things, construct them, make them into both a reflection of the subjectivity that assumes them and an impossible, persisting area of resistance, is the appearance in the work of art of just such moments where the characters stare at and are interested in things simply because they are things. It is not enough to know that all things surging in the language of the novel will automatically be assumed through that language: there is a doubling, and this assumption of things through qualities and their formulation becomes itself a subject for the novel, itself content, itself an event.

# CHAPTER FIVE

## *Transformations*

At a time when things were still fairly stable substances, when they had a static "nature" of their own that was quite distinct from the impressions and perceptions we saw them through, certain kinds of experiences were impossible. If a writer, no matter how acutely sensitive to the surfaces of things and the subtleties of the world, labels his descriptions "impressions" or through his manner and his syntax insists on the personal, the "subjective," the relative quality of these experiences, their presentation, no matter how vigorous or extensive, has been secretly vitiated: they are decoration, a lovely screen, mere play, they have an odor of aestheticism about them and the futility of merely beautiful words.

But the advantages of a new category of things are not only literary, they are in a way hygienic as well. The changing of a category does not change any single detail in the world: it remains as before full of the same objects, the same half-conscious swarming feelings, the same implicit awareness and inexpressed ways of seeing the objects. But in the earlier world these feelings were all rigorously "subjective," locked up inside our minds, invented in the chambers of our minds and only then projected out onto things to freshen them up. This first

world has some of the grayness which has been attributed
to the Cartesian world, where only extension was real,
and where the sensations we picked up through our various senses were nothing but a kaleidoscopic mirage playing on a blank and colorless substratum. In such a world
our daily feelings lose their importance, they are "subjective," are nothing but the twitchings of our several
senses; we pay no attention to them and our lives develop
some of the desiccation that characterizes the only reality
we recognize.

But when these sensations, these merely subjective
impressions are felt as "real" perceptions of real things,
even when nothing new has been noticed and no growth
in attention or sensitivity has taken place, the change is
felt as something far more intense than a mere change of
theories. This change in our distance from reality is the
same as a change in the way we think of consciousness:
what Husserl called the "intentionality" of consciousness, the idea that consciousness is a nothingness that
discovers everything outside of itself, in the things themselves, suddenly alters unrecognizably the texture of the
world. We can sense some of the excitement of such a
change in the pages that in attacking the old "digestive"
theory of perception outline Husserl's discovery:

> Don't you recognize in this description your own
> requirements, your own forebodings? You knew that
> the tree was not yourselves, that you could not make
> it enter your somber stomachs, and that knowledge
> could not without dishonesty be compared to pos-
> session. And at the same time consciousness is puri-
> fied, clear as a high wind, there is nothing left inside,
> only a constant movement out, a constant slipping
> away from itself . . . And now imagine a perpetual
> series of little explosions that tear us away from our-

selves, not even allowing time enough for an " ourselves" to form behind them, constantly hurling us
further ahead into the dry dust of the world, on the
harsh earth, among things; try to think of us as thus
flung out, abandoned by our very natures to a world
indifferent, hostile, uncooperative; and you will
have understood the full implications of the discovery that Husserl expresses in the famous sentence: "Every consciousness is consciousness *of*
something."[1]

Not only the tone but the very ambition of this essay
would have been inconceivable in the framework of the
older idea-world: at a time when real things were separate from the ideas we had of them, when our sensations
formed and dissolved without ever really having anything to do with things themselves, the replacement of
one epistemological theory by another is an event of only
limited importance, merely another page in the development of a specialized science; and it is no accident that
the period during which philosophy occupied itself almost exclusively with epistemology and with the categories of a kind of digestive perception of things, is also
the period when it had the least influence in human
affairs.

But now suddenly something happens. The world
that seemed empty suddenly seen through these new
lenses proves to be swarming with stirrings of all kinds,
sudden juxtapositions of colors and things, variations in
light, a perpetual instability where a face or an object
loses its identity and fades even before our horror has
had time to form into the unexpected and the unjustifiable. The world becomes open again, but in a new way:
not in the very early sense of huge geographical areas
into which the individual could escape, nor that of a

sudden social mobility that permitted access to buildings, the interiors of which were unimaginable, and to
groups of people whose luxurious customs had hardly
been visible before in the daily world. In our time these
issues that the frontiers or the fascination of other classes
provided are closed off, and a massive appearance of permanence restricts not only the development of individual
destinies but even the mobility of ideas and the spontaneity of our language. But just as stoicism, abandoning
any attempt to shake the solid facts of the prison, released the mind to circle in a kind of abstract freedom,
so here a kind of freedom is found among the unshakable
facts—a freedom in the facts themselves, an instability
in their appearances, a kind of second-best intoxication
offered by things themselves as a compensation for their
stubborn perseverance. So the most joyless visions are
defrauded by a secret exuberance of art:

> Brunet walked quietly along . . . He raised his head,
> looked at tarnished gilt lettering attached to a bal-
> cony; war broke out: it was there, within this lu-
> minous inconsistency, inscribed like an inescapable
> fact on the walls of the beautiful, breakable city; it
> was a motionless explosion that tore the rue Royale
> in two; people wandered through it without seeing
> it; Brunet saw it. It had always been there, but
> people didn't know that yet. Brunet had thought:
> "The sky is going to fall on our heads." And every-
> thing had begun to fall, he had seen the houses as
> they really were: arrested precipitations downward.
> This graceful shop supported tons of stone and each
> stone, fastened in among the others, had been fall-
> ing at the same point in space, obstinately, for fifty
> years; a few pounds more and the fall would set in
> again; the columns would bend out quivering and

they would fracture, horribly, in splintered stumps; the windowpane would burst; great loads of stone would drop down into the cellar crushing the bales of merchandise. They have eight-thousand pound bombs. Brunet felt sick: only a moment ago, on these symmetrical façades, a human smile had mingled with the gold dust of the evening. It was now extinguished: nothing but two hundred thousand pounds of stone; people were wandering among stabilized avalanches. Soldiers among ruins, maybe he'll be killed. He saw soiled furrows on the plastered cheeks of Zézette. Dusty walls, free-standing portions of walls with large gaping openings and pieces of blue or yellow wallpaper in places and leprous patches; red tiles among the debris, flagstones disjoined by weeds. Then wooden huts, encampments. And afterwards they would build great monotonous barracks like those on the outer boulevards. Brunet felt a sudden distress: "I love Paris," he thought with anxiety. And then the inescapable fact all at once disappeared and the city closed in again around him.[2]

The informing center of the passage is the definition of buildings as piles of stones pressing downwards, a pressure that has lasted fifty years and which cannot be detected except through scientific analysis or through the sudden inversion of the image: the downward hurtling stones frozen as if photographically into an ensemble accidentally gracious, masses of rock forming at a single point along their trajectory the rue Royale. There is a purely formal, a modern excitement in such an image: the construction of motion out of static parts like the "Nude Descending the Staircase," the artificial acceleration or sudden immobility of the movies. The motion

required in the description is discovered in the things
themselves, intrinsic; as in one of the Gestalt images we
merely alter our focus to see it. But once this premise is
given and explored, the form bursts, new conclusions
are drawn. We are given the fall in speed-up form so
that we can see it and then it really takes place, and we
are beyond the limits of the present, leaving the sense
data behind us; we see the waste of Paris destroyed, the
huts in its place, and the slight flick of the thumb that set
the motion going eventually pulls some of the future into
view along with it. And having thus stretched its life-
lines out too far, having entered the realm of the purely
imaginary, the vision begins to lose its obsessive power
and suddenly expires.

These sudden and unexpected transformations of the
whole world, like the perception of isolated things, compromise their witnesses: they are not gratuitous spasms,
they are ways certain subjectivities live the world. Like
the perceptions of things, they can be read in two different directions: they can tell us about the things themselves and their structures, or they can tell us about the
situation and the condition of the subjectivity who experiences them. In this moment Brunet suddenly manages to take the threat of war seriously. He had known
it would come, he had even been certain of it, and as a
communist, seeing in the war the promise of a kind of
autodestruction of capitalism, he lived in expectation of
it. Sartre has spoken of the way emotion, to strengthen
itself, to ratify the merely mental reaction with the solidity of the flesh, fills itself out with physical concomitants,
such as blushing, trembling, cold sweat: these are the
moments of "seriousness" in real emotion.[3] So in this
passage, as in the moments of belief which we discussed
in an earlier chapter, there is a distinction between the
thing merely thought, merely known, and the knowledge

of it that fills your whole being like an inescapable fact: the blinding realization of "really knowing" which the French describe with the word *"l'évidence."* Such a distinction obviously tends to devalue the purely epistemological problems that dominated nineteenth-century philosophy, and as we have already seen, the value that Sartre places on Husserl's revolution is that it converts knowledge from a purely mental act to a relationship of being, a coming into contact of two wholly different structures of being. So here Brunet does not merely "know" with one part of himself, he is suddenly transfixed by a tangible knowledge, and one that has to propose itself as true: "He had seen the houses *as they really were."* The violence of this burst of knowledge is necessary to break through an appearance that had become solidified over the years of peace: war "had always been there, but people didn't know that yet." The peaceful city that people think they live in is a kind of mystification. They are alienated from the nature of the city as something constructed, and destructible, by man; they live this historical moment in the development of the city as something as "natural" as a forest or a sunset. Thus only the most extreme of literary procedures are able to take these accepted surfaces of things and turn them into what they really are by shattering the habits through which we see them, in that tearing away of the veils of ordinary perception that Brecht called the *Verfremdungseffekt:* the revelation of the historical nature of something thought of as permanent and changeless. This insistence on the passage from an appearance to a reality, the necessity for the second term of the transformation to be *true,* is reflected in the frequency with which such expressions as "looking things in the face," and "things as they really are," recur again and again throughout the work. But the social and historical meaning of such a transfor-

mation has its parallel in an artistic necessity, for the
truth of the transformation serves also as a constant
check against merely aesthetic play, against the gratui-
tousness of these spontaneously developing forms, against
perceptions that would be merely decorative.

But in order to feel that fact with such intensity, Brunet has to feel it too much. Having generated this transformation out of his whole being, having paid the price
of feeling it with himself, he is no longer at liberty to
stand back and watch the spectacle with indifference, disinterested. He is compromised; a little area of not yet
extinguished nationalistic feeling begins to throb in this
mind that had wanted itself rational and supranational:

> Brunet stopped; he felt a craven sweetness in him-
> self and thought: "If there only would not be a war!
> If there could only not be a war!" And he stared
> passionately at the great gateways, at the gleaming
> shopwindow of Driscoll's, at the royal blue hangings
> of the Brasserie Weber. And after a moment he
> was ashamed; he began walking again, he thought:
> "I love Paris too much."[4]

The moment of transformation has called all of Brunet,
his very being and his life's work, into question.

Such moments have the artistic advantage of preserving the surface of the novel intact. In the recording of
mere impressions of things we constantly shuttle back
and forth between the colorless but real facts of things
and the rich elaboration they undergo on a purely subjective level. Here everything is equally real: the cat-
aclysm is as real as the calm architecture that preceded it.
Although this work follows by many years the movements
bearing that name, such moments may properly be called
*expressionistic,* and the passage from mere impressions to
such an expressionism is like the passage from the simile

to the metaphor (although the earlier uses of the metaphor are still hardly distinct from similes; they leave the "like" out but we experience them, and are supposed to experience them, as comparisons, only much more rapid and elliptical ones). And where the word "like" loses force, the verb "to be" gains staggeringly in impact, becoming a strong transitive verb: anger is not a reality parallel to redness of the face, not like it on another plane, it *is* precisely the shortness of breath, the rapid beating of the heart, etc. A colon form is present in which a series of approximations and distinctions, one-sided, imperfect, incomplete, struggle up toward the point at which they can be replaced by an affirmation. And the small almost inconspicuous verb is strengthened with italics, with adverbs, with the preceding negative qualifications that prepare it, so that when it comes we will feel the new force with which it can operate. This solution, functioning mostly in the philosophical works, is based perhaps on a forcing of the language, on the special emphasis given by the throat to the single weakened syllable; but its results in the work of art are precisely the kind of subjective event which we have already outlined: the raising of the merely subjective, of the change inside the mind that does not alter the "outside world," to the dignity of being, real being in itself. In the transformation of Paris, the city has merely been turned into what it already is, but this somewhat formal rectification has taken place in a burst of flame.

But the thing has to be turned into what it is, and this literature of transformations is an urban literature: the city is the place par excellence of these modern metamorphoses. The city is the ensemble of all the man-made objects which tended, as we saw in the last chapter, to shuttle back and forth between their uses and their material, their pure being, their apparently superfluous qualities. Unlike the individual objects of which it is composed, the city does not reflect merely a single human act, a single use, but all uses, all acts, all of human culture and human possibilities. Cities, in both Christian and communist eschatology, are the images of absolutes in human life, absolutes of either corruption or perfection. And in the private myths which writers of Western culture have invented to express, through their individual isolation, a generalized reality and truth, the city is like a man, *is* an Everyman. Among the many other things which *Nausea* is, satire, philosophical novel, rectification of the adventure novels of the nineteen-twenties, it is also the book of a city: Bouville is one of the main characters, a grotesque image of the absurdities of traditional bourgeois life; and the novel follows the city like a map. All of these different meanings of the city are so many terms into which it can be transformed; and since it is never wholly and concretely before us, since we always apprehend it through fragmentary parts of it that confront us in the present, in choosing the whole to which these parts and partial views belong, against the background of which they surge, we are also, by implication, choosing ourselves:

> First night of the war. No, not quite. There were still many lights attached to the sides of the houses. In a month, in two weeks, the first alert would blow them out; this was only the dress rehearsal. But even so Paris had lost its ceiling of fluffy pink. For the first time Mathieu saw a great somber haze suspended over the city: the sky. The sky of Juan-les-Pins, of Toulouse, Dijon, Amiens, the very same sky for country and town, for all of France. Mathieu stopped, raised his head, and looked at it. A sky that could have been anywhere, with no special con-

cessions for anything underneath. And beneath this
great equivalence, myself: anybody. Anybody, any-
where: a state of war. He focussed on a pool of light
and repeated, to see what would happen: "Paris,
boulevard Raspail." But these luxury names had
also been mobilized, they seemed to have been lifted
off a strategic map, or out of a news bulletin. There
was nothing left at all of the boulevard Raspail.
Routes, nothing but routes running from south to
north, from west to east; routes with numbers for
names. From time to time they paved them for a
mile or two, houses and sidewalks surged around
them out of the ground, and you called that a street,
or an avenue, or a boulevard. But it was never really
anything but a segment of a route; Mathieu was
walking, facing the Belgian frontier, along a stretch
of departmental route that had branched off National Highway 14. He turned down the direct and
manoeuverable road prolonging the railways of the
Compagnie de l'Ouest, formerly known as the rue
de Rennes. . . . Alongside this road, beneath the undifferentiated sky, the houses had been reduced to
their most primitive function: they were nothing
but registered dwelling areas. Dormitory-refectories
for potential draftees, for the families of those already drafted. And you could already sense their ultimate roles: they would become "strategic points,"
and then finally targets. So now they could destroy
Paris if they wanted to: it was already dead. A new
world was coming to birth: the austere, practical
world of instruments.[5]

This map-like world is the strict correlative of the Mathieu who has become a war statistic, a number, one
of the so-many-thousand French soldiers mobilized in

1938: his anonymity spreads through the landscape like a disease germ, infecting thing after thing in ever widening circles. First the sky goes out, then the little signs that hold up the names of the streets, the streets themselves, the houses, all of Paris. Paris outlives itself, surviving as a mere paved area not different in kind from the stretches of uninhabited road all over France, a mere thickening of the network of roads toward the center of the map. The image overflows the limits of sense perception, strengthens itself by enlarging itself to include the indeterminate that surrounds it and to the level of which the Paris beneath Mathieu's eyes is degraded. And then Mathieu walks a few steps in this new world, tries it out, and we are given a few sentences to show what it feels like: "He walked along a stretch of departmental highway . . ." But this sudden shrinking of the city into what it "really is," this shriveling and sudden dessication is a dehumanization in tone only. All the gracious, the most "human" qualities of the city are gone like a mirage, mere instrumentality remains, and yet instrumentality is in another sense the most human relationship of all to things: the rock that some early man seized to break something with or to loosen the tough earth was immediately transformed, became human, an extension of his hand, with its former being only clinging to it in those rough edges of its form that had not been adapted to their present purpose. The desolation of this change lies not in the nature of instrumentality but in the purposeless deployment of all the elaborate purpose which is war, an instrumental complex of the most elaborate kind which seems to develop gratuitously, feeding on and destroying itself without production, a kind of nightmarish parody of the complicated instrumental structure of industrial society.

We get mere glimpses in this passage of the term limit

of the transformation, of the ultimate underlying reality beyond which it cannot go, of the inhuman pure being which man-made things can show behind their final mask. This is the sky that no longer responds to the great complexes of buildings, or the farms, or the deserted areas beneath it, no longer an area and a special shade of color as familiar as the landscape itself but an emptiness, a gaping hole over our heads. And it is the monotonous earth suggested beneath the great stretches of roads and the sudden agglutinations of houses that had been known as cities: these lose their identity, becoming mere appearance. The single reality of the dirt beneath them makes everything equivalent, cities, country roads, all mere superficial forms darkened by the background that shows through them.

This last opposite into which the city threatens to fade is not exactly Nature. Nature is in some ways as human as the city, the rise of the city brings it into being around and outside of it; it is a conventionalized way of assuming an organic landscape, of humanizing it through the category of natural beauty, or in our day, in an even more symbolic ritual, through photography. And insofar as in densely populated countries this Nature has already been assumed and humanized through the work of farmers, insofar as it has become as utilitarian a construct as the city itself, even the apparently disinterested contemplation of "Nature" is the result of a transformation:

> At a given date the society of cities unwinds, and plays at disintegration; its members journey out into the countrysides, where, beneath the ironic gaze of the workmen, they are temporarily transformed into pure consumers. It is then that Nature appears. What is Nature? Merely the external world when we have ceased to have a technical relationship

to its things . . . reality becomes a décor; the righteous man is on a country holiday, he is *there,* simply
*there* without doing anything, in the middle of the
fields and the cattle; reciprocally the fields and the
cattle reveal merely their *being-there* to him. This
is what he considers coming face to face with life
and matter in their absolute reality. For a city-dweller to experience Nature, a departmental road between two potato fields is sufficient. Engineers laid
this road out, farmers cultivated the fields; but the
city-dweller cannot see the cultivation, that type
of work is foreign to him: he imagines that he has
glimpsed vegetables in a state of nature and minerals
untrammeled; and if a peasant happens to wander
across the field, he gets turned into a kind of vege-
table as well. Thus Nature appears on the horizon
of the seasonal or weekly variations in our society;
it reflects back to the righteous their fictive disintegration, their temporary idleness, in short, their
holidays with pay. They wander through the under-
brush as through the humid and tender soul of the
child they once were; they stare at the poplars, the
plane trees that have been planted along the road,
they have nothing to say about them since they have
no practical relationship with them, and they gape
at the marvelous quality of the silence: if they seek
Nature in the outside world, it is the better to reach
it within themselves: the tranquil growth of the
shrubbery offers them the image of a blind and certain finality; it convinces them that life in society
is merely a surface agitation: there is an order of
instincts which is basically no different from the
order of nature and which you find within yourself
when you surrender yourself to a gentle, mute swoon
before vegetation. But even childhood is social, and

the powerful natural instincts which the vacationers seek within themselves symbolize the legitimacy of their birth. The natural order they find both outside and inside themselves is simply the order of society. Nature is a social myth, the solitary enjoyment of one's self in Nature is a ritual moment of life in society; the sky, the water, the vegetation merely reflect back to the righteous the image of their untroubled conscience and their prejudices.[6]

The tone of this passage is partly dictated by its expository nature, but partly by the nature of the subject itself; for once, we witness a transformation in which the second term is not "true," in which the final result is not "things as they really are": an inauthentic transformation, a kind of running backwards of the process in which all the important elements are still present—the objective structure of things which reflects back the subjectivity of its witness. But we stand outside this subjectivity, with a certain cruel detachment we watch the insipid rapture of the city dwellers, unintoxicated we are able to judge the poverty of a moment green and magical to the people inside it. The transformation is a transformation for us alone: we alone are able to see the other term, the fields and the road "as they really are," products and reflections of human work. For the vacationers there is no moment of passage from one appearance to another; Nature surrounds them as a stable and persevering entity.

It is harder to get behind this Nature than it is to disperse the comforting appearance of the city: the simple juxtaposition of the constructed forms, "out of nature," with the inhuman backdrop upon which they surge was enough to shatter them appreciably. But although a plant may not be a natural object but the product of thousands of years of experimentation and gradual development, this sudden change in the plant, its suddenly human and constructed nature, is not the result of the passage from one sensory vision to another, but of the pressure of abstract knowledge which suddenly puts distance between us and what we see, like a description of ordinary daily objects in bizarre Latinate terms. These linguistic or intellectual shocks are ways of suddenly making us see the object again, new, yet they take place on the level of vocabulary, they are not so much the presentation of a sudden convulsion of the object into something else as they are direct challenges to our habits of language.

For the ultimate transformation of natural things is dependent on our habitual distance from them. The astonishing remark of Sartre, "they have nothing to say about the trees since they have no practical relationship with them, since they *do* nothing with them," a conception of the relationship between language and its subject matter which ultimately governs even the most rarefied literary languages and the development of the most specialized perceptions, here permits us to judge the extent of our normal perception of things in nature and of our language about them as well. The last linguistic contact which we can have with the things we do not use is the simple naming of them. Lucien named a tree and then looked at it, and in this most simplified relationship to things the sensory qualities which we may notice about the object suddenly come loose from the name, reveal themselves as brute sensation, unrelated to any words. The description of the tree root in *Nausea* is well known; but I am not sure whether this description would be able to convey anything at all if we had not ourselves just once *seen* the grotesque, the obscene quality of the roots of trees as they motionlessly disappear into the flat ground. There is a unique, historical experience which seems to oppose itself to the words with which we try to describe and convey it, a concrete perception which the words serve to recall, but which they could never "present" if it were not already known beforehand. So that the language seems headed for a kind of failure:

> This long dead serpent at my feet, serpent of wood. Serpent or claw or root or vulture's talon, no matter . . . this big gnarled paw . . . this tough and compact sealskin . . . a little black pool at my feet . . . Was I supposed to think of it as a voracious claw, tearing at the earth, wrenching loose its sustenance?[7]

The figures circle around the central reality, each abolishing its predecessor but not more complete than it had been. The succession of autonomous metaphors creates an empty space where the reality they glance off perseveres, unexpressed but outlined. There is no attempt to fix the thing durably in language; language is not supposed to be a total substitute for things, and its whole structure begins to break apart when the most basic power of evocation, the last rock-bottom of words and names, crumbles: "In vain I repeated: 'It's a root'—it wouldn't *take* any longer."[8] Now not even adjectives work any more: the unitary nature of the single words is wrong, the thing's qualities are not divisible like this, in small units, the object begins to slip away from all language altogether:

> Suspect: that's what all these sounds and odors and tastes were. When they sprinted rapidly in front of you like flushed hares, when you didn't pay too much attention to them, you were still able to find them simple and reassuring, still able to believe that there was a real blue in the world, real red, such a thing as a real almond smell or the smell of violet. But when you looked a little more carefully, the feel-

ing of comfort and security began to give way to a
kind of malaise: the colors, tastes, and smells were
never real, never wholly themselves and nothing but
themselves. The simplest, most indivisible quality
was always more than it should have been, excessive
to its very core. That black there, beside my foot, did
not seem to be black, it was more like a confused attempt at imagining black on the part of someone
who had never seen it and who couldn't moderate
his imagination, who imagined an ambiguous being
that overflowed mere color.[9]

We find ourselves almost back at our starting point, face
to face with a being so absolutely different from consciousness that it will not go into words, that language
slips and slides across its surface without gripping it: in
the moment of nausea things have turned into their
final reality, radical otherness.

The only difference is that the thing, the root, *has*
been presented, it has entered language, somehow, by
some detour, has even achieved the status of a famous
set piece. The mystics discovered that a language could
be constructed out of its own ruins, and that God, the
most stubbornly inexpressible entity, could at least be
circumscribed by negation, the "not this, not that." The
root has the advantage over God of being more tangible,
but its presentation is just as negative. Instead of steering
for a direct success, of taking the inadequate linguistic
instrument at his disposal and tightening it and working
it over until by some miracle the thing managed to be
fixed permanently in words, instead of trusting implicitly
in the powers of pure invention the way the earlier experimenters would have done, the writer seizes an indirection. He permits this language to show its failure from
the very beginning, reveals generously the collapse of all

the onesided imperfect formulations of the thing, moves in on the inexpressible with a host of partial approaches that in the end cause an absence to rise in front of our eyes. The unattainable object *is* this absence, it is there, solid, behind the veils of language. In being shown how everything that can be said about the thing is wrong, imperfect, we manage to reach the thing itself.

But the root is a mere individual thing, it stands in relationship to all of "things," to their inhuman being, as a kind of example to an abstract idea. The ingenious solution which caused the root to surge into literature before our eyes is out of the question when we approach pure being itself. We have already seen how this unitary category was able, with the help of an opposite, to provoke a whole system of images, a kind of myth. Without its opposite however it is as colorless and inaccessible as the pure nothingness which is its complement and equivalent, according to Hegel. We remember the three skimpy sentences of *Being and Not-Being* which proved to be all that language could express about this vast entity: "Being is. Being is in itself. Being is what it is."[10] The impotence of language seems again complete. The subjective correlative of the experience of being, the nausea that Roquentin experiences before it, is not enough to do the work of a presentation: the mere description of such reactions, the shying away from any attempt on the thing itself, would leave us once more in the middle of impressionism.

But being "is" also, as we have seen, *things*. The empty place of being suddenly begins to fill up with a host of indistinct forms, swarming, nodding, pressed thickly in against each other, yielding and surging; suddenly language has its subject matter back: "All things gently, tenderly, surrendered themselves to existence like tired women giving way to laughter and saying with moist voices: 'It does you good to laugh,' they sprawled out in front of each other, abjectly confessing to each other their own existence.''[11] The individual objects had come to assume human meanings; preserving their stasis, their facticity, their unattainable core of being, they had been used, put in motion, assimilated into language and subjectivity to the point of reflecting a subjectivity. Now there are no more meanings: meanings are human; the coming face to face with pure being is the discovery of that "something" which escapes all subjectivity, all language. And yet at this ultimate tension of language, when it reaches out for the absolutely other, the absolutely inexpressible, with a whirring like the Hegelian dialectic turning about into its opposite, this language that wants itself inhuman suddenly swerves into the human-to-the-point-of-obscenity.

This is the climax of the presentation of things. Here the final transfer by which things get into language at all becomes apparent: in themselves mute, stubborn, inaccessible, they have to be smuggled in through a process of humanization, they have to be rendered in the language of that which absolutely they are not, of consciousness. The point of this is not the obvious one of anthropomorphism:

> They didn't *want* to exist, only they couldn't help themselves, that's all. So they all went quietly and unenthusiastically on with business as usual; the sap rose slowly, halfheartedly, through the canals, and the roots slowly pushed into the ground. But at every instant they looked as if they were going to just give up and stop existing. Tired and old, they went on existing against their own will simply because they were too weak to die, because death could only come to them from the outside.[12]

The objects in question are in fact living organisms, so that the attribution of feelings to them runs along a channel already partially hollowed out; but we have only to recall the inorganic objects of *The Wall* that seemed to have "moved back, keeping their distance, discreetly, like people talking beside a deathbed," to see that this humanization is not dependent on any life-likeness in things themselves.

Sometimes the most subtle formulations are the most dangerous: they approach the essence of the object so closely that we swallow them whole, and with them the slight deformations of the object that they may imply; rather than attempt to shade off the color of the root, qualify it until it seems a perfect fit for the object, and thereby imply that such things as colors exist at all in a kind of pure state in nature, the entire category has been abandoned. So here the extreme humanization of things is the one formulation of them which will not falsify them: we know that they are not human, that they are the absolutely non-human, and the terms are sufficiently exaggerated for us to make no mistake about it. If all language is an assumption of objects, if all language is a kind of humanization, then the only safe formulation is one that pushes the humanization to absurd lengths, that labels and announces itself so blatantly a falsification that it can do no harm, and that behind it, behind this terrifying suddenly human mask, the inhuman being of things makes its presence felt. It is obvious that this literary solution, and the problem to which it was a response, are both dependent on the radical split of the world into two parts: only in a world where things were so divorced from consciousness and from its language would it be necessary for them to leap into their opposite to be presented; only in a world where language is an inevitable humanization of brute facticity would that facticity have to come to light deviously behind a too human expression of it.

But just as obviously, language stands in a more privileged relationship to consciousness itself, and it remains now to be seen whether its description of human reality can take place more naturally, without being affected by the mythical opposition that seemed to set things out of reach.

PART THREE

*Human Reality*

The most privileged manifestation of consciousness is the *cogito,* one of those rare and specialized thoughts that enjoys the luxury of a name. In the cogito consciousness is still consciousness *of* some object outside it, but at the same time is sudden blinding consciousness of itself. This is therefore the point where consciousness approaches the closest to self-sufficiency, to identity with itself, to a state in which it might "be." The cogito is thought reflecting on itself, but it is a pure kind of reflection: our self-consciousness suddenly illuminates all the shadowy corners of our minds, reveals for once exactly what we think, unlike some other kinds of reflection which are designed to shelter an unexpressed intention behind them and to make us think that a certain motive is complete in itself, our whole thought. The cogito is therefore a possibility of perpetually checking ourselves; and Sartre's philosophy, which is undoubtedly a reply to and a completion of Heidegger, a rectification of him and inconceivable without him (a relationship which almost all philosophical works entertain with their immediate philosophical past), differs from its rather oracular predecessor in that he insists on the relating of every individual detail to consciousness, on the submitting of these details to the surveillance of the cogito. The fact from which we have to start is the fact of our unique, individual, isolated consciousness; we cannot leap to a thought as large as the world itself and forget that this great entity is mediated through our own subjectivity.

But the cogito itself is a possibility which is based on a more profound structure of our consciousness; it could only take place if at all times there functioned what

Sartre calls a pre-reflexive cogito, a self-consciousness always capable of becoming reflected and thematized by the
official cogito but which was not itself reflection. What
this means is simply that even within action itself, in the
midst of a project where our consciousness is at one with
things, there must still persist a kind of self-consciousness
or we would be faced in these moments of action with a
consciousness which was not conscious. And yet this more
fundamental self-consciousness is in no way the kind of
pause in action which real reflection represents; nor is it
the kind of slyly divided consciousness where we act and
at the same time watch ourselves act out of the corner
of our eye. We are always conscious of ourselves and of
our acts and intentions; but we do not always *know* them.
Thematized knowledge is the result of reflection, and
the passage from consciousness of ourselves to knowledge
of ourselves is not always sure. We are always conscious
of the secret intentions of our acts but we do not always
want to "admit" them to ourselves: when we come to
think of them, to reflect them, with the consent of our
continuing consciousness of ourselves, we leave those
portions out; our reflection is impure, we have deceived
ourselves, although we are always conscious, in this curious subterranean consciousness of ourselves, of doing
so. It is through this structure of consciousness that Sartre
is able to account for the facts and discoveries of psychoanalysis without resorting to the inadmissible hypothesis
of an unconscious: the hypothesis is no longer necessary,
and nothing essential has been abandoned when it has
been abandoned. Even psychoanalytic treatment, which
seemed to be the bringing to light of buried motives and
complexes, remains a process of discovery; it is one long
attempt to perform a cogito, to find out what it is we
have been secretly thinking all along, and to thematize
those hidden reasons for our acts which we must have

been conscious of in some manner in order to perform
them.

These forms of consciousness are not only at the very
starting point of the philosophical study, not only the
fundamental structure in which all more complex
thought will develop; they are also at a kind of ultimate
point of language itself. The cogito, for example, sets
going a kind of complicated dialectic of naming. It has
to be named because it does not really have content and
cannot be described: the "I think therefore I am" formula is someone's attempt to put into words what in itself is not a set of words but a wordless "realization": a
sudden consciousness of ourselves so immediate that it is
too fast for words, so empty (except for its content which
would change every time it was performed) that there is
no matter for the words to seize on. To use another description, like "consciousness in its purest state," would
be to repeat the naming while losing the essential of the
process which is to separate this moment off from all
others, to insist on its absolutely unique character. But
with a name, the cogito becomes a historical experience:
something that Descartes had, that other people have had
from time to time, something recalcitrant to words but
even datable. The descriptions do not help us, and now
when the cogito happens inside our heads we cannot be
sure that it is really the same experience that took place
at certain times inside the heads of these philosophers.
We can give it the name, but we can never be sure we
mean the same thing the others have. Or else we stand
outside of it and look at it as such a unique and specialized experience that we are not aware of the fact that
we ourselves perhaps perform it daily in the course of
our lives. This dialectic of the inexpressible but nameable may seem exaggerated; there remains the fact that
the merely named cogito is the wordless, unexplained

center of Sartre's philosophy, otherwise so rich in explanations, so recklessly confident in the power of words. It is as if this starting point fell outside the tissue of language to be constructed around it.

The more fundamental consciousness of self is dependent on this earlier name: it is called the "pre-reflexive cogito," and the wordless center persists. Or it is defined through its relationship to what it is not: it is called a "non-positional," a "non-thetic" consciousness, in order to distinguish it from a consciousness which poses itself as content, from a reflexive consciousness. Or in a kind of final convulsion of language it is called the "consciousness (of) self," to distinguish it from the direct "consciousness *of* self" which is reflection. The inefficient language is buttressed by these extra-linguistic marks, which do not, as did the punctuation, underline something already there in the language but attempt to improve on it. And the mirror-image which attempts to penetrate to the very structure of this consciousness, the expression "reflected-reflecting" is only adequate insofar as it abolishes itself. This direct assault on the nature of consciousness is the most dangerous of all, for it offers us the possibility of a stable image, threatens to leave us with a hardened "idea" of the "nature" of consciousness, of its division in two interacting "parts," and thus completely falsifies that which it set out to illuminate. So that the words in this situation are useless unless we already know what they stand for: they do not express, they merely *stand for* or name.

There results from this dialectic, and from the inexpressible nature of consciousness, an important philosophical instrument. The mere names that we give consciousness, such as the "cogito," are not so dangerous because they are given us as empty names: we know that we have to perform a kind of leap to get inside them, we see how powerless they are in themselves unless we already somehow understand them. It is when language really attempts to express consciousness that the danger begins, for then we are liable to draw too many conclusions, to misunderstand, and to presume that since consciousness "is" this or that, it "is." Consciousness is inexpressible because it is not a thing, and because almost everything we might say about it has the result of making it look like one; even to call it "not-being" or "nothingness" petrifies it slightly. We can therefore draw a kind of negative profit from the situation: a critical instrument with which to test formulations about thoughts. Consciousness, its thoughts, are never things; and this ban on "thingification" is Sartre's major critical weapon. A book such as *The Imagination,* a critique of earlier theories of the image, is from beginning to end one long patient testing of the different theories to see whether they make of the image a kind of thing, a "content of consciousness," or imply in any way a "thingification" of consciousness.

But this critical instrument does not have to be limited to philosophical works; it is a way of bringing individual details into sudden relationship with the central problem of this world, the absolute split between things and consciousness. And just as the tension between humanization and inhuman objects inevitably imposed itself on our attention when we examined things, so now it is the degree of "thingification," its absence, or its avoidance, that must guide us through an attempt to see how human reality makes its way into this language.

## CHAPTER SIX

## *The Anatomy of Thoughts*

The reality of the novel does not exactly coincide, except in certain restricted forms such as the first person *récit,* with the reality of the human beings which are its subject matter. The novel's hero acts, suffers, thinks, feels; he is always in a situation, but because he is *inside* of it he does not experience it as something separate from himself. For him the situation is merely the pattern things take on as they rise up to meet him coming toward them. It is we who are able to separate the situation from the man in it, who are able to consider the content alternately as a human being or as the shape of a world; yet this separation of ours is abstract, it is not part of the reality of our reading but comes afterwards, when the reading is over.

For during the reading we also are involved in detail, and it is chiefly this distance that distinguishes the novel as a form from the epic, for example, the content of which is simple and static. The epic has complicated decoration but we see it as decoration, we discount it in order to come face to face with the single line of the narrative. In the epic the idea of the situation, the idea for the situation, its conception, shows through the concrete situation itself: we are not made to live a filled continuity of time but rather to contemplate a few huge and grand gestures, two mighty figures in combat, the appeasing imperial hand emerging from the toga, the flight of Satan through the dusk on the edge of the world. The sequence of words, the time of the sentences following and completing each other, ends up not in a real narrative time but in images that the mind preserves as spatial, and the epic pleasure is a pleasure taken in visual design.

Those novels whose plots have been admired for some rare perfection or ingenuity are generally on the other hand extremely complicated; and our admiration is on the contrary the result of a terrifically involved intrigue led to an almost unhoped for consonance, and takes place at the end of the book. Such plots are, in any case, like the well-made play, historical moments in the development of the form, and not possibilities accessible at all times to the novelist.

The writer of novels is therefore unlikely to wish to impose upon his continuity a moment of pause in which the situation can be apprehended in and for itself; and when his characters draw back to reflect on their situation, such reflection becomes itself part of the situation, itself detail and content. Nonetheless, from time to time there are moments in which we get some generalized sense of the situation as a whole: not a static, epic vision of the situation as, let us say, a grand loosening of chains, a passage from Bondage to Freedom, but rather a kind of sensitivity to the quality of a situation, an oblique perception of it reflected through something unique in the way it is lived. Thus, when Brunet and Vicarios flee the prison camp, they have no time to stop and reflect on what they face, yet in the midst of their action they live

a new disposition of the world: "There are two nights:
the one that sags out behind them, a great furious mass
now impotent, and the other, delicate, cooperative, that
begins on the other side of the barbed wire, a black
light."[1] This feeling about the world, about the night,
is a perception of its objective structure, as we have seen
to be the case in the perception of individual things: the
two men, through this apparently aesthetic apprehension
of the night, register the distinction between the place
they are leaving, the hostility of the other prisoners, an
interpersonal hostility alive and stirring intangibly even
when the others are all asleep, and the world of the outside, the new kind of danger they are about to enter—
an objective danger, a danger in the threading of their
way through things, across barriers, through zones of
impersonal peril. And in this new world the very darkness changes and becomes something not full of menace
but something that will hide them from their enemies, a
darkness now on their side. Yet all this is conveyed not
in abstractions, in an "everything will be different on the
other side of the fence," but in something that has happened to the night itself: the plural has turned this apparently omnipresent, unlocalizable time of day into a
unit no longer Night but *a* night, two nights, two different types of night-things. And with one set up in opposition to the other, the second night insensibly turns into
the opposite of the first: things cease to be swallowed
up and dissolved in it as in real darkness; they are there,
paths, obstacles, all clear as in daylight, except that this
light is pitch-dark; the night has turned into a kind of
blind day. Thus, through the revelation of a quality, the
situation itself has been implicitly crystallized; yet the
perception of the quality was possible only because there
were two qualities, opposites bringing each other into
focus, and this rare moment of the apparition of a situa-

tion-entity was itself possible only in the transition from
one situation to a new one. As long as the heroes are within a situation, no matter how intolerable, they are too
involved in its detail, too busy reacting to each of its individual manifestations, to see it; but as they step into
a new one, they are momentarily able to pause and turn
and gauge the whole extent of the old about to be abandoned.

In such moments the situation has been felt as time, as
something which can be characterized in terms of certain
qualities: it was not seen as a static set of problems, in
which certain choices were possible, certain others ruled
out, but rather as a continuity that had a certain feel: a
rapid-heart-beat eagerness of the moments succeeding
each other, or a long wilting and drooping of the very
objects themselves, a paleness of the world like the paleness of a face from which blood has suddenly drained
away, or a constant solidity to be molded or to be broken
against. And time is in fact the major instrument at the
disposal of the novelist to give an oblique feeling of the
quality of a situation in the place of that direct characterization of it which he dares not make. Time is somehow above the content of the narrative, beyond all the
incessant changes of detail which must make it up; it is
in a sense the writer's style, and we have already been
able to seize certain peculiarly shaped situations of this
work with the help of certain variations in time and
through the attention to different rhythms in that time.

But there is a difference between apprehending a
change in situations through a change in time, and feeling the essence of a single situation, from the inside,
through the mediation of the time sense. Within the
situation there are no longer any contrasts functioning,
and time risks losing its transcendent nature and turning
into content on its own:

Odette closed her eyes. She was lying on the sand
inside a dateless, ageless heat: the heat of her childhood, when she closed her eyes, lying on this same
sand and pretending to be a salamander inside a
great red and blue flame. Same heat, same moist
caress of the bathing suit; it almost felt as if it were
steaming gently in the sun, same burning of the sand
against the back of her neck in other years, she
faded into the sky, the sea, the sand, she no longer
distinguished present from past. Suddenly she sat
up, eyes wide open: today, there was a real present;
there was that anxiety in the pit of her stomach.[2]

We hardly recognize the process of remembering which
used to be so simple and familiar; it used to take place
inside the head, but here the world seems to be remembering for Odette: the heat is suddenly the same as it
was years before, not merely like it but the same identical
heat. And the structure of the human being, temporal
animal, suddenly reveals an unexpected suppleness: the
past is no longer irrevocable, the time of the animal can
be set backwards like a clock, Odette can suddenly find
herself really in her childhood again, until she finds herself once more "really" in the present. Yet this awakening
out of the past into the present is not the passage from
an old situation to a new one: the persistence of Odette's
past, her difficulty in living wholly in the present, is itself
her situation, and it has been indicated not by the sensitivity to two different qualities of time but by a single
peculiar event, which happens to be temporal. Here time
has become not the way in which all events are related to
each other and succeed each other but the subject matter
of one particular event; and once this has happened, the
time-quality can become simply one quality of things
among others, a quality of a rare and special nature, but

which is pressed into the service of an attention directed
on things:

> I hold the envelope in my hand, I don't dare open
> it; Anny hasn't changed her letter paper, I wonder
> if she still buys it in that little paper store in Pic-
> cadilly . . . The envelope is heavy, it must contain
> at least six pages. The hen scratches of my former
> landlady bestride this beautiful script: "Hotel Prin-
> tania—Bouville." Those little letters do not shine.
> When I open the letter, my disappointment makes
> me six years younger: "I don't know how Anny man-
> ages to bulge out her envelopes this way, there's
> never anything in them."[3]

These sudden whiffs of the past are more than merely
vivid, involuntary memories: the past suddenly revives
for an instant with all it entails, the love for Anny, the
situations which no longer have any application to the
world of the present. The indirection of the single sentence that tells us all this is a kind of gracefulness. Here
the pressure on things to reveal subjectivity, to express it
in a single datum which is then turned and developed, is
somehow achieved all at once through the paradoxical
effect of a piece of paper on time itself: it "suddenly
makes me six years younger," and the formulation is
complete and able to dispense with the progressive exploitations of the comma form.

And now that time has lent itself to this progress, has
become caught up in this constant objectification, it no
longer resists, and ends up by becoming itself a mere
thing within a situation which it had formerly struc-
tured:

> They had written to their families and so two days
> ago the time of cities had begun to flow again. When

the Kommandantur required them to set their
watches on German time, they obeyed in a hurry,
even those who had worn as a sign of mourning dead
watches on their wrists since the month of June:
this vague passing of time that had flourished like
wild grass was militarized, they had been lent German time, genuine victor's time, the kind that
flowed in Danzig, in Berlin: sacred time.[4]

But this line that has been drawn around a time-thing
takes on its incisiveness from the fluidity of the substance
it bounds: it is because time is not a thing, because it is
impossible to imagine time as a thing, that this image
of the borrowing and lending of real lived time, and of
the shamefulness of carrying around German time in
your head, is so striking. Time comes to be something
possessed as things are possessed, and marked and worn
by its possessors like a clear fluid suddenly permeated by
a coloring.

But now we are inside the situation, and its unity has
been lost from sight. We are no longer able to characterize it as a whole, and our attention is caught up in all
of the minute detail that makes it up. We must now
therefore begin to examine the different ways in which
human reality is presented within the situation: that
vast swarming of thoughts and feelings which is more
properly the content of the novel. But it is difficult to sort
these hosts of unique "psychic" events into categories
that will not impose some kind of preconceived "human
nature" on subjectivity. We have already discussed such
a category, that of the "thought," and found that in these
works, the old category was retained, with its "he
thought:" and the words that purported to represent it;
but we found also that the category of thoughts was, in
a kind of narrative sleight of hand, rescued from the old

psychology it seemed to suggest and treated as a thing in order that it might have some of the unitary value of an act, in the world and not merely inside the head. Yet such "official" thoughts are only the most obvious, the most easily detachable points in a situation that subjectively suffuses in more subtle modes.

### 1. The Taste of a Situation

The category of "feelings" is at least as suspect as that of thoughts: it imposes a whole psychology of its own, it reduces the reality of the work to an impressionism, pushes our perceptions of the world back into our own private minds. Yet we can be dissatisfied with the notion of "feelings" as separate, traditional entities without doing away with the word altogether. The verb "to feel" has in fact a completely different effect on the reading mind. A "feeling" is a token to which a familiar name is attached: anger, tenderness, sloth, and their equivalent adjectives; it reduces human reality to a gamut of universal experiences through which we pass in turn and from which we extract some of the comfort of no longer being unique. But the verb immediately attracts attention to itself, and the anger, when it is *felt*, suddenly begins to take place in time, as a flash, that surges and dies away. The next step is for this anger to lose its name entirely, for what is felt to be seized and registered as something utterly historical which has to be presented on its own terms, without any help from all those earlier and different moments of anger and all the easy suggestiveness of the generalized term. In Sartre's work these new demands are not felt as absolute imperatives: there are many moments when the older modes of speech continue to be used and when only a kind of timing, a "he felt *suddenly* ashamed," attracts our attention and makes us aware that human

reality is being described in a new way. But in certain
other moments something more striking makes its appearance:

> He had said: we; he had accepted a kind of complic-
> ity with this little kike. Us. We Jews. But he had
> done it out of charity. Schalom's eyes gazed at him
> with respectful insistence. He was small and scrawny,
> they had beaten him and run him out of Bavaria,
> now there he was, he very likely slept in a sordid
> hotel and passed his days in a café. And they had
> burned Weiss's cousin with their cigars. Mr. Birnen-
> schatz looked at Schalom and felt sticky.[5]

Here, for the "feeling" of unwanted involvement, the
annoyance and distaste of a hidden kinship revealed, a
kind of specialized emotion, something which can more
properly be called a feeling, is substituted: something
purely sensory, an uncleanliness and contact felt directly
by the pores. Yet this quality of stickiness is not developed, elaborated: it is apparently not interesting in itself, as a unique experience. It is merely named, and we
read its meaning from the situation in which it appears.
It can be a kind of shorthand for us that gives way at
once to such a meaning, that spares us the unnecessary
detail of such words as "unwanted involvement"; or it
can be an occasion for us to pause and attempt briefly,
using the meaning as an instrument for brightening the
sensation, to lend these few words some of the life of our
own sensations and give the passage a sensory vividness
that the words themselves have not really earned. This
shuttling back and forth between a sensation and a meaning is comprehensible in terms of a philosophy for which
sensations, tastes, awareness of quality, are profoundly
symbolic of the subjectivity that feels them. We have
already seen in the study of things how our perceptions

compromise us, how our sensitivity to certain qualities in preference to others reflects our original choice of being. Sartre himself has given[6] an astounding analysis of that viscosity which is one of the favorite sensations of his own works; and his presentation of the phenomenon is a careful mixture of sensory and moral language, letting the isolated sensation be enriched and made vivid by all that it turns out to mean. Such presentation is oblique: it is not the head-on attack we might have expected from some of the earlier modern writers, whom a great faith in language permitted to dwell on the sensation alone, wholly on its own terms, savoring it and finally inventing those combinations of words that would register it permanently.

Yet in general all such direct approaches to the sensation are illusionistic, *trompe-l'oeil;* for the sensation is nothing but brute physical experience on the one hand and a name on the other—sticky, sweet, green. We know what these names stand for because we have already had the experience; but here literature is deprived of its possibility of making us live through what we have never suffered in our own person, and the names would drop uselessly if we did not bring with us in the form of our own body a storehouse of all such experienced and remembered sensations. Moreover it is not in the nature of real literary work to ride easily on the help of such associations and to expect the reader to bring to life words that the sentence merely names in hopes that they will suggest something to him. There is therefore a kind of thinness in all simple naming of qualities, an inefficiency: when Mr. Birnenschatz feels "sticky," we have no way of knowing exactly what it is he feels; there is simply a blank space indicating that a feeling is taking place, we take note of it, imagine it as best we can, and pass on.

All this would be true if the individual sensations of this work appeared in absolute isolation from each other; but in fact, existing behind each of them is another rarer sensory phenomenon, a taste on the very limits of perception, one of those points at which the subject matter of this work is wholly new. This phenomenon is in a sense the opposite of all the unique sensations that appear upon the background of it: it is the not-sensation, but it must be sensed in some way for us to know that it is there at all. This extreme point in the awareness of qualities is the taste of tastelessness itself, the moment when the content of the original qualities fades away and leaves merely the pure empty form of something sensed, the blankness upon which the real qualities surge with a new brightness: insipidity, *"fadeur,"* one of the most insistent words in Sartre's books, recurring again and again with some of the fatefulness and suggestiveness of a personal language.

And yet this new quality seems hardly to enjoy even the benefit of a name, for the word "insipid," a sort of accident or ingenuity of language, stands for ... nothing at all. The content of the other qualities takes place at a point too fundamental for language; but here, in the very nature of the thing, there is no content at all. And yet the *process* of tasting, of attempting to sense, is going on even when it is empty of content, it continues in a state of purity, like a wheel unable to take against a surface and slipping and revolving uselessly upon it. Only a state in which nothing was felt and yet something was aimed at could tangibly represent this strange lack of feeling which is itself a feeling:

> And yet there were his hands on the white balustrade: when he looked at them, they seemed like bronze. But precisely because he could look at them,

they were no longer his, they were somebody else's
hands, outside, like the trees, like the reflections
that shimmered in the Seine, hands cut off. He closed
his eyes and they became his once more: against the
warm stone there was nothing but a slight, a familiar
acid taste, a faint very negligible ant taste. My hands:
the inappreciable distance that reveals things to me
and separates me permanently from them.[7]

On the outside of that vacant area which is his hands, on
the rim of the awareness not directed toward it but toward the feeling in the hands themselves, shimmers the
feeling of the stone of Parisian bridges, porous, warm
and prickly, "a petrified sponge." This prickliness is
content, the mere accident of having stood in that place
with his hands on that particular object while he tried
to feel the pure sensation in them; but there is an interesting parallelism in its quality. For the feeling of a hand
dangling free in the air, a sense organ detached and
floating without any object at all, is a kind of dizzying
foreshadowing of that pins-and-needles sensation of a
limb falling asleep which the French describe as the
swarming of ants *("avoir des fourmis"),* itself a kind of
prickling. It is as if at all times in our bodies, the "asleep"
feeling, the pins-and-needles, lay dormant, potential,
merely waiting to make itself felt, like the hum of a
phonograph that we cannot detect but which becomes
audible the moment the record stops. This unpleasant
but rarely tangible fact of the continuing existence of
our own bodies Sartre has named a nausea, and has
shown, in a passage already examined, how the secondary,
more obvious kind of nausea or physical illness is merely
an intensification of this dizziness, rather than the concrete term of a metaphor which tries to embody it in a
striking way; so that in a sense the literary problem of the

presentation of the first, the basic, nausea is likewise the problem of a state without content—the apparent content, the physical malaise, is only a kind of gross amplification of the first condition, that "perpetual awareness that consciousness has of an *insipid* taste, a taste without distance, which accompanies me even in my efforts to rid myself of it, and which is *my* taste." And in a kind of literary reversal, the gross physical fact does not help us to seize the more insubstantial one but must rather be understood *through* it and on the background of it. The very word "insipid" betrays the close kinship of the two experiences and in the presentation of that tasteless taste a similar kind of solution comes into play.

We spoke of the pins-and-needles feeling that tends to make its appearance when other sensations disappear and when we try to feel what the organ, the hand or the leg, feels like "all by itself"; but this pins-and-needles feeling is not yet completely content, not yet a sensation in its own right. If we could stand it long enough for it to intensify and to take on the amplitude of a genuine sensation, we would find that the organ had become numb. The feeling is rather something slightly dawning, about to be, something on the limits of what we feel rather than anything directly felt. But in this passage in which Mathieu suddenly tastes the taste of his own hands, the feeling of pins-and-needles is doubled by the outside world; for the stone outside of his hands is prickly as well, the slight bristling is there, real, on the surface of the balustrade, and this solid, but deliberately disregarded feeling of the bridge absorbs into itself the last remains of content within the hands themselves. If Mathieu had tried to make the experience without touching anything, the prickliness would have been there to trouble the purity, the emptiness, of his existing body; but as it is, he can think of any last shreds of sensation as being caused by

the ignored stone, and of his description, "a slight, familiar acid taste, a faint very negligible ant taste," all that
is left is the diminished volume, the familiarity; and the
insipidity is rendered pure. The pins-and-needles feeling
was there to draw our attention to the continuing fact
of *sensation* and not mere emptiness: this done, it vanishes and leaves us face to face with the sensation *of* emptiness itself.

Once tastelessness, *fadeur,* has been thus made accessible, it can become, in a conversion typical of this work,
itself a theme: it can be felt as a situation, a state the
whole world gets into which the characters try desper-
ately to shake off:

> Tears? I just hope they come back and get me and
> beat me so that I can refuse to answer again and
> ridicule them and intimidate them. Everything is
> so insipid here: the waiting, your love, the weight
> of this head on my lap. I'd like to be consumed by
> suffering, I'd like to burn, to refuse to say anything,
> and watch their staring eyes.[8]

The passion for extreme situations surges on the background of this tastelessness, which is the very taste of
time itself, as, unencumbered with any activity or passion, it keeps on uninterruptedly moving, and we look
into its emptiness without seeing anything at all. Pain
and suffering are preferable to this ennui, because in
them at least something happens; but the tastelessness is
the negative of real constructed time, of a freedom to
work in which consciousness realizes its nature as pure
activity, and the theme of insipidity here is intended not
so much to underline the passive necessity of going on
existing whether we like it or not but to bring into relief
all those forces beyond us that impose passivity upon consciousness and make its existence absurd.

But the rendered presence of the insipid also has implications for all the other more humdrum tastes and qualities of this world. This zero point of quality, always there even when something else is being felt, means that feelings will no longer be isolated events, spasmodic, occasionally noted. The world will be rather from this point of view one long continuous stream of sensation, and the life of the body one uninterrupted and endlessly varying taste. The stickiness of Mr. Birnenschatz must therefore be read not as a small detail which the author thought of enough interest to stand on its own as an event but as just one more sudden modulation of a body and a consciousness unable to escape sensation. The episode was too small to permit us anything but a snatch of this material; in others, it rises to the surface and begins to crowd everything else out of the narration:

> He swallowed his saliva painfully, it slid down into his throat with a horrible silky tickling and in his mouth insipid liquid already seeped, exhausting, exhausting, his ideas fled, there was nothing left but a great abandoned sweetness, an urge to rise and fall rhythmically, to gently vomit, at great length, to sink against the pillow, o-eess o-eess, without a thought, lifted by the world's great rolling back and forth; he caught himself in time: you don't get seasick unless you want to. He recovered himself completely, stiff and dry, a coward, a scorned lover, one of the coming war's dead, he regained all his lucid and icy fear . . . He raised a hand and passed it through the air with vacillating and somewhat solemn gentleness. Gentle gestures, gentle palpitations of my eyelashes, sweet flavor in my throat, sweet lavender smell and smell of toothpaste, the boat gently rose, gently redescended; he yawned and

time slowed down, turned sirupy around him; all he
had to do was stiffen, take a turn outside the cabin,
in the fresh air. But why *bother?*[9]

The approach of real physiological illness intensifies all
these sensations and makes them more immediately visible; but only few of them are genuine feelings in the
old limited sense of the word. The passage is an uneasy
oscillation between two groupings, two poles, of physical
awareness. Consciousness dominates one of them, the
body is here controlled, in retreat, at its command. At the
other pole it is the body which begins to replace thoughts
and decisions with its own sensations; and consciousness,
yielding to it, is no longer anything but the gentleness/
sweetness implicit in the word *"douceur."* Other moments of the work suggest the fascination of the word,
and the state named by it, for this writer: descriptions
of that sinking into the body which is sexual desire,[10]
the frequency with which the passage from one state to
another is rendered as a falling asleep, or a sudden waking up,[11] all show the crucial importance that such moments of the loss of consciousness possess for a novelist
whose theme is consciousness. And the growing gentleness of Pierre's gestures, of his body, a sluggishness which
is affirmed as pleasant, which is chosen, is the way this
passivity, slowly seeping into the last wakened places of
the organism, feels from the inside. But the usefulness of
the word is that it can mean at the same time activity
(the quality of gentleness in his bodily stirrings) and the
state, the static taste of sweetness which persists as the
unchanging symptom of his condition on another level
of perception. Thus the word "douceur," even before its
relationship to other sensations comes into play, acquires
already in itself the thickness of a mysterious sensation
that can never be reduced to the earlier, simple, unitary

feeling: it is two such feelings, it is the zone their intersection creates, an imperative to us to locate and imagine
a state which would be at the same time sweetness and
gentleness, and no other.

Yet it exists here as a taste among many tastes; it comes
into being, and will be abolished; it is caused, by the
backing up of sweet things mouthed at the moment before vomiting. Yet we are constantly aware that the illness
which it foreshadows is its opposite in all respects: neither gentle nor sweet, vomiting is on the contrary bitter,
experienced in spasms. And against this unspoken opposite, the sweetness ceases to be an everyday kind of
phenomenon, is distinguished in kind from all the ordinary sweetnesses of chocolate, orange, port, becomes
something rare, not sweetness in general, but an un-
nameable yet very specific kind of generalized sensation:
a concrete experience, but one whose name hardly suffices
to define it at all, which is defined rather by the movement of its appearance in the passage and by the presence
of its opposite. So true is this that before the opposite,
the threatening sourness of vomiting, makes its presence
felt, the sensation has no name, not even that of sweetness: it is merely "insipid liquid." It is as it will be, but
until it is able to identify itself against the sensation
negating it, the taste buds are bewildered, they register
a presence but are unable to say what it is, as in those
fleeting moments of the lapse of sense perception when
we are unable to judge whether something is burning
hot or ice cold.

Against these, the words describing consciousness itself strike us as being much more obviously figurative,
and each of them, taken by itself, could become a more
or less perfunctory and colorless manner of speaking:
stiff, dry, icy. But they are unable to persist in their isolation: consciousness, which felt so much as it began to

slip, can no longer stop feeling when it recovers itself. The dryness shows consciousness suddenly freed from the welling up of bodily liquids; it turns the sweetness into something humid, just as the iciness turns it into something fleshly and warm, but it is in its turn influenced and made something physical. The stiffness is not just a way of saying that the body is under control: it becomes the feeling of the entire body, as opposed to the sudden primacy of the digestive organs which is the illness. Moreover these feelings, clustering around the pole of consciousness, react on each other: they define a unique, existential state which is at the same time felt stiffness, felt dryness, and chilled by a persistent, motionless fear. Thus the words also tend to lose the simplicity they imply as names; they are no longer *general* as such words for qualities in their normal uses must be. Coexisting, each defining not the state itself but one of its limits, they are for us a sign of VIVIDNESS, lived density beyond any names; and the presence of many qualities overcomes the thinness and generality of each one taken singly, and becomes, through the very weakness of the instruments of language, a way of rendering a dimension of human reality that seemed too immediate for words.

Now once this thickening of feelings into unique states has been accomplished, these become part of the raw material of the narration itself and can be used not only for their own sakes and their own intrinsic meanings but to the benefit of events distinct from them. In the beginning the quality simply translated the meaning of the situation into new and more sensory terms: Mr. Birnenschatz' stickiness stood in no contradiction to the situation but turned out to be its aura for him, its essence. Now however, with the quality a unique state, it can seem to clash with the situation, and this dissonance can be felt as a kind of intensification of the narrative timing.

The flow, for example, of Mathieu's sensations as he watches the German soldiers approaching his tower, has an "inappropriateness" about it which is characteristically Sartrean and at the same time in the grand manner of bravura storytelling:

> A brake squeaked, car doors slammed. Mathieu heard voices and steps: he fell into a queasiness that resembled sleep: he had to struggle to keep his eyes open. . . . He sank into a kind of sweet gentleness; he loved everybody, the French, the Germans, Hitler. In a thickened dream he heard cries, followed by a violent explosion and shattering glass, and then the clattering set in again. He tightened his grip on the rifle to prevent it from falling. "The grenade fell short," said Clapot with teeth clenched.[12]

This now familiar condition of the body falling into somnolence, sweet, gentle, certainly has a meaning in terms of the situation: it is what Freud called the death wish, the instinct of the organism at moments of extreme tension to abolish itself, to retreat into unconsciousness rather than meet the danger head-on with open eyes. Yet in another sense it is only a way of presenting all the external noise and violence in such striking opposition of quality to it: the strength of the outside world is measured against the intensity of this physiological reaction to it; and the explosions, the rapid fire of the machine gun, the cries that are heard through this strange sweet sluggishness, are much more real than they would have been if they had had nothing to penetrate, if the narration had merely attempted to render them directly, define them through their own intrinsic textures.

Now finally this struggle of unique qualities against the names that both fix them and make them too general runs its full course; and instead of a plurality of qual-

ities that define each other and limit each other in a kind
of lapse of perception like that described above, the
name and the characteristics of one feeling get attached to
another by mistake, and the isolated feeling is able to
become opaque all by itself:

> Daniel looked with avidity at her shoulders and her
> neck. That stupid obstination irritated him; he
> wanted to break it. He was possessed by an enormous
> and opprobrious urge: to rape this consciousness, to
> sink with it into the depths of humility. But it wasn't
> sadism: it was more groping, and more humid, more
> fleshly. It was kindness.[13]

This astounding reversal is characteristic of Daniel and
the world of evil he has constructed himself, where there
is something obscene about all "positive" feelings. But
as a consequence this charity which does not know its
own name takes on some of the force and violence of
pure negativity, of evil, it loses its vapid moral flavor and
becomes an instinct, with the bodily solidity of all instincts. In this kind of imaginative puzzle played against
the readers, the process is the opposite from what has
been seen above: here the thickness and reality of the
feeling is first established and then, shockingly, named;
where before the weak and unsuggestive names of the
qualities were combined into a stronger and more mysterious entity. But the feeling always tends toward an
almost physiological intensity: it moves away from subjectivity, away from the transparency of meanings and
symbols on the one hand, and on the other, from the kind
of intentional pattern we might expect to find in the
context of a philosophy of freedom where emotions are
ways of acting, ways of experiencing the world, choices.
But the heavy atmosphere of these opaque feelings is
equally distant from a turning of feelings into mere

things: part of the price of our reading is the constant effort to discover the central term between two adjectives, not to freeze it into a sterile identification, a mere naming, but to bring it to life and vividness with the substance of our own life, our own feelings.

### 2. *Finding a Place for Meanings*

Thoughts have become solid like gestures, feelings thickened like a density of the atmosphere, things, in spite of the subjectivity they can reveal when stared at, are united in a kind of conspiracy of stubborn hostility, irreducibility: everything in this world seems moving toward a compactness of being that threatens to crowd the weak language of abstractions and simple understandings out of it altogether. And yet it somehow remains: we have already noticed the strange survival of all the old, ordinary value judgments, all the vocabulary of earlier moral wisdom that should have crumbled in this high-pressure zone.

There are ways of smuggling these words into the narration:

> "I said you can drink as much as you want to," Mathieu cried. "I don't give a damn." He thought: "The only thing for me to do now is leave." But he couldn't make up his mind. He leaned over them, he inhaled the rich sugary odor of their drunkenness and their distress; he thought: "Where would I go?" and he felt dizzy. He was not horrified by them— these losers drinking their defeat down to the dregs.[14]

The living center of this paragraph is the identification of drunkenness and distress. The few mild figures—Mathieu's dizziness, which like the single feelings threatens to become abstract, and the image of the "dregs of de-feat"—are caught up into it and become tangible when the identification is fixed. For the distress is not merely the cause and the meaning of this drunken orgy: when Mathieu smells the wine on their breath it is not merely an odor but distress itself that he apprehends, just as sometimes the glimpse of a particularly sordid room fills us, without a pause for thought, with an immediate and overwhelming sense of depression. The unhappiness of the men is not a separate entity, an interpretation that has to be placed somewhere in the crowded whole of the situation: it is a tonality of the situation, isolated just long enough to receive an abstract name, but continuing to preserve its concrete link with the realities of the senses.

The visible sign of this connection between abstractions and sense data, the yoke offered by language to tie together two entities that hardly seem to merge in any kind of organic relationship to each other, is the simile. But there is a kind of violence in this modern revival of the simile: it does not permit each entity to develop a kind of autonomous life of its own as the ancient simile did, it merely adds a second term of a different kind without reorganizing the movement of the first, simple sentence. "He got up, he went and sat next to her and took her hand. A hand soft and feverish as a confidence: he held it in his own without speaking."[15] The entire scene between Daniel and Marcelle is an exchange, a slow extraction of confidences, the intimacy of secret telling is slowly collecting in the room and at this point it begins to solidify: Marcelle's resistance is about to give way, the secrets are about to be revealed. The felt temperature of the hand is as meaningful, as certain an expression as a tentative look on someone's face. The warmth and the softness are no longer mere adjuncts of the situation, details added merely to fill in the necessary reality, ambiguous, caused perhaps by the temperature of the room itself or by Marcelle's physical condition: the simile limits their meaning and at the same time lends them some of the force of a gesture in a drama slowly building up. Yet looking back at this ambiguous entity from the point of view of the abstract term, there remains something gratuitous about the moment, about the fact that the abstraction should settle at that particular point, light on that particular sensation and not on another, attach itself here and not elsewhere, and not nowhere at all.

It is in the language of *The Flies* that we find the densest proliferation of such similes, many of them intended merely as signs indicating the epic quality of the play: "Her face seems a field ravaged by lightning and hail,"[16] empty and decorative similes that convey a certain stateliness of manner and whose archaic sound confirms our impression that there is something basically obsolete about this mode of expression, and that any modern use of the simile is likely to conceal some intention out of proportion with the antique appearance. From time to time in *The Flies* a different kind of reality rises into sight from beneath the older form: "This look burns into you, invisible and pure, a look more immutable than the memory of a look."[17] Within this description of the effect of the ghosts on the people of Argos, an astonishing tautology trembles. For the ghosts do not exist, they are brought to life by the living and fed with the irrevocable memories which are all that remain of the dead. The disguise which the comparison wears ("more immutable than") delays a sudden transparency in it, for the look the people of Argos feel upon them *is* the memory of a look; the reproachful staring that troubles the conscience of the living is brought to life by the strange ceremony, projected out of memory into the real world and received back with all of its original force. The machinery of comparison performs the feat of allowing the writer to formulate his reality in two distinct ways: since ghosts do not really exist, the modern audience is given a more tangible and satisfactory hold on the phenomenon ("the memory of a look"), while the mythical appearance it enjoys for the people on stage continues alongside it without suffering any diminution of its authority.

So that the formal appearances of the simile are merely an exterior that shelters the force of the verb "to be": "He was tired and nervous, he constantly saw before him an open suitcase in a darkened room, and in the suitcase supple and scented banknotes; it was like remorse."[18] The uncertainty of the first term of the comparison, whether it is the suitcase which is like a remorse or the whole process of seeing this obsessive image, again obscures the tautology, and retards the moment in which the statement that it was *like* remorse is exchanged for the announcement that it *was* remorse. We have already seen how this progressive development of an idea towards a climactic formulation with the verb "to be" is characteristic of the philosophical works: the verb "to be" functions as a kind of rhetorical seal on the reasoning which does not seem to be appropriate to narration. Yet whatever its form, such equations of an object to an abstract meaning become spontaneous and natural in the world of phenomenological analysis, where phenomena are comprehensible, where an analysis of an object does not add anything to the object but merely draws up into the light and formulates the meaning which the object had implicitly all along for consciousness. This philosophy depends not on proof but on recognition: its language tries to register as accurately as possible the faint tremors given off by the thing itself, sounds the normal ear is vaguely aware of but immediately forgets or ignores. Such an attention to things and to a language that will fix them becomes a common ground shared by philosophy and literature alike.

The verbal devices designed to connect the meaning to its object are therefore only the most obvious, and sometimes the most awkward, symptoms of a whole attitude towards things and their comprehensibility; the few scattered abstract words are not out of place in a world where things are in themselves a comprehensible language.

### 3. Inside the Mind

In recent years the texture of the novel has approached complete behaviorism as a kind of ideal: abstract thoughts or meanings or relationships ("his love for her had this odd characteristic, that he always tried," etc.) are felt as mere scenario, imperative to work, no longer sufficient in themselves. In his new passion for the concrete, the existential, the irreducible, the novelist attempts to dispense with such overt commentary, and to suggest it behind a unique gesture, or a unique spoken sentence. This, which can be thought of as a kind of progress in the history of writing, is probably partly caused by the heavy weight of past literature and past reading that jades the modern reader, and gives him a need for more fully realized, sharpened, and concrete sentences.

On the other hand it is obvious that consciousness is still the most interesting thing writers have to write about, and that the rendered gesture, the heard speech with its exact tones, do not exhaust the drama of human reality. There will still be a few "mental events" beyond the reach of the merely sensory. The thought was one of

these, but it is only one among many; and there are moments when some awareness has not yet reached the full
status of a thought, where something not yet identified
makes its presence felt on a stage no larger than the mind
itself: "Before me, settled in a sort of indolence, there
was a voluminous, insipid idea. I don't know exactly
what it was, but I couldn't look at it it disgusted me so.
All that was somehow mixed up in my mind with the
scent of Mercier's beard."[19] Almost any conceivable formulation of this strange looking but fairly common feeling would involve at least an implied dividing up of the
mind into parts: "something nagging at my attention"
freezes the division into a commonplace, a manner of
speaking, it subtly distracts your attention from the notion of separate mental functions which remains perpet-
uated in the bones of the sentence. But here the process
is brought out into the open, it does not stop, it goes on
developing towards a formulation even more concrete:
"That idea is back in front of me again, waiting. It's
curled up, it sits there like a big cat: explaining nothing,
not stirring, merely saying no."[20] The idea, the realization that there are no such things as "adventures," is
something Roquentin has secretly known all along, without admitting it to himself. But as he comes closer and
closer to admitting it, the object of his thought grows
more and more "objectified," makes it presence more and
more strongly felt like the presence of a thing. As soon
as he *knows,* the personification dissolves, there is no
more point to it, the mind is at one with its thought; but
until then this strange allegorical substance persists as
a reminder that we can know without really knowing,
that there is a level of consciousness which is not thematized and not directly admitted to the reflecting mind.
This solution is not unfamiliar to us: the experience presented in terms radically alien to it, its presentation so

exaggerated that we are not likely to be taken in, that we are in fact less likely to be misled by this gross treatment of a thought as a thing than by the restrained and insinuating formulation of it that we have suggested as an alternative.

But the force of the personification in this passage is dependent not so much on the way it treats the thought alone but on the contrast established between the thought-thing and the transparency of the directly known: the effect of the personification is not stable, it is given through the movement of the passage and through the contrast set up between two poles which can work just as well in the opposite direction:

> Ivich still didn't say anything.
>
> "She's judging me," Mathieu thought with irritation.
>
> He bent forward; to punish her, he brushed a closed, tightly shut mouth with his lips; he was obstinate; Ivich still said nothing. . . . "That does it," Mathieu thought, "it's irreparable." He hunched his back, wished he could disappear. A policeman raised his stick, the taxi stopped. Mathieu stared straight ahead, but he did not see the trees; he was looking at his love.
>
> It was love. *Now* it was love. Mathieu thought: "What have I done?" Five minutes ago this love did not exist; there had been between them a rare and precious feeling, something without a name, which gestures could not express. And he had gone and made a gesture, the one gesture he should never have made—in any case he hadn't meant to do it, it just happened. A single gesture and this love had materialized before him, like a great troublesome object that had already become rather vulgar.[21]

This perception is dependent on the language which permits a tacit, intangible relationship between two people to suddenly crystallize into a thing, an object that Mathieu can stare at while his eyes look blankly ahead. The perception is not the same as "falling in love," it is not even the same as realizing that one is in love, suddenly finding the word "love" for one's feeling, but is instead the passage from a rare and completely individualized feeling between Mathieu and Ivich to a state long standardized, with its clichés and its commonplaces, its name that accounts for behavior like a motive, the sense it imposes of participating now in something very ordinary. The personification of the feeling into a name is the same as this transformation into a routine thing.

It would somehow be symmetrical if we could attribute this new kind of allegory to the divisions of the mind psychoanalysis works with—themselves pieces of a complicated allegory; and no doubt the realities psychoanalysis discovered are partly responsible for the creation of this new language. We have just seen how the distinction between a profound, unthematized consciousness and a reflective awareness of what we are "really" thinking was able to express itself through a personification. But the allegories of psychoanalysis were designed as scientific hypotheses, as categories for new knowledge and new facts; these allegories of narration function somewhat differently:

> He clenched his fists and within his mind, with the seriousness of a grownup, a member of the middle classes, a respected member of society, the head of a family, he pronounced the words: "I wish to marry Marcelle." Rubbish! It was nothing but words, a vain, infantile resolution. "And that," he thought, "is just another lie: I don't need any will power to

marry her; all I have to do is drift into it." He closed
the phone book and stared, overcome, at the broken
pieces of his human dignity. And suddenly it seemed
to him that he could *see* his freedom. It was out of
reach, cruel, young, capricious as grace: it command-
ed him unequivocally to ditch Marcelle. It only
lasted an instant; he only managed to get a glimpse
of this inexplicable freedom that had taken the
shape of crime: it frightened him, and then it was
so far away. He remained dead set on this too human
decision of his, on the too human words: "I'll marry her."[22]

This moment, in which a kind of invisible boundary
line seems to be present, in which a man breaks out in
cold sweat at the point of making himself do what he
thought he wanted to do, is a privileged opportunity to
glimpse that "part of us" which says no, to feel the limits
of our original choice, or, if one prefers, to sense the
profound resistance of the unconscious. Just as value
proved to be most directly accessible, visible, at the moment of its disappearance, so here the choice turns out
to be something most easily measured by its limits. But
this apprehension of the "unconscious" is itself conscious; and it is not a merely intellectual figuring out
that because we cannot bring ourselves to do the act in
question, the act must have a profound symbolic meaning in terms of our whole life, our personality: that
would be a very indirect reading and interpretation of
the phenomenon. But the passage presents a direct experience of consciousness, a sudden tearing away of the
veils that permits us to see, for once, what we had known
all along, to realize not only that we will not do it but
that we had always known we would not do it.

The freedom-thing of this passage is therefore not a

closed, dead entity like the $x$ which is the unconscious in psychoanalytic symbolism. It is presented as something inhuman, something far distant from the humanity of Mathieu's resolutions, something so impersonal that it frightens him. But this entity is only one of the terms around which the paragraph is constructed; we are not at liberty to draw implications from it alone and disregard the way it interacts with the other elements with which the experience is composed. For we cannot even recognize the experience, it will not become living and organic for us, unless in reading it we travel the long distance back from the inhumanity of this freedom-thing to the realities of consciousness itself; unless we translate this personification back into the substance of consciousness and see it not as an independent entity but as a subtle, indirect way in which the complicated experience Mathieu is having must be presented. The personification permits the registering of the experience, but only on the condition that we in our reading abolish it: the mind is turned into parts and things only in order to be fixed the more surely as mind, as indivisible consciousness.

## 4. Problem-Words

But there are other abstractions which represent neither the psychic events that take place within human reality nor the meaning of a situation seen from outside and above: they are not the content of the speech of the novel but the content of the speech of the characters in a novel and of their reflections. The characters do not always talk and think about War, Life, Peace, and Freedom; but if they are going to, the novel faces a special set of problems. Such words, and the thoughts they generate, are of a different texture from narration; the fine

tissue of narrative is liable to be damaged by clumsy reflections and "thought" passages, or the concrete action
likely to be reduced to the status of an illustration, an
example confirming one of the thoughts. It is all the more
curious here, since these are the novels of a philosopher,
who is not likely to oppose the dense fabric of reasoning
of his philosophical works to sketchy approximates, isolated "ideas" of the kind that stud the so-called philosophical novels. The very names of these "problems" are
almost a compromise: in themselves they suggest prob-
lem-units and thoughts which would be solutions to
them, vulgarizations that exist in a kind of double standard with the real thinking; they are related to that whole
complex of older moral judgments, like courage, and
older moral problems, that continue to survive in a work
that has largely left them behind.

The very isolation, the very self-sufficiency which these
problems lay claim to by possessing names with capital
letters, suggests a development somewhat different from
outright thinking:

> A life. He looked at all those crimson faces, those
> reddish moons that were sliding across cushions of
> clouds: "They all have lives. Every one of them.
> Each has his own. They stretch out through the walls
> of the night club, through the streets of Paris,
> through France, they cross, they intersect, and they
> all remain as rigorously personal as a toothbrush, a
> razor, the personal effects you don't lend. I knew
> that. I knew that each of them had his own life.
> What I didn't know was that I had one too."[23]

Since a life is an idea, not something felt directly but a
concept that one arrives at by watching the lives of others
and realizing that our own apparently unlimited subjectivity has an outside too, an appearance that labels can

be given to and that can be described, this only indirectly
accessible life-idea lends itself immediately to description as a thing. No violence is being done the facts of
consciousness here because none are involved: an idea
has merely slipped down the narrow slope that separated
it from images. For a life is the external shape of a consciousness, it can remain after the consciousness itself has
disappeared:

> She was dead. Her consciousness was gone. But not
> her life. Abandoned by the soft and tender animal
> that had lived within it for so long, the deserted life
> had simply stopped, it floated, full of cries without
> echoes and ineffectual hopes, of somber flashes, of
> outmoded faces and odors, it floated somewhere on
> the edges of the world, between parentheses, un-
> forgettable and definitive, more indestructible than
> a mineral, and nothing could prevent it from having
> *been,* it had just entered its ultimate transforma-
> tion: its future was frozen.[24]

The simple notion of a life-thing is here loosed from the
ties that held it to time and to concrete content. Within
the circular motion of the comma form it begins to develop autonomously, rapidly, a growingly self-sufficient
image that nonetheless corresponds to an important philosophical development:[25] the idea that what remains of
human reality after death is merely our existence for
other people. This existence for others had been one
dimension of our lives and now it is the only one left,
we are forever in their hands. Out of that image, as part
of its implications, come the Sartrean ghosts, the ghosts
of *No Exit* and of *The Chips are Down.* The supernatural here has a curious and thin texture which can be
accounted for by its relationship to the idea that inspired it. For the ghosts retain the traces of an applied

idea, they are not the pieces of an impenetrable existential situation (as would be the case for example in genuine "ghost stories"), and each of the works could be summarized in a single sentence indicating the conceit to be exploited. What happens in these works is that the dimension of our being-for-others becomes autonomous and is replaced by the complete visible human being in the person of the actors. They then are made to submit to the vicissitudes which analysis has shown us that being-for-others is subject to. But a whole human being does not easily fit into the place of a reputation, and so a second supernatural is devised to make a platform for the first drama to take place on, and to fill in the chinks in the situation; thus we have the hotel-hospital-prison of the play and the very French bureaucracy of the movie, which are so distinct in quality from the special theme of the ghosts themselves, the problem of being-for-others, that our vague sense of something slightly out of joint in the situation tends to make its appearance at those moments when the ghosts are visibly superimposed on their décor like an image on a doctored photograph.

But this is by no means the only direction that the exploitation of a life-thing can take:

> Armand Viguier calmly continued in his supine position, all alone in his room, his yellow hands rested on the covers, his bony head with the tough gray beard and sunken eyes was thrown back, he smiled distantly . . . he was dead. On the night table someone had set his pince-nez and his false teeth were in a glass of water. Dead. And his life was there, everywhere, impalpable, finished, hard and full like an egg, so tightly packed that all the forces of the world could not have pressed another atom into it, so porous that Paris and the whole world

passed through it, scattered to the four corners of
France and entirely condensed in every point in
space: a great boisterous and immobile carnival; the
cries were there, the laughter, the whistling of locomotives and the burst of shrapnel, May 6, 1917, the
bleeding and humming in his head when he falls
between the two trenches, the noises were there, icy,
and the nurse listening heard nothing but a hissing
under her skirts. She got up and did not pull the
chain out of respect for death, she came back to sit
beside Armand's bed, passing through the great immobile sunlight that forever lights up a woman's
face, at the Grande Jatte, July 20, 1900, in the row-
boat. Armand Viguier was dead, his life floated,
closing in immobile pains, a great stripe running
right through the month of March, 1922, the pain
between his ribs, indestructible little jewels, the
rainbow above the quai de Bercy one Saturday
evening, it rained, the pavements are slippery, two
cyclists pass by laughing, the sound of the rain on
the balcony on a stifling March afternoon, a gypsy
tune that brings tears to his eyes, dewdrops shining
in the grass, a flight of pigeons on the Piazza San
Marco.[26]

This dead life, bubble filled with bright silent realities
that intersect like a collage, is a kind of figure of the
work of art itself: mute shouting page, movement fixed
forever before us. And to be seen as a unit, it is seen, like
Lola's dead life, from the outside: it floats free, placeless, and reduced entirely to a single point; its contents
are plurals that clash, cries and silences, bursts of light,
still generalized in order to be small enough to be retained in the mind as elements of a single whole and
to fight for a kind of place within it against the other

equally placeless elements. But then something new happens: these generalities begin to resolve into the individual events that they stood for, and the life-thing loses its strange unitary nature and becomes the more recognizable sequence of unique and individual details that we ordinarily think of as a life. But the bubble-like unity is constantly reasserted: "Armand Viguier was dead, his life floated," in order to avoid bursting under the pressure of the time sequence. The rapid alternation of the pictures flashing off and on is like a reel of film that projects violent, bright, and heterogeneous shots in an uncanny silence: they are no longer references from the outside to the contents of a life-thing, descriptions of the quality of the interior of this life, they suddenly are the content itself; and now a new opposition replaces the shuttling back and forth between the pictures and the unitary life, and the living nurse, coming back from the washroom in the empty darkened house, unwittingly walks through a patch of timeless light, the sun of July 20, 1900, shining there forever on a certain face, a brightness that has no one to see it any more, which remains, out of time and space, but *there;* and the two different realities, the nurse and the now placeless memory, intersect for a moment without knowing it and then separate again. Such a moment was obviously not possible in the world of *The Age of Reason,* from which came the earlier passage on Lola's life: it depends on a floating point of view, one that can register those instants when in the crowded world two lives, two different worlds, intersect and then part without being aware of each other: the very subject of *The Reprieve.* It is an example of the constant demands made on the individual elements of the work of art to intersect as much as possible, to entertain a multiplicity of relationships with each other. But the moment is real: it is not merely a reference to a meeting of two worlds, not merely a figure of that intersection (as are our own descriptions of it); this hardly tangible moment of contact has been seen, with all the reality of an accident or an explosion.

The executed passage stands in a different kind of relationship to its central "inspiration" than does the earlier one, which nonetheless has much the same subject. In the earlier moment, the notion of a life-thing was developed as an image: the unique contents of the life were not insisted on for fear the historical quality of such contents might prevent the freezing of history into an object. The idea remains present in such a development, it is itself the subject of the passage; but in the later moment it has gone out of sight, it has become not a kind of content but an imperative as to a kind of treatment of content, not an image to be developed but a requirement that the life be presented in a certain manner. Thus here unique and differentiated details appear in order to fulfill the life-thing, make it concrete; only these details never become autonomous, always retain a sample- , an example-like relationship to the life-unity of which they are a part. And the presence of the life-idea is detected in this very brokenness, in the fragmentary quality of the samples; for the more complete they got, the more we would lose sight of the unity. If a biography somehow began to develop out of such a moment, with its intrinsic interests and developments, we would have forgotten entirely about the life-thing that it had filled to the point of replacing it.

This is the characteristic solution to the problem of big words. After an initial tendency to become things and images, the words open up, they turn out to be the sum of everything included in them and not a separate, independent entity. Peace is the catalogue of all the things that happen in peacetime,[27] and trying to understand war, Mathieu comes to the conclusion: "You would have to be everywhere at the same time."[28] The words confirm the feeling of vulgarity that we saw in them by abolishing themselves, by bursting into a thousand pieces, and the mind, led down deceptive paths by the seemingly real problems posed by these words, suddenly finds itself face to face with something no longer exactly *thought,* something so close to sense perception that it can turn out to be impossible, unimaginable—a vain struggle to retain the details of the senses within the placeless infinite framework of abstract thought:

> An enormous body, a planet, in a space of a billion dimensions; three-dimensional beings could not even imagine it. And yet each dimension was an autonomous consciousness. If you tried to look at the planet directly, it would crumble to pieces, there would only be consciousnesses left. A billion free consciousnesses each one of which saw walls, the reddish tip of a cigar, familiar faces, each one of which constructed its own destiny and was alone responsible for it. And yet if you *were* one of those consciousnesses, you could tell from imperceptible contacts, insensible changes, that you were part and parcel of a gigantic and invisible polypary. War: everybody is free and yet the chips are down. It's there, it's everywhere, it's the totality of my thoughts, the totality of Hitler's words, of Gomez' acts: but nobody is there to add it up. It exists only for God. But God doesn't exist. And yet war exists.[29]

Here, within the individual consciousness, the idea has stopped short: it is still an imperative to be transformed into billions of unique and individual details, but the imperative remains a dead letter, one of the qualities of the image, just as the description of Lola's life ("full of cries without echoes and ineffectual hopes") failed to develop beyond the stage of a schematic image. But just as later on in the work another dead-life does manage to become concrete, so this image that Mathieu glimpses becomes the invisible center for an enormous materialization, that of the whole novel *The Reprieve,* which is the broken fragmentary sum of all the lives that make up a world about to go to war.

And even freedom itself, in the novels, abolishes itself; unlike the oblique and exhaustive treatment of freedom in the philosophy, the word, obsessing Mathieu, seemed to be an indicator pointing toward something to be found, seemed to promise a discovery. He makes it:

> Outside. Everything is outside: the trees on the quay, the two houses on the bridge that tint the night rose, the frozen gallop of Henri IV over my head: everything that has weight. Inside, nothing, not even a whisp of smoke, there is no *inside,* there is nothing. Myself: nothing. I am free, he thought, his mouth dry. In the middle of the Pont-Neuf he stopped, he began to laugh: I've been searching for freedom in such out-of-the-way places; it was so close I couldn't see it, I can't touch it, it is nothing but myself. I am my freedom.[30]

This is the same process of equation that took place in the earlier passages; but here, instead of there being details which could make up a sum, there is only the consciousness of Mathieu into which the freedom-entity fades until the two are one. Again the verb "to be" fuses the abstraction into the solid realities of the narration: it had seemed to be something separate, it was only an appearance, it resolves once more into what had been there all along.

Thought comes to a curious end in such passages. We

had had the impression that the motive of abstractions was to withdraw us from concrete reality, to purify it so that we could distinguish its lines and forms without being lost in its immediate presence; but at this most sophisticated point in the development of thinking, the primitive once more makes its appearance. The purpose was not to remain with those hard won entities, those carefully constructed abstractions: having been formed, they immediately dissolve into the sensory reality upon which they had been performed, just as the idea of the whole situation constantly fell back into the realities of the situation itself. So that all of the discoveries, the final understandings of the great problems, turn out to be nothing: the attention is awakened, everything is transformed after the passage of the abstraction, and yet the same concrete things are there as before; it was merely the abstraction which had seemed to promise an event and which indeed provided its own event, a momentary flash and glitter as it sped overhead and burnt itself out, leaving us once again alone with things.

# CHAPTER SEVEN

## *The Anatomy of Persons*

Human reality has an outside as well as an inside, a solid visible material shell that seems much closer to the world of things than do these facts of consciousness which are radically distinct from them. But somehow we never make any mistakes, we always treat these "things" which are other people in a very special way:

> The being of other people's bodies is a synthetic totality for me. This means: 1/ that I can never seize the body of the other person except on the background of a total situation which indicates it; 2/ that I am never able to perceive in an isolated state a given organ of the body of the other person, that each singular organ is indicated for me against the background of the totality of *flesh* or *life*. Thus my perception of the other person's body is radically different from my perception of things.[1]

Objects are infinitely divisible, they can be looked at from many angles, made to juxtapose with many different kinds of things, made to *transform*. But we are never in any danger of wondering what the series of heads with hats on moving past the window sill is; we understand them immediately as parts of people whose bodies are out of our sight.

The implications of such analyses of perception for
the work of art are strikingly different now from what
they once were. It is because we are made with two eyes,
set at a certain distance from each other, that we see
three dimensions. The artists of the Renaissance were
stirred by this discovery of the nature of perception to
imitate its results, to put together paintings which
would somehow double the perspective that human reality brought with it into the world: the achieved perspective had been fixed there on the canvas, it would linger
on even when no one was there, into the future. And instead of passively remaining an isolated element in the
three-dimensional vision of the spectator approaching
it, instead of submitting to a position within that vision,
the painting inside its four edges presents a second, imitation depth to which the eyes are attracted and into
which they fall.

Modern art is more consequential. The viewer brings
his sense organs, his structure of perception, with him
to the painting. Why try to add it in for him beforehand?
Supposing, as long as the mind automatically registers
the parts of the body as parts of a whole, we let the mind
have merely the part and let it perform its customary
function on that single datum, without building in a
dimension that indicates the whole beyond it: "His eyes
are glassy, in his mouth I watch a somber, rosy mass
stir."[2] The name, the word "tongue," would have added
in itself that dimension we wanted to avoid, for it names
not only the isolated organ but its connection with the
body; "tongue" does not mean merely a special kind
of object but a part-of-the-body. The sentence simply
notes the raw material of perception, and lets us figure
out what is being seen.

And yet no one actually sees things this way. The artist
is not doing the easiest thing, setting down the most

immediate perceptions: he is breaking the immediate whole perceptions down into their parts, fragmenting them, and these fragments are as strange to him as they are to us. Some stimulus undoubtedly comes from the movies. In the early period camera men and directors were not very attentive, either through choice or through clumsiness, to the habits of perception of their audiences. The jerkiness of transitions, the almost gratuitous shots of details like hands moving and lips stirring, figure a broken world which is far from what we experience in ordinary life. But the total effect of these gleaming and rapid bits of vision is instructively different from what happens in words. In the fragmentation on the screen the various limbs, mouths, eyes, float past us clearly: we have no doubt what they are, that they belong to bodies. We sense a violence in these grotesque fragments, the autonomy of the medium over its material, the will to fragmentation of the director, his high-riding freedom over his story and over matter itself.

Since the camera speaks directly to the eyes, the whole dimension of words and naming is absent; and we saw that some of the strangeness of the sentence quoted above depended on the withholding of the name. The camera is incapable of registering such moments when a name comes loose:

> The door of the room was half open; he pushed it. The air smelled stuffy. All of the day's heat had accumulated within the room, like dregs. Sitting on the bed, a woman looked at him smiling, it was Marcelle.[3]

That split second when a very familiar face is unrecognizable, when the structures of habit suddenly dissolve and leave us momentarily without a past or memory, is dependent on the words that mark the transition back to

the familiar, the names that surge and abolish the suddenly new.

But although the camera cannot register such moments, it can sometimes cause them:

> I hear rapid breathing and from time to time, out
> of the corner of my eye, I see a reddish flash covered
> with white hair.[4]

Everyone has at one time or another experienced in the
movie theater that sudden bewilderment caused either by
being too close to the screen, or by a too rapid transition
of images, or by a close-up too huge and too unexpected,
in which we are aware of nothing but the masses of light
and darkness on the screen: what are they? The eyes re-
fuse to focus; it is the irritation at not being able to locate
the giant face concealed in the trick landscape. And then
suddenly, recognition:

> It's a hand.

The verbal equivalents of these blur-moments, when all
the details are given but the name is withheld, function
in the midst of the prose like a small form: tension is
built up, confusion, curiosity, the mind flutters about the
puzzle, and then the releasing of the name stills and satis-
fies our expectations. We have already described this
form in our discussion of the colon and what it symbol-
ized: the possibility for the reality (and for the narrative
speed at which it is revealed) to slow down, to become
divisible, to be separated from itself for a split second
until the withheld elements finally spring back into place
and leave us once more with a totality.

And yet there is a distinctive difference in quality between the parts and fragments into which the reality is
divided, and the whole which results from them: such
fragments are, in their naked state, ordinarily not acces-

sible to perception, they are in a peculiarly sensory way abstract, they are, in short, facticity, the facticity of our bodies, and the perpetual necessity for us to assume this facticity is imitated by the constant resolution of such sense data into comprehensible wholes. Just as the pressure of our attempt to understand could be counted on to bring the personifications of mental processes alive, to turn them once more into pure consciousness, so here the assuming of facticity that we are at all times engaged in prevents these notations of human reality from freezing into broken pieces of mere things. It is the impossibility of our treating human beings as things which permits the artist to register them that way, solidly.

But we have exaggerated the puzzle-like quality of such moments by restricting ourselves to those parts of the body which are static, merely seen and then recognized. There can be a kind of fragmentation even when we know already what it is we are seeing, when we are given the name right away: "Her mouth pinched together on the last words: a varnished mouth with mauve glints, a scarlet insect busy devouring this ashen face."[5] The comparison isolates the mouth like a close-up, makes an insect-unity out of it. Yet although we know what it is we are looking at, there is still a confusion to be resolved: we have been given clearly labeled parts, a mouth, the pinching of the lips, the lipstick like a scarlet insect against the pale skin, but we have to somehow visualize them. The fragmentation here does not strike the isolated part of the body, it seizes on the act that part of the body is engaged in; it demands that we manage to *see* the expression on the mouth, having been given all the necessary information.

This process of visualization does not necessarily imply the discovery of a name that will solve it, as, for example, irritation. The abstract word is itself a kind of shorthand

for something sufficient in itself. Just as we did not need
to stop and figure out the relationship of isolated organs
to a body, so we never take up all of the details of someone's gesture into ourselves, to mull them over and decide
what it is these details express: the body is itself immediate meaning:

> That knitting of the brow, that redness, that stam-
> mering, that slight trembling of the hands, those
> tentative looks that seem both timid and menacing,
> do not *express* anger, they *are* anger. But it must
> be clearly understood: in itself a clenched fist
> is nothing and means nothing. But we never do
> perceive a *clenched fist:* what we perceive is a man
> who in a certain situation clenches his fist. It is this
> meaningful act which, considered in relationship to
> the past and to possibility, understood against the
> background of the synthetic totality "body in situa-
> tion," *is* the anger. . . . Thus it is not necessary to
> resort to habit or to deductions by analogy, to ex-
> plain the fact that we *understand* expressive con-
> duct: such conduct is from the very origin given to
> perception as comprehensible; its meaning is part of
> its very being, as the color of the paper is part of the
> being of the paper.[6]

This immediate comprehensibility of the body's gestures
and expressions, of its acts, permits them to be used both
as a point of departure and an ultimate term. Now the
most complex gestures can be broken to pieces and fixed
in the language, and our minds go to work on them with
the sudden feeling of comprehension as the test of the
work:

> On the opposite sidewalk, a gentleman holding his
> wife by the arm has just whispered a few words in

her ear and begun to smile. She at once thoroughly eliminates all traces of expression from her creamy face and takes a few sightless steps forward as if she were blind. There is no mistaking the signs: they are about to exchange greetings. And sure enough, after a moment, the man tosses his hand into the air. When his fingers are at close range of his hat, they hesitate a second before delicately alighting on the brim. While he gently raises it, lowering his head slightly to assist the extraction, his wife gives a little leap, inscribing a young smile on her face. A shadow passes them by, bowing: but their twin smiles do not immediately disappear: they remain on the lips in a kind of residual effect. When the couple finally pass me, they have reassumed their expressionlessness, but there are still traces of gayness around their mouths.[7]

These exquisite notations require a certain cooperation on the part of our reading mind: they are not a soft, already imagined matter into which we can comfortably sink. The demands are being made, not on our quickness of mind, like puzzles, but on our imaginations. Sartre has spoken of the way the reader chooses the work, the way he creates it along with the author, bringing it to life with himself or letting it sink back to the state of mere printed matter with the lapsing of his attention, the way we are compromised by the intensity with which we make the characters in books live in our minds.[8] Here, it is as if this analysis were not permitted to remain as a simple description of how we ordinarily read, as if it were pressed into service as a purpose; and the normal act of creation on the reader's part is doubled with a second, heightened one, where the reader does not merely re-create but has, himself, to create an act out of mere indications. And this creation is compromising because it is at the same time a judgment: if out of these absurd gestures we are able to visualize the ordinary scene of people greeting each other, we have already admitted that the scene is absurd.

The fragments, the raw material out of which we construct the scene, have a relationship not only to the recognizable scene itself but also among each other. They are given to us through the continuity of language, and this imposed continuity may scatter them, arrange them differently, put them back together wrong:

> He saw Ménard, seated, legs hanging down, on the top of a small wardrobe, swinging his boots in the crimson of the setting sun. He was the one who was singing; his eyes crazed with gaiety rolled around above his gaping mouth; his voice came loose out of him all by itself, it lived on him like an enormous parasite sucking out his guts and blood to turn them into songs; inert, his arms hanging loose, he stared with stupefaction at this vermin coming out of his mouth.[9]

The details are primary here, the fragments each undergo a kind of autonomous treatment in order to make them as vivid as possible and this treatment may work against the unity of the act. So here the eyes of Ménard are rolling, drunk and loose in his head. They do not change, but after the development of the voice as a parasitic entity, a new and more vivid formulation for these eyes seems in order: the showing of the whites, the rolling around in the orbits, seem to be rendered even more strikingly by the figure of astonishment, he seems to be staring at the monstrous voice. This astonishment is merely an illusion: the eyes are exactly as they were

when they were described as "crazed with gaiety," but
the new formulation, while it helps us to see the detail
more intensely, threatens to lead us further and further
away from the whole situation of which it is a part, risks
throwing us permanently off the track.

The confusion is inevitable: there are only a limited
number of expressions the human face can twist itself
into; but within a concrete situation we are rarely confused, we know that this appearance of hysterical merri-
ment is really an agony of grief, because we know the
context in which it takes place. But when the context
has been broken up, things begin to look like each other:
"Mathieu noticed that her face had become gray. The
atmosphere was pink and sugary, they were breathing and
eating pink: and then there was this gray face, this fixed
look, you would have thought she was trying not to
cough."[10] This new confusion eliminates the last traces
of a picture-puzzle quality from the writing: now it is
no longer necessary to fit isolated pieces together. The
comparison requires of us a purer kind of visualization;
we have to see precisely the kind of look people have
when they are trying not to cough and this look must be
individualized in the right way to fit into its new context. Once it has materialized, the old name and interpretation is dropped, and the concrete situation is present before us.

The "as if" is here the sign of a renewal of visual description, yet a renewal from an unexpected direction.
For it has some of the same tautological quality that we
have found in the simile: an expression on a face turns
out to look like what it is, except that the sense of the
expression is different, misunderstood, or inappropriate.
The "as if" does therefore not represent any powerful
dose of metaphor added to the situation, but simply the
creative power of subjectivity working within the given

situation, breaking it to pieces and putting it back together again its own way. For it is the sign, not only of
fragmentation, but of fusion as well: an imperative to
the reading mind to bring life back to the heap of visual
data, to return the offered sensations to their status as
described human reality. This fragmentation of human
beings therefore only partly reflects the destructive, negative dimension of the Sartrean "look," that mode of
consciousness whose very reason for being is in a sense
revenge, the neutralization of those other human beings
whose sudden appearance in my world is a fundamental
and permanent trauma. This negative force has also a
built-in rectification; like any destruction its results are
positive, and the Sartrean world remains a human one.
For what is done to these faces and expressions is not a
depersonalized malice, passing itself off as what the world
really is, but a human gesture: the writer's gesture, his
sentence, but also in a sense our own. For the style does
not show itself to us as polished and complete, indifferent
to our reading; on the contrary, it exists only in the moment of our reading, it requires our participation, and
this respect for us as human beings involved in a relationship with the writer puts in perspective the severity
visited on certain types of human beings in the content
of the work. The satire no longer issues from some disembodied point above humanity but from a writer within it, in his concrete situation; and it does not permit us
as readers a sheltered enjoyment but makes us witness
a treatment of human reality to which neither the writer
nor the readers are themselves immune.

As was the case with the opposition between the
unique feeling and the general name it bore, these descriptions of the outside of human beings have become
precise not through attention to a single word that would

point toward the expression (an *angry* face, *trembling* lips, etc.) but by locating the one unique expression of this face midway between two general expressions, and forcing the reader to discover the exact point of intersection, and with it, the concrete expression itself. Yet the expressions of faces in this world are not all equivalent, equally powered and therefore equally lacking in self-sufficiency. Just as certain feelings, through a kind of special density that they possessed, tended to become ground-feelings in the work, and to be used frequently to evoke and strengthen other, lesser feelings, so here from time to time we stumble across a facial expression that seems to set up reverberations throughout the entire work, that is somehow not simply limited to the situation to which it is a response and which lends it its immediate meaning, but that rises as a kind of generalized atmosphere to float over the work, a sudden obsessive look on a face which persists long after it is gone from the sentences and which seems to us a privileged vehicle for the tone of this world, something "typically" Sartrean.

Such a ground-expression will automatically begin to be pressed into the service of weaker expressions, it will become the reinforcing term of an "as if" clause designed to spring them more adequately onto the mind. It is therefore no accident that Ménard's eyes, in the passage examined above, were described in terms of *astonishment*. It was essential that the staring bug-eyed look be rendered in terms of some second expression, but nothing in it dictated this particular term of comparison; we might have been readily satisfied with some other, such as horror, at the sight of the vermin image of the voice. Yet in a cumulative reading of Sartre's work, the expression of astonishment comes to be enriched with special, obsessive, private overtones, like those leitmotif words of the poets which come to spread about them, each time they are pronounced, zones of greater meaning than their isolated appearance on the page, among many other words, would seem to justify. At this point it is no longer possible to account for the force of the recurrent expression through the special kind of language which presents it; on the contrary it is itself one of the elements out of which effects of the language are built, and its evocative quality has to be traced to some peculiarity in the structure of this world, to themes and content rather than the words that are able to register them. Yet it is related to a special type of content: consciousness is active, the books are full of its various ways of acting on the world, its motives, values, the kinds of thoughts it thinks, the way it gives to the things it does and feels the very sense of action, of "something happening," all phenomena we have been able to examine elsewhere. But in astonishment there is apparently a kind of pause in the relationship of the human being to his world, a manner of judging it and of feeling something about it which extends beyond the unique, particular cause of the astonishment and ends up in a kind of sudden stupefaction at the world itself. Or at the human reality which is a correlative of the category of a "world."

It is as if something like fragmentation occasionally took place within human reality, so that our awareness of ourselves faltered and groped with the same tentativeness as our perceptions of other people's faces, destroying the authority of self-consciousness and letting us misunderstand our own gestures in the same way that we misunderstood those of others in the outside world. And we are astonished at having been wrong, and at being able to be. A word, for example, that suddenly escapes us: "If it were not a question of *recapitulation . . .* "

"Recapitulation." Pierre had suddenly had a stupid expression on his face and the word, long and whitish, had slid out of his mouth. Pierre had stared ahead with astonishment as if he saw the word without recognizing it; his mouth was open, loose; something seemed to have broken inside of him.[11]

This description of the breakdown of a mind has implications much wider than its immediate, limited subject; for insanity can only work with and deform, exaggerate, tendencies already present in every consciousness, and the possibility for human reality to break into pieces, into a mind watching astonished as its unbidden word gets spoken, is somehow perpetually present. The body in action is spontaneous and whole; we are not even aware of it as a body since we are at the moment only aware of that upon which we are working. But when something disturbs and shatters the unity, when reflection makes its appearance in the midst of what was spontaneity, the clumsy hand, immediately magnified, is seen as a hand, and our being breaks down into a mind with its purposes and the body-instrument attempting vainly to carry them out. Our surprise is the shocked recognition that this hand, which stirs so effortlessly at the taking of a thought, that these spoken words, still warm from the mind that hardly had a chance to conceive them before they were uttered, are also no longer parts of us, but outside of our subjectivity, things in the world now somehow separate from us.

So also in the world of our emotions. In this work, for which emotion is not an isolated zone of irrationality constantly threatening to take the conscious mind by surprise but rather a mode of consciousness as freely chosen as any other, the emotions of the characters are

nonetheless not transparent and immediately meaningful. In earlier novels of analysis the emotion, watched
for greedily by the narrating consciousness, seemed to
blossom amply and easily under the weight of the expectation; it can sometimes surprise—especially in the analyses of love—but its interest and its truth are in its
depth and its persistence, its opaque presence that permits the sentences to descend ever more deeply into it
without its being shaken or suddenly fading away. The
Sartrean emotion lacks this cavernous resonance, it is a
burst and nothing more, but a burst apparently at cross
purposes with the conscious mind. Just as there was a
staccato quality in the events of this world, an angular
shuttling back and forth of pieces of episodes and of time
itself, so also emotions tend to make unexpected appearances, to rise up fast and strike us with full volume, and
then to disappear again just as unexpectedly, before we
have had time to adjust to them:

> He offered us English cigarettes and *puros,* but we
> refused. I looked him in the eyes and he seemed em-
> barrassed. I said: "You didn't come here out of com-
> passion. Anyhow I know you. I saw you in the court-
> yard of the barracks with a bunch of fascists the day
> I was arrested." I was going to go on, but all of a
> sudden something happened to me that surprised
> me: the presence of this doctor abruptly ceased to
> interest me. Ordinarily when I'm after a man I don't
> let him go. And yet the urge to speak left me; I
> shrugged my shoulders and looked away.[12]

Such moments seem to figure consciousness as the empty
place through which emotions violently pass, a stage cha-
otically peopled with feelings and sometimes empty of
them, as the man relaxes exhausted from the agitation
that had taken only momentary possession of him. When

the phenomenon is not focused on directly, verbs remind us in passing of this obligatory suddenness of what
is felt: feelings *surge, die out, invade* consciousness, and
*fade* rapidly out of it again. And when there is no possibility of replacing a calmer verb with vocabulary of
enough violence, the adverbs continue to insist on how
"abruptly," "suddenly," and "without warning" the
feelings take place. These mannerisms, which we might
ordinarily tend to see as a way of tightening up an otherwise bland sentence, are here the visible signs of the
conception of emotion in general as that which takes
human reality by surprise.

It is perhaps not so incomprehensible that a philosophy
of freedom should be fascinated by what seems to contradict it, and should grapple directly with the problems
that seem to pose the greatest difficulties for it. Insofar
as the work has a secondary polemic purpose, that of
bringing us face to face with our own freedom, figures
who are clearly free and who openly control their destinies are less useful than people who *seem* trapped by
something, whether it is sexual malfunctioning, insanity,
the "second nature" of people who "are" cowards or col-
laborators, felt compulsions, or simply the helplessness
and sterility of people like Mathieu before the forces of
history pressing in upon them. Such destinies, which the
theory of freedom sees as choices, pose literary as well as
philosophical problems: the felt determinism, the fa-
tality, must be presented as well as the real freedom and
choice which is responsible for it. A story like ***The Room***
is therefore not a clinical study of insanity from the outside but a way of showing both the erratic outside surface of the psychosis and the game of self-deception, the
slow withdrawal from an intolerable reality, that is the
choosing of it. We have already seen how Sartre's formulation of the "unconscious" was dependent on the dis-

tinction between reflective and unreflective spontaneous consciousness. It is on this second level of consciousness that our choice takes place, which the reflective mind lives as something somehow imposed on it. But the narration must be able to give the sense of passively suffering a destiny as well as the meaning of its having been chosen, otherwise images obviously untrue to experience such as someone "deciding" to be insane will suggest themselves.

In the same way, the violence of the verbs of feeling, the insistence on the suddenness, the surprise, of emotion, guards the lived truth of the experience. The emotion is chosen, but not in terms of a kind of vulgarized will power philosophy: we do not decide to feel a certain emotion but put ourselves into a passive state in which for us the emotion is able to seize us, and is able to seem to.[13] The emotion is necessarily felt as something submitted to, undergone; it has a lived density which is a necessary characteristic of it, and in order to "choose" an emotion we must necessarily be stunned and overpowered by it. Our surprise is our recognition of that part of emotion which is facticity, irreducible brute content. That is why the characters of this universe of freedom never are able to turn into mere transparent symbols of a meaning or of a kind of choice, as they have a tendency to do in the works of Malraux for example: each of them has his choice, his drama, which is his meaning, each of them feels emotions which are themselves ways of acting in a given situation and as such have intentional meaning, but the meaning remains abstract and derived through the mediation of the unforeseeable thickness of lived experience.

Thus these moments of astonishment can be traced to types of fragmentation, but what they all have in common is a sudden jog in the apprehension of reality: the habitual ordinary reality suddenly breaks to pieces under our eyes, becomes unreal without being replaced by a more stable reality, and the whole notion of reality, now that it is gone, proves to have been nothing more reassuring than habit. It is at this point that a more profound drama of astonishment begins and that the opposite of astonishment comes into play, not stolidity or imperturbability but rather a dazed, sleepwalking kind of apprehension of the world. In *The Age of Reason,* at the moment when Mathieu without knowing exactly what he is doing leans forward and kisses Ivich, instantly regretting it and amazed at the spontaneity of this gesture that has results for the feeling between them out of all proportion to its weight in time and decision, an anecdote suddenly suggests itself:

> He remembered the gesture of a man he once saw in the rue Mouffetard. Fairly well-dressed, with a face gone completely gray. The man had walked up to a food stand, he had stared for a long time at a slice of cold meat on a plate in the display, then he had stretched out his hand and taken the piece of meat; he seemed to think it was all very simple, he must have felt free too. The owner had shouted, a policeman had led away this man who looked astonished.[14]

This little story is too complete to be simply a one-to-one commentary on Mathieu's feelings: it has the autonomy of any solid anecdote surging into a continuity of which it is not a part; it illustrates something and as an illustration fits into the narration, but as a narration on its own right it is also concrete and the fascination it exercises is irreducible like any fact. The story is a parable of social life in general and of the alienated individual within it. The hero, the man with decent clothes on his way down and out, has ceased to understand even the most fundamental social signs. The notion of property, which for us is so habitual that it is inscribed in things themselves and needs no tickets or warnings to attract our attention, has become utterly incomprehensible. Instead of threading his way through other people's belongings according to well-defined rights and limitations, the privileges of the coins in his pocket, the instant differentiation of wares from things not for sale, the man wanders among nothing but separate objects, sense data with no categories to link them to each other. The shopkeeper's face turning toward him slowly, interrogative and with at the same time the indifference of the vendor and the rapid sizing up of social status based on the quality of the clothing and the condition of the man's personal hygiene—this face has nothing whatsoever to do with the stale meat lying before him, no logical relationship to it, the two are merely pictures, separate things visible at the same moment. The meat being there, he picks it up; he is not insane but merely in a state of nature, and his astonishment is a kind of waking up to social realities long forgotten.

The child stands in a similar dream-like relationship to the world around him (and Sartre's description of Genet's first theft, his original trauma, is very similar to the little story we have just examined). For the center of gravity of the child's world is outside of him, in the grownups: his first awareness of values is the distinction between what is "serious" and what is properly his own permitted sphere of behavior. When these intersect, the world's lighting fluctuates and becomes problematical:

> The parish priest, who lunched at the house every Saturday, asked him if he loved his mama. Lucien adored his pretty mama and his papa who was so strong and kind. He answered, "Yes," looking the

priest in the eye with a cocky little look that made
everybody laugh . . . The priest said that it was good
and that he should always love his mama; and then
he asked who Lucien loved the most, his mama or
the Lord in Heaven. Lucien could not guess the
answer right away and he began to shake his locks
and kick his feet in the air crying "Taraboomdiay"
and the grownups took up their conversation again
as if he didn't exist.[15]

This rather pompous catechism, which for the grownups
is merely the expected sign of the priest's profession, his
appropriation of that conversational subject which is
his speciality, is for Lucien one of those privileged moments in which the grownups turn their attention to him,
in which all the play-like solitary child's behavior is suddenly invested with real seriousness, and in which the
child has a sudden foreshadowing, in this new quality
of his being, of what adult action is like. But there are
limits to the situation: Lucien knows very well that he
is only being treated "as if" he were a grownup, and he
has to answer "as if"; his answer has to fit in, it has to
be what the grownups want to hear, he has to *guess* the
right answer. And the second question awkwardly seems
to tear him between two loyalties and two different persons in the room: one or the other is bound to be angry
—his mother, or the priest, who seems to have some
vested interest in the Lord in Heaven. The child prefers
in his confusion to abandon his new position and revert
to infantile behavior, and then something bizarre takes
place. We can assume that these sentences, which register only as much as Lucien sees of the world, do not dis-
pose of the means to pick up the more delicate realities
of the situation: his mother's humiliation, the priest's embarrassment, the fluency with which some other person,

to cover matters over, begins to converse again. Lucien is too busy shaking his head and kicking his feet to notice any of this, so that for him the transition is as abrupt as the shift in a dream: the adult conversation on the fringes of which he was playing a little while before, only vaguely listening to it, opens up for a moment around him and then closes again without a trace. Lucien is not astonished by this sudden autonomy of the conversation that seems to hold the grownups within itself and permit them only momentary lulls and then sweep them on; he has no points of comparison, the law of his world is to be unreal and a new irreality is not surprising. But we as readers are the ones who are surprised at the way this seemingly stable world can grow thin and two-dimensional without warning, how this social gathering can suddenly fade into something as distant and mannered as a ballet.

These moments of the fluctuation of reality express themselves for the normal man in the form we have described as a transformation, and at this point they can no longer be accounted for by any peculiarity in the situation of the viewer, his position on the edge of society as a child, or his utter isolation. There must be, in order for them to take place at all, something more fundamental wrong with human reality itself:

> "You want to die for the Sudetens?" asked the man with the beard. "Shut up," said Maurice. The man with the beard looked at him with a baleful and hesitant expression, it looked like he was trying to remember something. All of a sudden he shouted: "Down with war! . . . Down with war! Down with war!"

Here is the now familiar structure of the Sartrean environment: the expression that looks like something else, the suddenness with which the shout pops out as if it had happened all by itself, the jerky quality which we analyzed in a formal way in our description of the period. But suddenly something happens to the scene:

> The bearded man continued to shout, with a tired urbane voice—a rich man's voice; and Maurice suddenly had the unpleasant impression that the whole scene was rigged. He looked around him and his joy disappeared: it was the others' fault, they weren't doing what they had to do. At the meetings, when somebody starts yelling a lot of goddam nonsense, the crowd just moves in on him and blots him out, you see arms in the air for a second and then nothing at all. But instead of that the others had moved back, they had left an empty space around the man with the beard.[16]

The event is not strong enough to take place all by itself: all of it is there, it is serious, and yet somehow, in a kind of "internal hemorrhage of being," its reality has been drained away. No one seems to believe in it, not even the bearded man, who looks like he is merely going through the paces of an arrangement prepared for him, without conviction. The mere outside of the event is not enough: it is as if we were watching, behind glass, a struggle in an uncanny silence that turns all the violence into something visual, a series of gestures without significance, a grotesque moving pattern. But this is not something that affects the observer alone: each of the actors, in the moment of raising his fist, or shouting, or backing away, feels secretly that he is playing a part and that he is suddenly no longer engaged in this gesture that the whole of him seemed to propose spontaneously. The weakness is no longer in the situation, but in some lack of reality within consciousness itself:

Take for example this waiter. His gestures are quick and studied, a little too precise, a little too rapid, he comes toward the customers with too quick a step, he bows with a little too much alacrity, his voice, his eyes express an interest a little too full of solicitude for the client's order, and then here he comes back, trying to imitate in his walking the inflexible rigor of some kind of automaton, carrying his tray with some of the daring of a tightrope walker, setting it constantly in an unstable and ever broken equilibrium that he constantly retrieves with a slight movement of the arm and the hand. His entire conduct looks to us like a game. He is busy trying to link his movements together as if they were mechanisms that set each other in play, his mimicry and his voice itself are like mechanisms; he imitates the alertness and rapidity of things. He's playing, amusing himself. But what is he playing at? You don't have to watch him long to realize: he is playing at *being a waiter*.[17]

That resolution of our being into an "inside" and an "outside" ends up ejecting from consciousness everything that is not an act on our part, all of the labels and qualities that it seems to us we *are*. Status, the profession of "being" a waiter, the fact of "being" Jewish,[18] of "being" a thief, all these words we can never feel from the inside. We go through the motions they seem to require, make the gestures appropriate to such conditions, but the moment we stop and, inactive, attempt to feel some of the feeling of "being" this or that, it vanishes, and we are nothing but pure consciousness again. We have seen earlier that this was the case with moral adjectives, with bravery and cowardice, good and evil. What now becomes apparent is that this distance between consciousness and what it is supposed to be is not limited to the static descriptions of qualities and labels alone: it exists even in the heart of action, prevents our very expressions and gestures from ever being the direct spontaneous revelations of our being, and makes the act, even before it is completed, separate itself from us and go unreal, unrecognizable, infected with a lack of seriousness, a kind of play- or dream-like quality. It is enough to have once had the experience of being looked at for us never to be able to get rid of a kind of staging of our person, even in total solitude; and the most violent emotions, with nobody around to watch them, remain tinged with a secret embarrassment because we never suffer them passively enough, we are always busy acting them out even when we would like to be completely submerged by them. The astonishment that we have noticed is the perpetual reaction of consciousness to this lack of reality that bides its time at the heart of everything we do. The strangeness, the body's autonomy, the rushing into being of an unplanned gesture, the loss of belief in a situation we were strongly committed to moments before, the fading of the reality of waking life—all these are moments that can have their own unique historical causes, their meaning in terms of the individual drama being lived through them and the society they take place in; but they rise upon the distance within all consciousness, the distance which prevents consciousness from coinciding with itself.

We have examined these moments before, approaching them through the demands they made on sentences, through the formal inventions that had to be made for them to be seized and articulated; we showed the new kind of drama that the insufficiency of moral labels and descriptions, the need for acts to be constantly assumed, imposed, and we showed also how in the novel new kinds of narration told the story of events so slight in volume as to require the massed force of subjectivity to bring them into focus. These were at first questions of form. But now, after a long detour through the world of things, such formal peculiarities prove to be justified by the world from which they spring, and by the very nature of consciousness itself: a scenery of unattainable things, a consciousness constantly set in doubt, unstable, and unable to be.

## Conclusions

It is obvious that the literary results we have been considering in these pages would not take place and would not even be possible in every kind of work, in every kind of style: they are not "techniques" but parts of an indivisible whole, the language reflecting the themes, which are in their turn materializations of what is already in the language itself. It is more dangerous to try to locate a single center from which these things issue: a kind of original choice which has no geographical or historical position but which constitutes the final irreducible reality behind developments whose relation to each other is back to it first and then out again. In a formal way it is evident that both the necessity for things to come to language in human terms and the way human reality seemed to need a "thingification" to remain human are dependent on the vision of the world that sees it as an opposition between being and existence, between objects and subjectivity. Without this first premise the dialectical relationship between the two terms would disappear, and the presentation of the raw material (assuming it could survive) would alter beyond recognition. This seems a very sterile point to reduce a rich work to; but one reason for its poverty is that it would be necessary, so as to give this central choice the development it requires, to situate it in Sartre's own concrete life in the manner of an existential psychoanalysis: something we have no means of doing. All we can do is indicate what implications the persistence of this abstract starting point has had for the work we are considering.

In *Being and Not-Being* it seems to me that this opposition takes on the form of what I would call an arrested dialectic, or the imitation of a dialectic. Whenever opposites are established, they enter into a dialectical relationship with each other, and such is the case in this book, except that the terms are so defined that their very nature consists in not being able to synthesize with each other in any way. They have to interact: the world, and human experience, is just such interaction. But only one of them, consciousness, is dependent on the other: pure being can easily do without consciousness. And at the same time the attempt to do without the unparticipating term of the dialectic, the non-human, was already once made vainly in idealism. It is the idea of facticity which as we have seen assures the perseverance of brute being in the humanized world consciousness generates around itself; but what is this idea except a way of cutting the dialectic off short with a kind of empiricism, a kind of rough common sense, after it has permitted the problem to arise? It is as if the dialectic were useful in setting up the problem, as a framework for developing it; and once the problem has been expressed, the expression takes on the quality of an answer to it: the dilemma is ratified, its *recognition* by the reader is the purpose of the exposition. The apparently dialectical apparatus is not permitted to pursue its course under its own power and create the illusion of a synthesis, or of a solution; it springs the problem onto the screen of our minds and then is choked off. This procedure can be seen for example in the discussion of the *Mitsein,* where every formal instrument in the discussion of the relationship of one consciousness to another indicates the possibility of a first person plural subject in which the consciousnesses would participate . . . except that it does not exist, and the relationships between different human beings, all conflict, are resumed empirically under the forms of love, hatred, sadism, masochism, etc. None of this, of course, holds true for Sartre's most recent work in the Marxist dialectic, which has another basis altogether. Nor should it be construed as a regret that the dialectic had not been preserved. What interests us here is that, just as we have seen in narration, the philosophical work uses a kind of inherited structure through which to present its new perceptions, so that it would be possible to imagine a new philosophical development, which would take this as its point of departure, and which would preserve this content, in which we recognize ourselves more adequately than in any other modern system, at the same time that it abandoned the form and the arrangement of the material around the split between being and consciousness. Such a progression of a similar reality through books that look very different from each other would be characteristic of the history of philosophy since Descartes.

In the novels and plays there is a realer, lived synthesis between the two terms, one that is familiar to us since it was with it that we began: the so-called "subjective event" itself, where the word subjective and all that it suggests merely shows that we had introduced the opposition too early, for expository purposes, into a phenomenon which takes precedence over it and suppresses it. For in fact, all action, all human experience in the world, precedes the separation of the world into two static terms. When we use instruments in a project directed into the future, we are at one with things, and even this way of putting it is inadequate, since there are no mere things and there is not even a consciousness aware of its isolation from them, there is merely a human project developing itself. Language is the moment of rupture of this indivisible phenomenon, and the distance from it that causes it to fall apart into what appear to be separate entities coming into fleeting contact with one another; it is the need to say the personal pronoun and to name the things and the setting; it is also the place of a gymnastic effort to restore some of the unity within the limits of its means. It is only after this moment of the appearance of language that some events take on the illusion of being purely subjective in contrast to others that we accept as real without question, so that it is here that the verbal opposition between objective and subjective, between being and consciousness, arises: it was in the language all along, an inherited syntax, part of the residue of a long Western philosophical development that we cannot think away or suddenly ignore, a tendency even intensified in an alienated world to discriminate between the human individual and the things around him that seem to him to have been always there, and to reduce the apprehension of the world by his consciousness to mere images and psychological "subjective" responses. Instead of attempting to suppress the distinction in a utopian poetry, this work as we have seen pushes it to its limit. The synthesis is the content of the narration itself: lived human experience, but it remains there, in the content; and the language that expresses it oscillates back and forth between the two terms that it is incapable of abolishing. It is at this point that we must grasp the relationship between this event and its language, and the major form in which it takes place.

*Nausea,* which is unquestionably Sartre's most perfect novel, is cast in the form of a diary: it has the advantage of preserving Roquentin's solitude, implying readers as does every kind of sentence, but only obliquely, much later, after it is all over, as a kind of historical accident.

The diary permits the isolated daily experience to dispense with the prejudice of a continuity that the memoir, or the chapter novel, would automatically impose on it. Its fragmentation, its purely empirical succession, is precisely that "walk in a night empty of premonitions, a night that offered [the hero] its monotonous riches indiscriminately." He does choose among these riches, but we watch the choice being made, we see before our eyes the gradual development of the idea-instrument, the notion of a nausea, that lets him express them and permits them to increase in intensity and fully reveal themselves.

The unity of the book is therefore dependent on the structure of this cumulative experience that it describes, or on the structure of the idea in terms of which the experience is grasped; and the distance between this book and others whose contents are related in one way or another to "ideas" is a function of the unique shape of the experience, the idea, which is itself distinct in quality from all other "ideas." The following sentence of Maurice Blanchot underlines the rare movement of the book's development:

> When Roquentin finally meets existence face to face, when he sees it, understands it, and describes it, what really happens is that nothing new happens, nothing changes, the revelation does not illuminate him for it has never stopped being present to him, and it puts an end to nothing, because it is in his fingers that feel and in his eyes that see, that is to say continually absorbed by his being that lives it.[1]

The curious solitude of *Nausea* as a great novel, the feeling of a tour de force that we have in spite of ourselves, of an absolutely unique occasion rather than a book whose success is easily integrated into the history of the form, is perhaps a kind of optical illusion in which we apprehend the book both as a "novel of ideas" and as the novel of an idea so unique that no other idea could have "worked" in its place. This feeling corresponds to something real, for although here the idea of existence is absolutely identical to Roquentin's own individual existence with its unique historical contents, it remains, through the very fact of persisting as an abstract word, something that can transfer itself to any other life, with its own special contents, and be at one with the new life as well. The book is therefore at the same time a self-justifying whole and an unjustifiable, contingent body of contents: nothing can make the facticity of Roquentin's life a more privileged vehicle for the revelation of existence than that of any other life, but once we have passed within the book's framework, once, standing within this life, our attention is diverted to the drama it is about to undergo, the feeling of a contradiction weakens because one of its terms is accepted and out of sight. This presence of facticity is in one way or another the formal problem of the other novels as well.

After the special case of *Nausea* the later novels have to be a beginning again, in a formal void. The idea of freedom which they seem to deal with and which is present in their titles does not stand in the same relationship to their contents as did the idea of existence in the earlier work. It tends to imply in spite of itself an opposite, a condition of not being free, which lends it a didactic movement and threatens to turn the earlier discovery which was not a discovery of anything new into a real revelation, a real moment of truth or of the appearance of an "idea"; and because these works are a series of dramas rather than that of a single individual, the problem of freedom threatens to reduce itself to the preoccupation of a single character, no more privileged than the quite different preoccupations of the others. And just as the shape of the idea in *Nausea* seemed to dictate its form, so here each novel, the evocation of a historical moment of distinct quality, crystallizes into a form different from each of the others: the progressive dramatic organization of *The Age of Reason,* the formal innovation of *The Reprieve,* and the chaos and loose ends of *Death in the Soul* that finally resolve themselves into a simple linear narrative in the story of the prison camp.

*The Reprieve* is a kind of great reaching out for everything, an expansion of the novel's ambitions until they seem to reach the point of an equivalence between the work of art and the world itself: everything in Europe at this moment in time is supposed to leave its traces here, for the moment of crisis is not only related to those actors directly concerned with it but also profoundly influenced by all the personal dramas that deliberately ignore the danger of war and pursue themselves in indifference to it. Just as the great catalogues of the individual events of a life, or the things that happen in peace time, fill in the abstract words Life and Peace, so *The Reprieve* is the working out in solid details of the abstract vision Mathieu had of an unimaginable world full of autonomous consciousnesses. Yet as vast as the published book is, its ambition is in its very nature impossible: *everything* cannot possibly fit into the work, and since it deliberately invites a comparison between everything and what manages to be there, the individual episodes turn into samples and examples of an unrealizable totality. Nothing controls the selection of detail; after it is all over the episodes and the characters have become part of a historical moment meaningful in its own right, but while it is going on, there is no reason why there should at this point be a transition to this drama rather than that: and the drama itself would not be missed if it had happened to be replaced by an entirely different episode before the book's publication; its presence is accounted for merely by the fact that it *is*. Yet these loose ends are themselves a part of the book's plan. It is in a way necessary that they be individually unnecessary, for the book is not intended to constitute a fixed place from which the world can be seen "as it really is," it is not supposed to replace our individual isolation with the reality of interpersonal relationships seen in some "objective" way, but rather to preserve the primacy of the individual consciousness within a world that transcends it and of which it can only have but the most fragmentary conception. In a sense there is an abstract idea around which the book is organized, but it stands in a different relationship to the executed novel than did the idea of existence to *Nausea:* this is the notion of a kind of simultaneity of consciousnesses, the awareness of the individual consciousness that its private world has an unattainable outside, that its time is simultaneous with the times of unnumbered other consciousnesses of which it can only be abstractly aware, or in another sense, the feeling of our participation in a history (or a society) far larger than we are of which we will never see anything but the limited reverberations our life permits it to cause, the limited face it turns toward our own isolated existence.[2] This simultaneity, out of sight, informs the novel like a kind of imperative: the details, the episodes, must be absolutely concrete and individual, as unforeseen as all those aspects of other people's simultaneous lives that shock us on account of that core of them that can never be reduced to the idea we first tried to form about them. The contents of those other lives are less important than their sheer facticity for us: the astonishment at finding a world beyond our own is more important than what that world turns out to be, so that it is precisely this necessity for things to be absolutely unique that prevents them from being absolutely necessary in terms of the organization of the work of art.

It is in *The Age of Reason* that this contradiction between facticity and artistic inevitability is most accessible. The book is organized on the order of a well-made play, it finishes with a *coup de théâtre,* the sudden satisfying of all the anticipations, the untying of the melodramatic knot. Such a climax is supposed to return upon all the earlier episodes and justify them by turning them into points in an inevitable movement: a playwright's novel, except that in the plays, as we have seen, there is only an appearance of melodrama, they tend to find their fulfillment not in the objective coming together of the situation but in words and speeches, in the taking up of the situation into language. This "dramatic" organization is moreover very different in quality from the reality of what we have called the "subjective event": the coup de théâtre is the autonomy of the situation itself over its parts. After it has been developed to a certain point, the situation takes over on its own momentum and rapidly and inexorably evolves toward a climax. The material, the brute content, provides its own movement: it has to happen, the characters can do little about it, it is not dependent on any quality of perception, which then becomes merely part of the embroidery, details of the execution, of a fixed pattern; and when the characters seem to have a relationship of freedom to the events taking place, the disastrous climax returns upon them to turn them into "character" or psychological destiny. The hollowness of melodrama as a form is precisely this illusion that the shattering and explosive events are *intrinsically* interesting, self-satisfying and satisfying to the spectators in their own right: the story of a murder does not have to be justified when murder itself is a perpetually fascinating phenomenon. The subjective event, on the other hand, was dependent on a kind of passiveness of the material, the constant possibility for consciousness to make its events out of anything, no matter how "intrinsically" banal or inconspicuous—the necessity, in fact, for consciousness to assume responsibility for the things it sees as events and as worth telling.

The coup de théâtre is therefore old-fashioned, as the problem-words were old-fashioned, as the moral problems of cowardice and bravery were. In the new atmosphere of the Sartrean world such patterns seem survivals; and yet they have to entertain some kind of organic relationship to the new perceptions. Sartre has frequently insisted on the importance of "extreme situations," and most of his works are organized around the moments where the problems facing consciousness are intensified, purified, made more surely authentic, by the imminence of death. The coup de théâtre of *The Age of Reason* is a way of evolving an extreme situation out of a situation where death is not present; it is a way of imposing a continuous progressive time upon a series of "subjective events," perceptions, moments of transformation, which threaten to be self-sufficient (and our analyses of such moments were made possible only by the secret autonomy of the moments themselves). There is a contradiction between two kinds of time, the time of the individual event and the time of the book, or between what Coleridge called fancy and imagination, the minute execution of the work and its first general conception, between the style of the book and the "idea for" the book. It is only in *Nausea* that Sartre seems to have had the possibility of letting the specialized perceptions organize themselves without an imposed framework, without a "plot." Yet the extreme situation is not simply an extraneous framework that does violence to the reality of the works: we remember that within the subjective events themselves, in the transformation, for example, there was a kind of regulatory agency inserted; the transformation had to be "real," things had to turn into "what they really are," and the event had to have its necessary facticity recalled and insisted on so as not to fly off into purest subjectivity and aesthetic play. The insistence on the extreme situation performs a similar regulatory function on the events as a whole: the perceptions experienced in danger are more surely "real" perceptions, the fact that we compromise ourselves, that we choose and commit ourselves, through any perception of the world is doubled and intensified when the difficult situation makes the perceptions really count. The extreme situation is a kind of gross intensification of our everyday existence, our everyday assumptions, in the same way as the parable of Hugo reflected symbolically through itself the structure of every act.

This curious doubling, this superposition of the old upon the new, is repeated at a more fundamental level in the treatment of people themselves. The basic category of the older novel was the "character"; and the word suggests not only a kind of representation of human beings on which a novel or a play is built but a special relationship to human beings as well. A "character" is someone contemplated at distance, from a purely aesthetic point of view. The overtones of comedy in the word reflect the distance; the curious amalgam of mannerisms that is a "character" is usually apprehended through amusement. But the oddity of the person is only a function of his conspicuousness, his isolation, the fact of his having grown away from an abstract "universal" idea of Man, from a fixed and permanent "human nature." The distance we have from him is the result of divisions and classes within the society: we ourselves are separate and sheltered by the class or status to which we belong, and we are therefore able without compromising ourselves, in the literature of "characters," to watch human beings from the outside, safely, as a kind of grotesque ballet that confirms us in our own privileged standing, unless, by some accident, that standing turns out itself to be the object of derision of another class. This literature is in its very nature prolific: there are as many subjects, as many novels, as there are characters in a crowd or in a city; and a Balzac has only to see the face of an old man hobbling past him in the street to be in possession of a book.

A literature of consciousness reflects an entirely different disposition of the world. Consciousness is pure, impersonal; even the feeling of having a personality is external to it, a kind of mirage that vanishes altogether when we are directly engaged in our projects, and reappears upon the horizon of our consciousness when it rests and enjoys a meditation upon itself. For such a consciousness there is no longer any possibility of protective distance from others. The apprehension of them that once included their whole face, their body and all of its reassuring private mannerisms, is shrunken and reduced to their eyes alone; and the eyes are abstract, they merely indicate our vulnerability before the other consciousness; and the face, the personality, to which the eyes belong, is less real than the fact of being seen itself. It is when the grotesques, the "characters," begin in turn to look at *us* that a literature of characters is done for: in this new kind of society we cannot hide, the groupings and the classes are too weak to protect us any more, and every consciousness becomes unique, privileged, dangerous.

This book has been a study of a literature of consciousness. There were no passages that we had to explain in terms of the "personality" of the actors in them, no per-

ceptions that had to turn into manifestations of a character in order to be understood. The notion of personality is here replaced by the idea of the original choice,
but insofar as that choice always is a choice of being it
can always, no matter how bizarre its form, be made intelligible when its development is complete: we do not
merely "understand" from the outside the gluttony of
Mme. Darbédat, we feel it directly as one human possibility among others, we *recognize* it, we are made to
choose it briefly ourselves in the very reading of it, and
such recognition, which compromises us and makes us
assume all other human reality, even what we would
prefer to keep our distance from, as our own, is the object
of such a literature.

Only it turns out that in these works there are *also*
characters in the older sense. Mathieu is a consciousness
at odds with the problem of freedom: impersonal and
absolute, what he perceives is an ultimate reality. There
is no other truth of things behind his perception unless
we make the leap into a second consciousness and its
truth and world, the reality of his consciousness is limited
only by that of others, and there is no privileged place
where these worlds finally meet and correct each other
and form a single objective real world. Mathieu *is* his
situation, his reality is a constant present developing itself; but at the same time, above that present in places
we find traces of older recurrent character problems that
remind us of their existence before our attention to the
present sweeps them away again, and rise again later on
as planned but forgotten elements of the book. The
"personality problem" of Mathieu is his distance from
people, an attempt to approach them through understanding them which constantly risks the professorial or
the condescending. The very opening of *The Age of
Reason* announces this theme: Mathieu's refusal of a

chance meeting, of the revelation of another consciousness, his regret afterwards. And it is as if the theme had
been able to show itself so nakedly here only because the
continuity of presented consciousness had not yet had
time to set in with full force. Mathieu's regrets about
the Spanish civil war are another reflection of this difficulty; the episodes of the war of 1940 are another; and in
the very last page in which Mathieu appears, in the moment of the firing from the tower, it is there again:
"Here's one for all those guys, every last one of them,
whom I felt like hating and whom instead I tried to understand."[3]

This is not an isolated example: Boris, for instance, is
obsessed with the distance between the generations; he
deliberately surrounds himself with people older than
he is, both in his social life and sexually. And even Roquentin, the hero of a novel which is almost wholly pure
consciousness, without intrigue, has his "personality":
he is visited by the nausea because he is "somebody"
who likes to *touch* things.[4] These "problems" are never
borne down upon and developed as they would be in a
"psychological novel": it is difficult for us to keep both
them and the descriptions of consciousness in focus at
the same time, so that we tend to notice them only when
we step back from the sentences and our engagement in
the reading of consciousness is interrupted. We think
of them as something extra added to the novel, something
we would not miss and which reflects the survival of an
older notion of complete presentation of characters.

These personality patterns are therefore both independent, mirage-like entities and at the same time the
raw material that consciousness is consciousness *of*.
Mathieu lives the problem of fraternity in anxiety, and
in another perspective "is" someone who "has" the problem of a certain kind of distance from people. The

themes of his original choice at certain points become frozen into mere aspects of his character, qualities of his essence. This doubling, this alienation of a newer by an older manner of presentation, in one sense reflects the facticity of all consciousness: its necessity to be always "in situation," to have a certain body, be caught in a given moment of time in a unique place, with certain problems—the absolutely individualized, irreducible, contingent face of a consciousness which is also pure and impersonal. So that Mathieu is consciousness, but he also has to "be" somebody, and he happens to be a teacher in a *lycée,* who lives in a certain apartment, knows and consorts with a given group of people, and who has pre-occupations of a certain order; and these are the unjusti-fiable facts, the core of chance or contingency that the work of art carries within itself, unable to assimilate them to the transparency of a "pure" art form.

There is one perspective in which all this is of course terribly obvious: books have to be *about* something, their characters are at least no more contingent than the peo-ple we actually do end up meeting, and in terms of common sense we are saying nothing that could not be said about every novel when we stumble over a zone of chance in this particular work. But in this perspective the very notion of contingency is incomprehensible, and in its turn the common sense perspective itself is possible only before the idea of contingency has made its presence felt. There is of course no reason why the world should be felt as "absurd," unself-justifying, somehow excessive in its very nature, unless the world is being measured against some standard of intelligibility in terms of which it becomes absurd. Such a standard in medieval times was the idea of the perfection of God, and it was at this mo-ment that the world's contingency was first grasped and given formulation. The re-emergence of this experience

in our own time is the result of a different kind of intelligibility: the massive humanization of the world in the
industrial age and the glimpsed possibility of a complete
humanization of the world that permits its present contingency to be once more painfully vivid. This experience is reflected most accessibly in the problems and ambitions of those modern artists who lived their art as an
absolute: it is the horror of Mallarmé before chance, and
his attempt to eliminate as much of it as possible, to purify the work of art to the point where it could revolve on
its own momentum, without any contact with the world.
It is the reason for being of the twelve-tone system, that
leaves no single note to chance or to extraneous laws, but
reaches down to determine every last element of the
work, as well as of the elaborate planification and overdetermination of Joyce, where the facts are not purged
out but abundantly admitted and then justified to their
very color or moment of appearance by large general
schemes. It is in the light of these absolute solutions to a
common problem of facticity and of artistic necessity
that this aspect of Sartre's works takes on its meaning.

The form of these works is not a product of the
"naive," unproblematic aesthetic that dispenses with
dealing with contingency simply by remaining unaware
of the existence of the problem and thinks it is describing
things as they are when it turns out to be merely using a
ready-made inherited language. But on the other hand
the problem, which is present in the works, is not the
object of an attempt at a total solution as in the earlier
generation; it is merely preserved as a dilemma within
the structure of works that remain deliberately imperfect,
and which therefore, no longer attempting in their com-
pleteness to stand in rivalry with the world itself, find
their place within the world, in direct action on the reader. Sartre has often spoken of the novel as a machine to

work on its reader; and the genesis of his novels is very often the result of a described content suddenly turning into a motivation for the work as a whole. Those moments, for example, in which a character begins to feel the unseen presence of the simultaneity of other people, in which he tries to fix with his imagination the great zones of the unknown around him at distant points on the earth's surface and succeeds only in painfully ratifying his own isolation, his own small place in a real but unrealizable universe: such moments are at first episodes, content, subjective events. Yet in terms of them it is not only the origin but also the purpose of *The Reprieve* that is suddenly apparent: the book is designed to lift the experience out of the heads of characters *inside* the book and make it happen to the readers themselves, in the real world, to make the imaginary suddenly happen. So also *The Age of Reason* has for its subject anxiety: the characters experience it, it is described; but anxiety is not something that can be aesthetically contemplated from the outside, and the book is designed to be precisely a machine to release anxiety in us, to bring us suddenly face to face with our own freedom. This effect is made possible only by the structure of facticity within the work that we have examined: it is not the product of that "empathy" which earlier theoreticians invented to explain our astounding escape, during the reading process, from the monad. For the concrete situation in which Mathieu is engaged is obviously very different from our own, foreign and exotic, in spite of the cultural affiliation. We remain at a distance from the facts of his life; but Mathieu's anxiety is precisely *his own* distance from those facts as well. It is the moment in which a pure consciousness suddenly becomes aware of its own facticity, realizes that it has "a" life, "a" character, which it recognizes as its own, to which it is inextricably related, and which is nonetheless somehow distinct from it. So that as readers, pure consciousness and unique situation at the same time, we are no further away from that destiny as a teacher in a particular *lycée* in Paris than Mathieu is himself: we meet him on the plane of pure consciousness, pure anxiety, and the accidental content of his life is less important than the fact that it is set in question *as* facticity, and along with it, our own life as well. The very effects of the novel as a major form are therefore dependent on their internal contradictions, on that lack of synthesis between consciousness and facticity, the survival of an older kind of literature within the literature of the subjective event, that we saw as the result of the split in the world between being and not-being, of what we called the arrested dialectic. And what happens in the larger dimensions of the form is necessarily reflected and repeated in the microcosm of the language itself.

In the philosophical works this deliberate imperfection of the form can often be apprehended in the language as a kind of word-play: the verb "to be" becomes the instrument of a verbal prestidigitation and yields formulas that resolve the problems on an unexpected plane of language. Thus, for example, in the problem of time, the question of the nature of the past, of its relationship to the present, is entirely a question of finding the right words to describe this phenomenon of human experience which everyone necessarily knows already. The earlier theories are found both to illuminate certain unquestioned aspects of the past's reality and to be deficient in what they go on to *imply* over and above those aspects. The words of them either insist so strongly on our separation from our past that there is no way to connect it to our present again, or they underline the continuity of past and present time to the point where it is hard to see the difference between them. Both of these twin faces of the past must be preserved for a description that does justice to our lived experience of the past; but once we have reached this point in the analysis the problem has been for all intents and purposes solved. We have found what our lived experience of the past consisted in: the past is both separation from our present and continuity with it, we *recognize* the phenomenon. When the official formulation arrives therefore—the past as something which we both "are" and "are not," temporality as a structure only possible for a being that can be-what-it-is-not and not-be-what-it-is—the formula has the shock of an unexpected truism because we were waiting for language of a different kind, we were waiting for the phenomenon to turn into philosophical terms, terms like Bergson's *"durée."* We were not aware that the real philosophical work was already over, and that the formula is not designed to register the phenomenon in language but merely to serve as a kind of convenient peg to hold the glimpsed reality behind the words in place. The philosophy only has the appearance of a system: it does not find its fulfillment in an achieved terminology but in eclipsing itself once the reality of the phenomenon has been evoked by words ephemeral enough to fade out once their work is done.

This philosophical presentation is dependent on the unique situation of the verb "to be," which is in its turn made possible by the relationship between consciousness and things, or rather by their separation which requires a new kind of relationship to resolve it. In this new relationship which is the verb "to be," the meaning of the verb is itself infected in its very structure by the negations in which it is so often called to function. When it is a strong verb, attempting to preserve the unity of human reality by replacing more divisive relationships with a new identity (the trembling is not an expression of anger, not a symbol of it, does not merely reflect it, it *is* the anger) nothing new has been said, and the two terms are merely returned to the unity they originally had in lived experience but enriched by their temporary separation from each other. The equating of the two phenomena is possible only when we have become convinced of their distinctness, otherwise they would have already faded into each other and the sentence would not even be possible. And when the verb "to be" is negative, the description of the relationship of consciousness to things as that which it *is not* is as violent a relationship as identity, since consciousness cannot possibly exist at all without the things it is consciousness of. The verb "to be" is itself a kind of subjective event, where both something and nothing happens; it is the point of an ineffectual slipping across things by language which always says the opposite of what it means, implies unity where it is trying to distinguish, and separates what it is trying to join. But it is also the possibility of correcting that defect, since within itself it is both strong and weak, both able to express something new and to show through its very colorlessness that nothing new is intended and that the reality behind it is to be grasped directly, as immediate lived experience, beyond the imperfection of the words.

We have already seen this process at work in the language of the novels: how the affirmed identity of things with subjectivity permitted us to grasp the inhuman reality of the things, how a blatant "thingification" of human reality was the only way to let us come into contact with that reality without damaging it. Such an attempt to restore the unity of experience through the play of a false kind of identity obviously precludes any aesthetic of a wrought, permanent language which achieves an equivalence with the things it describes. In such an aesthetic, where the work of art is an object, laboriously set together by a skilled craftsman, the sentences attain the autonomy of their content: precious things, it is no longer really necessary that they be read, they go on existing whether they are being respectfully contemplated or not, and no reading is ever enough to make them as transparent as subjectivity, they are always partly out of reach and have some of the resistance of things themselves. But in this work there is a kind of engagement in the world implied upon which all later more obvious "engagements" take place: the reader is built into the style, the deliberate imperfection of the sentences requires the corrections his mind will perform on them to make them express reality. The distance between the sentence and its meaning must be filled with the subjectivity of the reader himself just as in the form the distance between consciousness and facticity drew him into complicity, and made him assume and live that facticity instead of abolishing it through some unique organizational vision.

It is therefore apparent that Sartre's works face the same situation, the same cluster of aesthetic problems, that the older generation of moderns attempted to solve in a different way: the place of chance and of facticity in the work of art, the collapse of a single literary language, a period style, the expression of a relatively homogeneous class, into a host of private styles and isolated points in a fragmented society. They share with the older experimentation a kind of provisional, unofficial quality as well, that absence of even the possibility of some "classic" status which Roland Barthes describes as follows:

> We find in the novel the destructive and at the same time resurrectional apparatus which is peculiar to all modern art. What has to be destroyed is the passage of time, the ineffable continuity of existence: order, whether it be the order of the poetic continu-

um or that of the novelistic signs, is always an intentional murder. But the passage of time reasserts
itself over the writer, for it is impossible to develop
a negation in time without elaborating a positive
art, a new order which must be in turn destroyed.
Thus the greatest modern works pause as long as
possible, in a sort of miraculous suspension, on the
threshold of Literature, in a waiting room situation
where the density of life is given and extended before us without having yet been destroyed by the
confirmation of an order of literary signs: hence for
example the first person of Proust, all of whose work
is one prolonged and retarded effort in the direction
of Literature.[5]

Yet that deliberate stopping short before an official Literature, that refusal of an effort toward a completely
expressive and self-justifying language which would immediately become Literature if it were possible, is here
achieved in a manner, in a "style," quite distinct in nature from that of the earlier generation. The very existence of such a generation, with the multiplicity of new
roads traced, the apparent exhaustion of the possibilities
of direct experimentation, constituted in itself a new situation for the writers following it: a situation to which
many of Sartre's contemporaries responded with an attempt to revive old archaic forms—and we have seen
how in Sartre's works themselves these forms tend to survive and to coexist with elements genuinely new. But
what is unique in his works is the fact that they somehow
ought not to exist at all, that they arise on a place which
should have made them impossible. They are not *natural*
works; behind them we sense a motive-power of great
violence bringing them into being, the mere feeling of
the uniqueness of a personal world pushed and extended

until it becomes work, until it generates out of itself the narratives through which it can come to expression. This will to creation is, it seems to me, characterized by the turning of description into prescription, the straining at a fixed "set of conditions" until it yields a temporal expression of itself, the transformation, by fiat, of a static dilemma into fable and action. Such a will is apparent in the famous unanswered questions at the end of *Being and Not-Being*, where the philosopher implies the possibility of authentic consciousness, constant awareness of ourselves as freedom, turning into a new style of life, into a new kind of morality and value and action. It is apparent also in the very ambitions of the literary works themselves; and we have seen many such moments in the course of this study, where the mere experience of a simultaneity of other consciousnesses and other worlds, at first simple content, turned into the reason for being of a whole novel; where the simple analysis of anxiety gave way to the intention of causing it in us, and the description of freedom to the didactic purpose of forcing an awareness of our own freedom upon us; where the observations on the use of objects turned into a new literary moment in which the writer impatiently "used" his object as many different ways as possible all at once; where the mere idea of our being-for-others generated out of itself the whole scheme and content of the Sartrean ghosts; or where the abstract idea of a life turned into an image, and then into the imperative of a new literary development. Throughout these very different examples the pressure of a single hand can be felt, the constant presence of a single, special style of doing things and a will power moving through all of them in the same characteristic direction.

This will is present even in the language itself, in the very possibility of a voice through which such content can come to light. For as we have seen, the vision of the world from which all more progressive content springs, the split between being and consciousness, seems to render language powerless. Language, one of the most fundamental syntheses of things and consciousness, falls useless between them when they are too radically separated. Yet a language is forced up into existence in the very silence which ought to take its place, and the imperfection of language does not inspire an attempt to correct it, or become the grounds for an utter failure, an abandonment of any speech and a silence, but is made the very instrument for speaking: the inhumanity of things is revealed through the humanized language, and the purity of consciousness unveiled at the very moment when consciousness is intolerably being treated as a thing. Thus action, both in the subject matter of the works, and in the work itself of elaborating it, is resolutely undertaken in a situation which seemed to make it impossible; and the very imperfections of the works are merely another face, the negative dimension, of their vastness; for when all forms are impossible, no single one is any more impossible than any other, and suddenly they all come into being, all possible, criticism and plays, philosophy, novels, and political and historical and biographical analyses, bringing us face to face with the image of a consciousness for which everything can be understood, and of an unintimidated language for which there is nothing that cannot be said.

## Afterword

Whatever its merits, this book had the originality of attempting—not merely to analyze Sartre's work formally, from an aesthetic perspective—but above all to replace Sartre in literary history itself. The readings and analyses I made over twenty years ago still strike me as plausible (nor do they need to be modified in the light of the two or three "literary" or storytelling works Sartre was to write in the intervening period). But I feel that I am in a better position today to *interpret* those findings, that is, to articulate Sartre's historical moment in somewhat less impressionistic or intuitive ways than I did then, although even then I seemed to have grasped the matter accurately enough as an antagonism, or at least a tension, between the modernist tradition and Sartrean narrative or stylistic procedures. Let me therefore tell this story over again in what seems to me today a more satisfactory terminology.

I should add, as a matter of historical interest, that in the late fifties, when I was working on these texts, what has come to be called theory (or perhaps I should specify it as *French* theory, since my formation was in French) did not yet exist. The advanced cutting edge of literary criticism in those days was the still very phenomenological work of Jean-Pierre Richard (my own conception of style study, however,

derived more from Spitzer and from my teacher Erich Auerbach, as well as from Sartre's own early criticism, collected in *Situations* I). Or rather, the theoretical existed, and it was a heady and intellectual
period indeed, but that conceptuality was drawn almost exclusively from the very Sartrean existentialism whose linguistic expression made up the subject
of this book. (That Sartre's work also included a theory about itself will have already become clear in the
preceding pages.) My own references to the few
emergent theoretical texts of those years—Barthes'
*Writing Zero Degree* (1953) and Adorno's *Philosophy of
Modern Music* (1958)—were to say the least prema-
ture; and the more appropriate coordinates—the essays of Walter Benjamin, first collected in the two-
volume edition of 1955)—were lacking, but can now
be reintroduced.

For the basic propositions of this study turned
around the question of narrative, or more exactly,
around the relationship between narrative and narrative closure, the possibility of storytelling, and the
kinds of experience—social and existential—struc-
turally available in a given social formation. This is
of course Benjamin's great theme—the formal unfolding or disintegration of storytelling as a reflex of
village society, the great industrial city, and the world
of the media respectively.

Yet such a problematic at once raises preliminary
theoretical difficulties of its own. We have to do here,
clearly, with what the Marxian tradition loosely des-
ignates as the relationship between base and superstructure, between concrete social relations and their
(in this case essentially) cultural forms. Benjamin
himself told us that "the superstructure *expresses* the
infrastructure"[1]; but the underscored term merely

dramatizes the enormous historical distance that has come into being between the thought of Benjamin (and of Sartre himself) and that of our own "post-structuralist" age, for which conceptions of expression and expressivity count among the most stigmatized ideological ruins of the thinking of the past. (For the Althusserians, the category of "expression" is a Hegelian one, while the relationship between levels—such as this one between social organization and cultural production—is never to be grasped analogically or homologically, but rather in terms of determinate distance *and* difference, each developing at its own rate of speed and under a dynamism and a logic specific to it alone, or, as they liked to put it, *semi-autonomously*.)

The limits of this problematic can also be evoked in the framework of an influential non-Marxian view of expression, the so-called Sapir-Whorf hypothesis, namely the idea that the structure of a given language limits the possibilities of thinking available to the speakers of that language. This view (which derived from inspection of non-European and more specifically American Indian languages) was only one of a number of historically significant efforts to break with the traditional Western identification of logical categories with the categories of Indo-European language from Aristotle to Port-Royal, but it clearly still presupposes that combined distinction and recoordination between language and thinking which characterizes the concept of "expression" in general; and is in any case unverifiable (it constitutes, in other words, what Collingwood would have called an "absolute presupposition" rather than a testable hypothesis). Benjamin's problematic (and the one which underlies the present study) amounts to something like an extrapolation of the linguistic concept to the larger field of narrative: the opposition language/thinking here becomes an opposition between *storytelling* and *experience*. Some such view strikes one as being implicit in the central Sartrean analysis of storytelling (in *La Nausée*, quoted above pp. 22–25), even though Sartre's exposition modifies the simpler linguistic proposition by proposing an ontological interpretation of the two levels: now the linguistic and storytelling level will be seen as a mirage and a form of inauthenticity, while "experience" will prove to offer a truer and more authentic glimpse of the meaningless and sheerly additive nature of human time. What is lacking here, by comparison with Benjamin's various approaches, is history itself, that is, some recognition of the social relativity of the opposition itself and consequently any reflexivity about the historicity of the Sartrean discussion itself, about which one would at least minimally want to say that it is a peculiarly modern experience of the influence of storytelling or anecdotal schemata. The other seeming inconsistency in this great fragment from *La Nausée* will also have become explicit: namely that (unless one wants to describe this passage as "philosophical discourse," distinguishing this last radically from "narrative discourse") the attack on narrative is conducted by narrative means and with the equipment and instruments of storytelling, something which can mark a first approach to that Sartrean linguistic optimism which is the omnipresent subject of the book at hand. Sartre's more general view of language is no less traditional and no less "expressive" than those of Sapir, Whorf or Benjamin (it is essentially a gestural conception of language, involving notions of context or "situation" and presupposing our empathetic pro-

jection into the standpoint of the speaker or "sender");
but it would seem to be substantially modified by a
sense of the absolute elasticity of language itself, which
is perpetually able to reabsorb the limits (grammatical or semantic) which it confronts (but which in fact
it sets for itself). Thus, the moment in which a given
language is able to become aware of and to register
its own constitutive limits (what it cannot say: the inability of English to convey Hopi temporality or space,
the inability of Hopi to handle Western conceptions
of time and space), these limits are no longer bind-
ing in the older way. Language is thus always a matter of the identification and simultaneous transcendence of its own constitutive limits (in that, the Sartrean
conception of language presents curious analogies with
Marx's account of the dynamism of capital, in the
*Grundrisse*); and this perpetual possibility of linguistic
self-transcendence stands in striking contrast to the
pathos of contemporary Derridean or de Manian
notions of an imprisonment in the shackles of ideological closure or quasi-material tropological structures. (It is probably no accident that the other writer
to whom I have devoted a single book-length study,
Wyndham Lewis, was also characterized in terms of
the same linguistic optimism or elasticity.[2])

But I would today want to stress the advantages of
Benjamin's historicism by contrast with the narrower
ontological framework of the Sartrean approach.
These advantages are on first glance perhaps only too
readily grasped as ideological weaknesses and as the
scars of the inevitably nostalgic features of historicism as it is generally understood. For the Benja-
minian "stages theory" would seem to suggest, not that
all storytelling is an artificial and illusory reordering
of some more fundamental experience (which ought

perhaps no longer even to bear that name, since it is if anything an "experience" of the meaningless and of the emptiness of time, an inauthentic "essence" having forcibly been imposed on "existence"), but rather that once upon a time, in a distant precapital-ist past, real storytelling was possible, and this owing to the real possibilities of "experience" in such social formations. The reproach of a golden-age narrative is therefore a telling one, but in my opinion by no means as damaging as might at first appear. I cannot here suggest the ways in which Benjamin's "linear" narrative of social and aesthetic forms can be opened up by replacing it within the more properly Marxist framework of a *multiplicity* of modes of production. Suffice it merely to observe that even this simple view of the three fundamental historical moments[3] changes complexion when we grasp it as a negative and crit-ical, diagnostic instrument. What is at stake is less some full and positive notion of what achieved storytelling is, than a means by which to detect and to articulate what we may call the psychopathologies of later nar-ratives: their artificial closures, the blockage of nar-rative, its deformations and formal compensations, the dissociation or splitting of narrative functions, in-cluding the repression of certain of these, and so forth. It is therefore essentially as an instrument for the diagnosis of the various modernisms, of those forms which emerge after the crisis of the older sto-rytelling possibilities, that Benjamin's reflexions will be useful to us.

We thereby find ourselves confronting the central question of the nature of aesthetic modernism itself, a topic everywhere presupposed in my discussion of Sartre, but never engaged directly (an omission which goes a long way towards accounting for the debility of this book's *interpretive,* as opposed to its *analytic,* capacities). For if Sartre's unique narrative and stylistic *gestus* is to be grasped in the situation of hegemonic modernism, then we obviously need to have a clearer sense of what this last is and how it historically emerged, something I will now try to convey under the twin headings of a social crisis of narratable experience, and a semiotic crisis of narrative paradigms.

What is paradoxical about the first of these—the extinction of traditional storytelling and of traditional narrative categories of experience—is that, in spite of the language I have just used, such a development is by no means exclusively to be seen as loss, privation, catastrophe, impoverishment, but can also be celebrated as a very palpable liberation. We will not do justice to this immense historical transformation without a keen and constant awareness of its essential *ambivalence* (which the ideologically forewarned reader will at once associate with Marx's own account of the ambivalence of capitalism itself—at one and the same time negative and positive, a historically unparalleled force for the simultaneous liberation and alienation of human beings). And yet, surely, a people without stories would seem to be in the unenviable position of being a people to whom nothing ever happens; how is this to be understood (let alone celebrated) as a joyous matter?

I follow Benjamin (who in turn follows a whole traditional German reflexion on the *Novelle*) in seeing the story or tale as the commemoration of the *unique,* and that in the two senses of the temporally irrevocable and of the unaccustomed, unanticipated, unparalleled stroke of fortune, whether good or bad (storytelling is presided over in general by categories

of fate, destiny, providence or fortune, it being relatively more indifferent whether these agencies are
benevolent or malign: categories whose historical
dissolution accompanies that of storytelling itself).
Death is only the most fateful and emblematic of such
events, which must be grasped against the background of a repetitive or cyclical social life scarred
and marked only fitfully by the New. Extrapolating
Benjamin's account of Baudelaire back into an older
village culture, we may suggest that what will come
to be called Experience is a complicated process of
absorbing and defusing the shock of novelty, and inventing those great narrative categories and abstractions—Adventure, Grace, Fortune, Ananke, Love
beyond death, Retribution—which can then serve to
pull the sting of the unforeseeable, if not for the
person involved, then at least for those spectators who
listen to his story. For these are irrevocable things,
that happen once and for all and for good, and mark
their victims forever: and this whether in the triumph
of the captain, the great good luck of the peddler
whose ships return from the East with an unhoped-
for bounty, or in the miseries of the turning wheel,
of capital execution or definitive enslavement. Such
events, such prodigious reversals of fortune in either
direction, are then also to be grasped in vivid relief
against the immemorial patterns of a hierarchical and
traditional social order, in which your life path is laid
out in advance by the caste, status or calling of the
forefathers, an immense frozen ice flow that will split
and crack thunderously under the warming dynamism of capital, releasing a new wealth of existential
content which can no longer be organized in storytelling categories.

Having had something happen to you, "having" a story to tell—Todorov terms the protagonists of the older tales "des hommes-récits," narrative bodies, story-persons [4]—this feature of the narrative mark or scar is not necessarily an attractive fate for contemporary people, for whom the very absence of fate means perpetual possibility, lability, freedom, lack of ultimate definition. In that sense, perhaps, Henry James' fable, "The Beast in the Jungle," strides the divide and constitutes at one and the same time the last traditional story and the first anti-narrative: the shock of discovering that your unique fate is to have no fate, that the one thing destined to happen to you and only you in all the world is that nothing was ever destined to happen to you at all. What now may seem reassuring and optimistic about this otherwise grim novella springs from our sense that stories (and destinies) are incurable, that were you to "have" one, you would have to live with it the rest of your life. Nor is the medical reference gratuitous, in a world in which, at least in principle, everything is supposed to be curable (except death). Whence the horror of the infirmity of old Miss Thompson (in Paule Marshall's *Brown Girl, Brownstones*)—her "life-sore" as the others call it, the thing you are destined to suffer the rest of your earthly existence. Our panic before such forms of the irrevocable is comparable to that of Peer in the realm of the trolls: the troll princess's future groom can look forward to a long life full of laziness and all the wealth and privileges imaginable, on one little condition—that he allow himself to be horribly mutilated so as (out of solidarity) to become as ugly as his hosts. But why should anything—a wandering life full of privations—be preferable to that; why do we bless the wonder drugs that cure us of our destinies, of our chance to be the protagonist of some genuine tale?

The reaction of Sartre's own characters in this situation is an exemplary one: flight before the horror of the wheel of generations, in which Mathieu might vanish into the species; and the general sense everywhere that any decisive form of action is like a ball and chain you will have to drag about with you for the rest of your life (even writing books—especially writing books—can become an "ideological interest"[5] that inflects and commits your future, so that if you have to write them, it may be preferable to leave them unfinished and incomplete, as Sartre was wont to do his whole life long). Official Sartrean thematics formulates all this in terms of the concept of "freedom" and of a brutal shift from freedom as the unmarked, the uncommitted, the permanently "disponible" to freedom as choosing the life-sore and the scar. In our present context, however, all of this suddenly takes on a somewhat different appearance: the choice, the free act, is now tantamount to shouldering a fate or destiny, that is, to acquiring a "story." Sartrean characters are modern in their horror of just this narrative self-definition; yet everything urges them to dare to become again the protagonist of the traditional tale. They are characters whose destiny is to *become* "hommes-récits"; and the Sartrean text always ends on the edge of that great mutation, on the point of becoming a tale. A curious reversal in which modernism becomes the antichamber to traditional storytelling; in which the modernizing situation with its dilemmas is repudiated in the name of a world of tales and destinies that cannot come into being.

Such are the social and existential determinants of

the crisis of narrative in the modern age, and of Sartre's peculiar and ec-centric response to it. There would, of course, have been another way of describing this "realm of freedom" under capitalism, this lifting of the traditional burdens of narrative destiny: for from another perspective, we might have evoked something like a repression of narrative time from the span of individual biological life. The rhythms of capital that emerge in modernity are indeed the great fifty year cycles of the Kontratiev wave. These enormous patterns are the basis for the narrative intelligibility of History, for its possibility of being "scientifically" reconstructed; yet such long waves are clearly out of synchrony with the briefer periods in which the individual subject lives his or her "existential" experience. There slowly comes into being in modernity therefore an absolute dissociation between "existence" and narrative intelligibility which cannot but empty traditional human stories of their significance. The crisis called modernism is a result of this structural dissociation on the temporal level (while something analogous begins to happen on the plane of space itself, with the increasing disjunction of a global world system from the smaller spaces in which individuals live out their immediate destinies). We cannot here further develop this analysis of modernism, which should however correct the impression that the illusions of freedom evoked above tell the full story of human life under capitalism.

We therefore now turn to the other determinants of the crisis of narrative in modernity, which have to do with the inner crisis of the narrative paradigm itself and of its more general form, in the crisis of the sign. For it is most convenient[6] to model the dissolution of the latter in terms of the increasing dis-

junction of its three fundamental components: signifier, signified and referent. This is the sense in
which one may posit some initial stage in which the
sign as a whole is felt to be "natural" (that is, its relationship to reference is as yet unproblematized),
followed by a second moment—that of modernism
proper—in which the referential relationship, in-
creasingly the object of philosophical skepticism, becomes rarefied and attenuated to the point of now
constituting the minimal ultimate link between the sign
and its various referents. At this point, the realm of
the sign has acquired a kind of free-floating autonomy (which classical aesthetics designated as the
sphere of culture). What we have called traditional
storytelling is then clearly at one with the first, unproblematized moment of the sign's "naturality": but
it is equally clear that the more conventionalized
paradigms of older elite cultures also belong to this
"linguistic," as do the novels of what Lukacs was still
able to call "the great realists." The problematization
of narrative and of its relationship to reality (the
problem of its epistemological value, as we shall see
in a moment) is then the drama of the next moment,
and it is in this sense that modernism in general may
be identified as the very culture of capitalism itself,
its "organic" culture, historically new and specific to
this particular mode of production. (Finally, we must
note the possibility of a third stage of moment which
is implicit in our model of the sign: namely the further logical possibility that the forces which disjoined
sign from referent may also be capable of penetrating the structure of the sign itself, and separating
signifier from signified. This is in fact, on my view,
what characterizes what has come to be called "post-
modernism," something which only became visible as

a whole new cultural logic since the writing of the present book in the late 1950s. This third stage is worth noting here, if only because the work of Sartre—in distinct tension and antagonism with the strategies and solutions of the modern movement— is clearly also to be sharply demarcated from the styles and solutions of post-modernism, which become culturally dominant, institutionalized and hegemonic, in ways in which the eccentric Sartrean gesture never could be.)

It will be convenient to understand the increasing sense of the artificiality of narrative paradigms in general as a shift in which aesthetic value and inspiration are displaced onto the moment, the illumination, the epiphany, first in that astonishing explosion of new lyric poetry called Romanticism, and only later on within the novel itself (where little by little the commodification of desire and of success is felt to contaminate the well-made plot, and to condemn the now modernist novelist to the anti-novel on the one hand and the lyric or plotless novel on the other). This newly emergent authenticity of the instant, however, demands the imposition of relatively external or extrinsic overall reunifying forms, in order to arrest the break-up of the work into sheer fragments: these external forms will most often involve an appeal to "myth," as in Joyce's *Ulysses*, if not to mythic ideologies, as in Lawrentian vitalism. Meanwhile, such intermittent authenticity requires an appeal to some new kind of authority, which will for the most part be staged in terms of inspiration, genius and later on, the Unconscious (and will of course generate a whole series of new roles for the poet or the great writer).

The peculiarity of Sartre's own aesthetic gesture can perhaps most immediately be grasped in the light of this last feature. That Sartrean existence philosophy can be seen as a culmination of modernism in philosophy proper only underscores the peculiar uncertainty of this writer's position in aesthetic history, where, from the vantage point of modernizing values, it has been only too easy to stigmatize the narrative or dramatic works as thesis plays and mere novels of ideas. I have tried to show in the preceding study that the characterization is apt, only on condition we recognize the unusual structure of such "ideas" by contrast with older kinds of philosophical theses: "concepts" such as those of freedom or of being are to be seen as something like empty forms, which no longer have the content of the traditional philosophical notion, for reasons to be developed further below.[7] Nonetheless, that there is a kind of brutal instrumentality in Sartrean narrative, a pressing impulse to make points and to "say" something, which overrides the modernist surrender to inspiration; and that the "experimental" moments in Sartre's work have little in common with the desperate projections of new form in modernism—all of this seems accurate enough, on some impressionistic level. *La Nausée* is staged under the sign of Céline; yet no one is likely to read the later text as post-Célinian. Nor does the crosscutting of *Le Sursis,* which owes so much to Dos Passos and to the American novel generally, strike us as being "original" in the sense of these last. It is, however, Sartre's relationship to Surrealism which is the place in which all this lights up most sharply; for as has often been noted Sartre is one of the very few writers of his generation never to have been touched even minimally or fitfully by the great surrealist revolution. Here, as also in his ambivalent relations with Freudian psychoanalysis itself and with the very conception of a genuine Unconscious, the Sartrean valorization of praxis, intention and activity over the more passive-receptive vocations of the various modernisms is unmistakable.

Yet this is not, in my opinion, an old-fashioned reversion to pre-modern conceptions of reason, so much as the anticipation and foreshadowing of an experience that will only be articulated clearly in the light of the post-modern age. This is an increasing and asphyxiating sense of the reification of modernist culture as it becomes canonized and institutionalized. The double-bind for younger writers (who thereby at a certain point feel themselves to be epigones) lies in the contradiction between the powerful dereifying impulses of the modernist unconscious processes and the rigid monumental forms into which the latter tend to congeal. Not Sartre but post-modernism will point the way out of this dilemma; yet in its early stages Sartrean aesthetic voluntarism is also felt to be a welcome and indeed a liberating, iconoclastic gesture, even though what I still had to call a "literature of consciousness" in 1961 was to remain as unrealized a program as Sartre's own utopian ideal of a "literature of praxis" (announced at the end of *What is Literature?*).

This said, the other feature of high modernism evoked above—the increasing primacy in it of the instant over the older narrative paradigm or plot—strikes one as being uncomfortably similar to the descriptions of Sartrean narrative offered in the present book, something which must now be rectified if "Sartre" is not to fold back into the modernist aesthetic without a trace. The Sartrean version of the "epiphany" or instant is generally differentiated from the high modernist one by the apparent option of paraphrase that it enjoys: the seeming availability of two distinct discourses, a narrative or aesthetic one, and a philosophical, discursive, or finally *phenomeno-logical* discourse or register. What is meant by thesis or propaganda art—as these epithets are applied to Sartre—is evidently the possibility for any given narrative moment to be recoded in abstract philosophical form. No matter that the same reproach has frequently been made the other way around, so that the weakness of phenomenological discourse from a technical philosophical standpoint has often been identified as its secret "literary" vocation and its scarcely veiled narrative procedures. It is however at least certain that the modernist instant, as it finds itself incarnated in language, projects the claim that only that unique style—born miraculously out of the most absolute and oppressive silence—allowed the thing itself to find speech. (Ideologies of the modern—most notably the American New Criticism—pressed this claim again and again, in their differentiation of scientific and poetic languages, and in their well-known stigmatization of paraphrase and translation.)

I think that the radical differences between the modernist and the Sartrean instant or moment have to be sought in a somewhat different place, in the types of *content* vehiculated in each of these distinct languages. But before offering a fresh characterization of the specificity of such Sartrean "content," it is worth noting that the two aesthetic paradigms must also be sharply distinguished according to the ways in which each seeks to *reunify* its discontinuous moments in the final form of the organic work. Here a paradoxical juxtaposition of Sartre with another late

writer who has most often been assimilated to the
modernist paradigm—Vladimir Nabokov—may be
helpful. In Nabokov also one has the sense of instan-
taneous perceptions which are only later on, in some
second moment of construction, sewn back together
in the form of the seamless narrative. Indeed in both
writers—as in Lewis also, at least as I read him—we
seem to witness, far more dramatically than in the
achieved monuments of a henceforth classical modernism, that peculiar dissociation between the verti-
cal and the horizontal, between synchrony and
diachrony, between the time of language and the time
of narrative, between epiphany and tale, which Coleridge already, at the dawn of the modern era, diagnosed as an interference between fancy and imagination, or decoration and architectonic. This tension
is more visible in Sartre and Nabokov because its
"resolution"—the wilful reunification of fragments—
does not, as in high modernism, appeal to ideologies
of myth, but rather seizes on dead, preexistent, heterogeneous paradigms which are then visibly imposed from above: in Sartre's work, these are for the
most part the "unities" of melodrama, boulevard
theater, and the "coup de théâtre" (most obviously in
the "dramatic" moment at the end of *L'Age de raison*
in which Mathieu reenters the room [or stage] with
the pilfered cash), while Nabokov will appropriate the
machinery of the detective story for unconvincing yet
tantalizingly metaphysical reidentifications and unexpected slip-knots. The ostentatious application of
such artifice then leaves Sartre free to demolish the
illusions of storytelling from a philosophical standpoint (see again the passage from *La Nausée* referred
to above), where the moderns—who *believed* in their

procedures—were obliged, each after their own fashion, to evolve whole worldviews to justify their formal solutions.

This was possible because the "instants" of high modernism were felt as emergence and as the stirrings of a Novum which—as was everywhere hoped during that great transitional era—was to transform everything around it—both self and world, the body and city space—into an as yet unimaginable Utopian new world. Modernism is finally not comprehensible without this passionate sense of impending transformation, this protopolitical hope and appetite for renewal. What strikes one in the Sartrean instant is not only the disappearance of these Utopian premonitions (the great moments of historical promise in Sartre's experience—the Liberation and May 68—remain dead letters); but even more paradoxically in the philosopher of the *project* and of *praxis,* the static, retrospective and immobilizing character of such empty visions. One is therefore tempted to associate such lucid narrative paralysis with the key Sartrean conceptual category of the *situation*—whose rigid limits are at one with the very force of the perceptions it enables.

The very great merits of the concept of the situation are indeed almost exclusively operative in the field of retrospective and historical interpretation. It allows one to cut across the sterile opposition between determinism and individual will: if for example certain local ideologies, a certain whole "period" style, is detected in a range of people of very different backgrounds, this is now no longer to be explained by recourse to the *Zeitgeist,* nor either to some spurious notion of individual influence, but rather by the re-

construction of a common social and historical situation to which the gestures, acts and texts of contemporaries were bound to be so many (divers) symbolic
responses.[8] But historiography seems always to have
been for Sartre a subordinate field in what now strikes
us as one of his fundamental impulses, namely the
*biographical* passion. From Roquentin's archival interests through the various versions of "existential psychoanalysis" to the full-blown biographical effort of
*L'Idiot de la famille*, the reconstruction of a dead life,
out of its multitudinous traces, into a series of fresh
acts *in situation* was an operation whose fascination for
Sartre perhaps more adequately explains that commitment to the *cogito* and lifelong ideological attachment to the framework of the individual consciousness (even in the *Critique*). Yet at the present time,
when a post-structuralist intellectual climate is still
hostile to the older Sartrean and phenomenological
heritage (and when such obvious things as the debt
of early Lacan to Sartre remain unexplored), it is
worth repeating one of the points made strongly in
the present volume, namely that "consciousness" as
Sartre understands it is very far from being a matter
of the ego, of personality, of character, and the like.
These features, qualities and experiences, which we
normally associate with the "individual subject" are
rather all so many responses to and reflexes of the
*situation*, of which "consciousness" in the technical
Sartrean sense is but a rigorously *im*personal correlative. (Meanwhile, the wonderfully stimulating and
innovating misuses Sartre made of that theory for
which he had so little sympathy—psychoanalysis—are
also to be grasped here, as modes of enrichment of
the concept of the situation, new enlarged to include

childhood itself and the family space.) So many roads, therefore, which lead back to this central and symptomatic concept.

Indeed, after the powerful onslaught on "retrospective illusions" staged in *Les Mots,* it no longer seems particularly paradoxical to assert that the very idea of the situation in Sartre is presided over by the Hegelian conception of historiography as the retrospective reconstruction of Necessity: "the owl of Minerva flies at dusk." Even more is this the case for the biographical project, whose retroactive mirages Sartre himself often liked to characterize by quoting Mallarmé's well-known line: "tel qu'en Lui-même enfin l'éternité le change . . ." The moment of truth of the great Sartrean instants, as they have been laid out in the preceding volume, is therefore not at all a matter of self-consciousness, let alone of any radical conversion to some new and energizing possible future: it is the stark discovery of the imprisonment in the situation itself, whose spatial analogues range from the room to the death cell (we now know that "sequestration," far from being a convenient philosophical symbol, was something closer to a life-obsession and a pathological behavior pattern for Sartre himself). "Self-knowledge" at this point thus ceases to be a subjective matter in which we acquire some better sense of our own "character" or psychic habits or even of our own "Desire" or fantasies about the future and change: it is resolved into a stark and architectural confrontation with the situation itself, as the latter organizes childhood experience and continues to preside over the acts and choices of adult life. In this sense, the situation has become coterminous with more extensive conceptions of ideological closure, with this difference, that "situation" is a peculiarly diachronic and dialectical notion from which we can also read the very formation of those ideological impulses and practices. The concept of situation therefore promises to restore both the transparency and the opacity of individual symbolic action: it promises to account for everything that is alienated and reified in our attempts to think and to change the world, at the same time it deconceals that earlier moment in which such attempts were fresh, immanently meaningful gestures.

The full development of this concept will therefore not become visible until, in the *Critique of Dialectical Reason* of 1960 Sartre will name and specify this play of spontaneity and reification as the *practice-inert*[9]: the process whereby intelligible action, through its very success in modifying the world (and the "current" situation), survives in the form of objective, inherited, institutionalized traces which now oppose so much incomprehensible inertia to the activity of people in some new stage of things. The concept of the practice-inert thus suggests that the concept of the situation strangely includes the moment of the latter's own dissolution in time, and a perspective in which the time of a sequence of modified situations conflicts with the more persistent learned habits organized to deal with one of those moments, which is now no longer present. One should perhaps therefore speak of some introjection of the situation itself, which first presents objectively, as the way we organize a state of things that freshly confronts us as problem, dilemma or contradiction, is then absorbed into the subjective procedures and choices it generated, now living on as the ghostly schemata of a long-dead world that continues to persist within ourselves. Alongside notions of freedom, the project and praxis (about which we will have more to say shortly), there is then also posited a different mode of radical escape from this situational confinement, Sartre's conception of radical conversion, which seemed to offer at least one viable resolution to the problem of narrative, in constituting moments or instants (such as Mathieu's "illumination" on the Pont-neuf) which could be read as the climax of a whole set of narrative developments. But "conversion" in this sense is an empty and purely formal experience (since the content of the new choice is omitted or at least not yet articulated): it strikes one as being little more than the other face of the notion of the situation itself. If in other words the situation is both closed and discontinuous, then it follows necessarily that there are breaks and gaps between "situations," and it is for these that the word conversion would seem to have been devised and reserved. (The conceptual dilemma here is not unlike the historiographic problem of discontinuous moments, whether in the Marxian debate over modes of production or in such histories as those of Foucault, from which a mirage of the "break" is conjured up which is itself little more than the obverse and compensation for the category of a "total system" itself.) Moments of conversion are therefore in Sartre only extreme cases of the Sartrean instant in general; they can seem at best to provide a formal pretext for the ending of a work (of which, however, we have already seen that few enough of them are really finished or concluded), but tend to disappear altogether from narratives such as those of the psychic development of Genet or Flaubert in which the continuum of events is too strong for such moments of suspension to appear plausible any longer.

Conversions now therefore tend to fall outside the work, either in the form of suicide, as at the end of *Les Sequestres d'Altona,* or as that enigmatic silence which at the end of *Les Mots* gives us to understand that the childhood Sartre of that work has today passed away altogether. Indeed, one is tempted to pursue the "logic of the signifier" explored in the present book (the colons, commas and typographical breaks of various kinds) to suggest that Sartrean effects of closure may well in this sense be projections of material breaks rather than the other way around (the alternative formula, in which material signs and breaks would be taken as the *expression* of more non-material forms, is however also still at work in the preceding text).

Still, the formal function of the "situation" in Sartrean narrative can be observed at work more concretely in Sartre's last extended narrative, the three-thousand-page unfinished psychobiography of Flaubert. This is, as Sartre liked to point out, "a true novel," and it does tell a story and eventually reach a shattering climax, only not necessarily where one might first expect one (Godard is supposed to have remarked, on being asked whether his films had "beginnings, middles and endings," that they did, only not necessarily in that order). For *L'Idiot de la famille* will develop along great spirals and loops, which tend to recapitulate analogous movements on distinct levels, which vary from Flaubert's childhood situation in the family to the status of intellectuals in the mid-19th century, the nature of post-Romantic ideologies, the history of language and form, and so on. In the Genet book these spirals followed a still relatively Hegelian architectonic, each stage in Genet's spiritual career recapitulating the earlier ones on distinctly "higher" levels—so that the vocation of the aesthete will subsume and transcend that of the thief, the vocation of the writer will "fulfill" that of the aesthete, etc.: here a kind of symbolic "sublimation" is clearly visible in the movement from one level to the next. In the Flaubert narrative, the relationship of the various spirals to each other is more synchronic, a matter of multiple determinants or what the Althusserians liked to call "overdetermination." The organizing oppositions are still roughly those of subject and object, but this alternation is less governed by ontological presuppositions of the Hegelian type than it is dictated by the existence of distinct *methods:* most notably psychoanalysis, as Sartre now understands it, and class or ideological analysis (particularly as it isolates the related but distinct "objects" of the contradictions of bourgeois ideology in general during this period, and the dilemmas of the aesthetic ideology of that class, as these last are observed in the problem of the status of the 19th-century artist).

With these separations the term of telos of the narrative movement is given in advance; it will drive towards the convergence point of the various loops or levels, that is to say, towards that moment in which, in a henceforth unified symbolic act, *Madame Bovary* will be produced. The act bearing this name (which one must distinguish from subsequent readings or reifications of the novel by later publics in radically distinct social and historical circumstances) is then the place at which the subjective determinants of the personality and talent of "Gustave" become at one with the objective determinants of class ideology and aesthetic possibility—and it was the story of this confluence and coalescence of the various determinants that the unwritten fourth volume of *L'Idiot de la famille* was to have told (Sartre projected it as a "structural analysis" of *Madame Bovary*): a moment of luminous intelligibility in which the multiple "situations" of "Flaubert"—both objective and subjective—coincide at the point at which they generate a complex yet meaningful act. The theoretical problem of whether this symbolic act constituted a transcendence of those situations or rather simply their *expression,* their translation into a distinct and more active set of thematics, can of course now never be raised, let alone solved: but that the symbolic act into which *Madame Bovary* was to be rewritten was to have been grasped and read through the elaborate reconstructions of Flaubert's situations that preceded it is obvious enough. This is them if you like, something like a "happy ending" for the drama of the situation, a resolution of the latter's constraints into the creative production of a new gesture, no matter how desperate this last may have been ("neurosis," Sartre once said, being "an original solution the child invents on the point of stifling to death").

But the narrative—truncated as it is—has other narrative climaxes which are no less revealing in the present context; only their slow curve must be plotted on a gigantic scale, great hundred-page segments serving as the building blocks of a momentum which the reader needs a change in metabolism to grasp with the naked eye. If such a readjustment is possible—one in which exasperating prolixities and often tedious digressions are kept in perspective—then the various "themes" of Flaubert's childhood can be seen as coming together, over some two thousand pages, in that cataclysmic private trauma generally known as the "crisis of Pont-l'Evêque."

Gustave is at this point twenty-one: his mysterious

seizure, on his way home on vacation from his legal studies in Paris, has no particularly crippling after-effects. Dr. Flaubert will nonetheless conclude that his second son will never be able to live an active life and should remain in the care of his family. The father's own death shortly thereafter leaves Gustave materially secure; the "hermit of Croisset" is born, and the novels of Flaubert can now be written.

Gustave's convulsion has been variously diagnosed (on the flimsiest of evidence), most often as an epileptic fit; biographers have considered it a minor episode, at best an obstacle to Gustave's later, literary career. For Sartre, however, it was the central event of Flaubert's life and of a piece with his literary vocation. The philosopher of freedom reinterprets this seemingly physical trauma as an intentional act whose intelligibility greatly transcends the "psychosomatic." Faced with the intolerable prospect of "real life" in a secular, business society, Gustave is now seen to use his body as a way of inventing the ultimate solution to an unresolvable dilemma: the "crisis" of Pont-L'Evêque is thus a way of committing suicide without dying. After that, Gustave is able to live a *posthumous* life (the similarity to Sartre's account of his own childhood illusions in *Les Mots* is obvious)—to die to the world, to bourgeois ambition, to money and profession, and above all, to a *self* he loathed and detested. How this personal or psychic "resolution" then offers a miraculous "preexistent harmony" with the more "objective" resolutions of collective ideology—critical negativity, misanthropy, the ideal of classlessness (that is, of privilege), the defense of the autonomy of the intellectual (now "mistranslated" into art for art's sake), and a quasi-religious conviction of the nothingness of the world and the emptiness of life—

this astonishing "fit" between psychic or subjective form and ideological and socio-historical content, which will be developed through the third volume of *L'Idiot*, can only briefly be sketched here, but is also modelled in the language of the collective situation.

Flaubert's more objective dilemma as an artist will then be read at one and the same time as the crisis of the middle-class writer in a market system, faced with a disappearing public; and the ideological contradiction of the French bourgeoisie, which at the time of the great Revolution had invented the notion of a universal human nature as an aggressive arm against the aristocratic culture and values of the *ancien régime*, only to find itself confronted during the 1848 revolution with a new proletarian underclass it was reluctant to recognize as forming a part of that universal humanity. The French bourgeoisie of Flaubert's period will "solve" this new ideological problem by becoming "Victorian," by repressing the bodily, animal "nature" it had seemed to share with the proletarians, and transforming its earlier humanism into a misanthropic positivism.

This last and most extensive of the great Sartrean narratives thus continues to turn on the supreme category of the situation itself, whether this declares itself negatively in the form of physical collapse, or positively in the symbolic act of the production of *Madame Bovary*. What remains essentially retrospective in the famous "progressive-regressive method" Sartre borrowed from Henri Lefebvre, is then this elaborate reconstruction process whereby what looks like a free act, a project, a commitment to an emergent future, is suddenly reread and retransformed into the triumph of the past and the omnipotence of its frozen contradictions.

Far from dissolving or transcending the stasis of the various modernisms, therefore, this unique Sartrean narrative must rather be seen as something like a "negation of the negation," a moment in which a prodigious shift in narrative perspective and optics allows the paralysis of the event and of the act to be turned inside out and experienced, actively, in the form of historiographic or biographical reconstruction. Is this to say, then, that the other well-known Sartrean themes of the project, the act, praxis, the perpetual transcendence of present and past towards a future in course, are merely formal and empty compensations for this concrete, but immobilizing view of the imprisonment in the situation?

This is certainly the case, since the appeal to the project and to the creative innovations of action and praxis must remain open and unspecified, if the new moment is to constitute a radical break with the older situation and its multiple determinants. Yet those themes, as purely formal as they remain, must also be reckoned into any account of the Sartrean moment, the Sartrean contradiction. The Maoists with whom Sartre surrounded himself during his last years disapproved of this elaborate and seemingly endless anatomy of bourgeois neurasthenia to which he had voluntarily but stubbornly committed himself, rather like some self-punishing and meaningless exercise he had taken upon himself for reasons of private justification in the later years; they often liked to suggest that he would have done better to write a proletarian novel. Yet in retrospect, Sartre's life work can be seen to be an alternation between two great themes: those of praxis and of the Imaginary, whose passive modes of derealization and of the transformation of the world into sheer images are first analyzed in the early philosophical texts only to reach their climax in this account of Flaubert. These distinct and antagonistic modes are not only radically different ways of living the world, they also ideally project two incompatible types of culture and literary production: no matter if the "literature of praxis" described at the end of *What is Literature?* could never find realization in Sartre's own work. For these modes of existing and of writing are finally explicitly identified in class terms: the aesthetization of the immobile instant, the death of the future and of action or Event and its curious expression in the Imaginary mode, becomes the cultural style of a stagnating bourgeoisie, while the future-oriented commitment to praxis suggests some radically different type of culture which can only be achieved by the new class of active industrial workers who see the world as a space of productivity and of human transformation. This second kind of culture would then clearly once and for all spell the transcendence of the modernist dilemma and the passage into some new realm in which the traditional event and the modernist instant would both alike be replaced by the act itself: a prophetic vision which finally has much in common with the equally visionary stance of Benjamin's account of the mechanical work of art. To grasp the immobilities of Sartrean narrative against this larger Utopian projection of History is then to restore its "moment of truth" to Sartre's own historical situation, which must otherwise today seem remote and a peculiar backwater in literary and aesthetic history.

# Notes

## PART ONE: THE EVENT

### Chapter One: The Problem of Acts

1. *Théâtre*, p. 158.
    ESTELLE: Enfin tu dois bien te rappeler; tu devais avoir des raisons
    pour agir comme tu l'as fait.
    GARCIN: Oui.
    ESTELLE: Eh bien?
    GARCIN: Est-ce que ce sont les vraies raisons?
    ESTELLE: *dépitée.*—Comme tu es compliqué.
    GARCIN: Je voulais témoigner, je . . . j'avais longuement réfléchi . . .
    Est-ce que ce sont les vraies raisons?

2. Ibid., p. 158.
    GARCIN: Estelle, est-ce que je suis un lâche?
    ESTELLE: Mais je n'en sais rien, mon amour, je ne suis pas dans ta
    peau. C'est à toi de décider.
    GARCIN: *avec un geste las.*—Je ne décide pas.

3. *Les Mains sales*, pp. 55–56.
    OLGA: Il a réussi. . . .
    HUGO: Il a réussi. Avant la fin de la semaine, vous serez ici, tous les
    deux, par une nuit pareille, et vous attendrez les nouvelles; et vous
    serez inquiets et vous parlerez de moi et je compterai pour vous. Et
    vous vous demanderez: qu'est-ce qu'il fait? Et puis il y aura un coup
    de téléphone ou bien quelqu'un frappera à la porte et vous vous
    sourirez comme vous faites à présent et vous vous direz: "Il a réussi."

4. Ibid., pp. 184–185.
    JESSICA: Toi, tu vas tuer un homme.
    HUGO: Est-ce que je sais ce que je vais faire?
    JESSICA: Montre-moi le revolver.
    HUGO: Pourquoi?
    JESSICA: Je veux voir comment c'est fait.
    HUGO: Tu l'as promené sur toi tout l'après-midi.

JESSICA: A ce moment-là, ce n'était qu'un jouet.
HUGO: *le lui tendant.*—Fais attention.
JESSICA: Oui. *(Elle le regarde.)* C'est drôle.
HUGO: Qu'est-ce qui est drôle?
JESSICA: Il me fait peur à présent. Reprends-le. *(Un temps.)* Tu vas tuer un homme.

5. Ibid., p. 185.
"Ce n'est pas ma faute: je ne crois que ce que je vois. Ce matin encore, je ne pouvais même pas imaginer qu'il meure. *(Un temps.)* Je suis entrée dans le bureau tout à l'heure, il y avait le type qui saignait et vous étiez tous des morts. Hoederer, c'était un mort; je l'ai vu sur son visage! Si ce n'est pas toi qui le tue, ils enverront quelqu'un d'autre."

6. Ibid., p. 259.
"Si je reniais mon acte, il deviendrait un cadavre anonyme, un déchet du parti. Tué par hasard. Tué pour une femme."

7. Ibid., p. 259.
"Je n'ai pas encore tué Hoederer, Olga. Pas encore. C'est à présent que je vais le tuer et moi avec."

## Chapter Two: The Nature of Events

1. *L'Age de raison*, pp. 54–55.
"Mathieu s'était approché du vase, les mains derrière le dos, et l'avait regardé en se dandinant avec inquiétude: c'était effrayant d'être une petite boulette de mie de pain, dans ce vieux monde rissolé, en face d'un impassible vase de trois mille ans. Il lui avait tourné le dos et s'était mis à loucher et à renifler devant la glace, sans parvenir à se distraire, puis tout à coup, il était revenu près de la table, il avait soulevé le vase, qui était fort lourd, et il l'avait jeté sur le parquet: ça lui était venu comme ça, et, tout de suite après, il s'était senti léger comme un fil de la Vierge. Il avait regardé les débris de porcelaine, émerveillé: quelque chose venait d'arriver à ce vase de trois mille ans entre ces murs quinquagénaires, sous l'antique lumière de l'été, quelque chose de très irrévérencieux qui ressemblait à un matin."

2. *La Nausée*, pp. 57–59.
"Voici ce que j'ai pensé: pour que l'évènement le plus banal devienne une aventure, il faut et il suffit qu'on se mette à le *raconter*. C'est ce qui dupe les gens: un homme, c'est toujours un conteur d'histoires, il vit entouré de ses histoires et des histoires d'autrui, il voit tout ce qui lui arrive à travers elles; et il cherche à vivre sa vie comme s'il la racontait. Mais il faut choisir: vivre ou raconter. Par exemple quand j'étais à Hambourg, avec cette Erna, dont je me méfiais et qui avait

peur de moi, je menais une drôle d'existence. Mais j'étais dedans, je n'y pensais pas. Et puis un soir, dans un petit café de San Pauli, elle m'a quitté pour aller aux lavabos. Je suis resté seul, il y avait un phonographe qui jouait *Blue Sky*. Je me suis mis à me raconter ce qui s'était passé depuis mon débarquement. Je me suis dit: 'Le troisième soir, comme j'entrais dans un dancing appelé la *Grotte Bleue*, j'ai remarqué une grande femme à moitié saoule. Et cette femme-là, c'est celle que j'attends en ce moment, en écoutant *Blue Sky* et qui va revenir s'asseoir à ma droite et m'entourer le cou de ses bras.' Alors, j'ai senti avec violence que j'avais une aventure. Mais Erna est revenue, elle s'est assise à côté de moi, elle m'a entouré le cou de ses bras et je l'ai détestée sans trop savoir pourquoi. Je comprends à présent: c'est qu'il fallait recommencer de vivre et que l'impression d'aventure venait de s'évanouir. Quand on vit, il n'arrive rien. Les décors changent, les gens entrent et sortent, voilà tout. Il n'y a jamais de commencements. Les jours s'ajoutent aux jours sans rime ni raison, c'est une addition interminable et monotone. De temps en temps, on fait un total partiel: on dit: voilà trois ans que je voyage, trois ans que je suis à Bouville. Il n'y a pas de fin non plus: on ne quitte jamais une femme, un ami, une ville en une fois. Et puis tout se ressemble: Shanghaï, Moscou, Alger, au bout d'une quinzaine, c'est tout pareil. Par moments—rarement—on fait le point, on s'aperçoit qu'on s'est collé avec une femme, engagé dans une sale histoire. Le temps d'un éclair. Après ça, le défilé recommence, on se remet à faire l'addition des heures et des jours. Lundi, mardi, mercredi. Avril, mai, juin. 1924, 1925, 1926. Ça, c'est vivre. Mais quand on raconte la vie, tout change: seulement c'est un changement que personne ne remarque: la preuve c'est qu'on parle d'histoires vraies. Comme s'il pouvait y avoir des histoires vraies; les événements se produisent dans un sens et nous les racontons en sens inverse. On a l'air de débuter par le commencement: 'C'était par un beau soir de l'automne de 1922. J'étais clerc de notaire à Marommes.' Et en réalité c'est par la fin qu'on a commencé. Elle est là, invisible et présente, c'est elle qui donne à ces quelques mots la pompe et la valeur d'un commencement. 'Je me promenais, j'étais sorti du village sans m'en apercevoir, je pensais à mes ennuis d'argent.' Cette phrase, prise simplement pour ce qu'elle est, veut dire que le type était absorbé, morose, à cent lieues d'une aventure, précisément dans ce genre d'humeur où on laisse passer les événements sans les voir. Mais la fin est là, qui transforme tout. Pour nous, le type est déjà le héros de l'histoire. Sa morosité, ses ennuis d'argent sont bien plus précieux que les nôtres, ils sont tout dorés par la lumière des passions futures. Et le récit se poursuit à l'envers: les instants ont cessé de s'empiler au petit bonheur les uns sur les autres, ils sont happés par la fin de l'histoire qui les attire et chacun d'eux attire à son tour l'instant qui le précède: 'Il faisait nuit, la rue était deserte.' La phrase est jetée négligemment, elle a l'air superflue; mais nous ne nous y laissons pas prendre et nous la mettons de côté: c'est un renseignement dont nous comprendrons la valeur par la suite. Et nous avons le sentiment que le héros a vécu tous les détails de cette nuit comme des annonciations, comme des promesses, ou même qu'il vivait seulement ceux qui étaient des promesses, aveugle et sourd pour tout ce qui n'annonçait pas l'aventure. Nous oublions que l'avenir n'était pas encore là; le type se promenait dans une nuit sans présages, qui lui offrait pêle-mêle ses richesses monotones et il ne choisissait pas. J'ai voulu que les moments de ma vie se suivent et s'ordonnent comme ceux d'une vie qu'on se rappelle. Autant vaudrait tenter d'attraper le temps par la queue."

3. Ibid., p. 59.
"J'avais oublié, ce matin, que c'était dimanche. Je suis sorti et je suis allé par les rues comme d'habitude. J'avais emporté *Eugénie Grandet*. Et puis, tout à coup, comme je poussais la grille du jardin public, j'ai eu l'impression que quelque chose me faisait signe. Le jardin était désert et nu. Mais . . . comment dire? Il n'avait pas son aspect ordinaire, il me souriait. Je suis resté un moment appuyé contre la grille et puis, brusquement, j'ai compris que c'était dimanche. C'était là sur les arbres, sur les pelouses comme un léger sourire."

4. Ibid., p. 59.
"Ça ne pouvait pas se décrire, il aurait fallu prononcer très vite: 'C'est un jardin public, l'hiver, un matin de dimanche.' "

5. *L'Etre et le néant*, p. 404.

6. *L'Age de raison*, p. 24.
"Son côté gauche lui faisait mal à force d'être regardé."

7. *Saint Genêt*, p. 349.
"Que s'est-il passé? Rien. Rien sinon qu'un acte utilitaire, par sa précision et par son rhythme, par les souvenirs aussi qu'il évoque, a paru tout à coup se suffire à lui-même . . . Du coup, le but pratique de cette action n'en est plus que le prétexte. Le temps s'invertit: le coup de marteau n'est pas donné *pour monter le manège*, mais la foire, les gains futurs que le forain escompte, le manège, tout cela n'existe que pour provoquer le coup de marteau; le futur, le passé sont donnés en même temps pour produire le présent . . . Les baraques, les maisons, le sol, tout devient décor: dans un théâtre de verdure, dès que les acteurs paraissent, les arbres sont de carton, le ciel se change en toile peinte. D'un seul coup, en se transformant en geste, l'acte entraîne, avec lui, dans l'irréel, la masse énorme de l'être."

## Chapter Three: The Rhythm of Time

1. *L'Age de raison*, p. 94.
   "Daniel s'emplit d'une eau vaseuse et fade: lui-même; l'eau de la Seine, fade et vaseuse, emplira le panier, ils vont se déchirer avec leurs griffes. Un grand dégoût l'envahit, il pensa: 'C'est un acte gratuit.' Il s'était arrêté, il avait posé le panier par terre: 'S'emmerder à travers le mal qu'on fait aux autres. On ne peut jamais s'atteindre directement.' "

2. Ibid., p. 96.
   "Les chats miaulèrent comme si on les avait ébouillantés et Daniel sentit qu'il perdait la tête. Il posa le cageot par terre et y donna deux violents coups de pied. Il se fit un grand remue-ménage à l'intérieur, et puis les chats se turent. Daniel resta un moment immobile avec un drôle de frisson en aigrette derrière les oreilles. Des ouvriers sortirent d'un entrepôt et Daniel reprit sa marche. C'était là."

3. Ibid., p. 95.
   "C'était une place populeuse avec des bistrots; un groupe d'ouvriers et de femmes s'était formé autour d'une voiture à bras. Des femmes le regardèrent avec surprise."

4. See *L'Etre et le néant*, p. 181 ff.

5. See *L'Etre et le néant*, pp. 554–55.

6. See *Saint Genet*, Chap. 1: "L'enfant mélodieux mort en moi."

7. *L'Etre et le néant*, pp. 554–55.

8. *La Nausée*, pp. 16–17.
   "Je fixais une petite statuette khmère, sur un tapis vert, à côté d'un appareil téléphonique. Il me semblait que j'étais rempli de lymphe ou de lait tiède. Mercier me disait, avec une patience angélique qui voilait un peu d'irritation: 'N'est-ce pas, j'ai besoin d'être fixé officiellement. Je sais que vous finirez par dire oui: il vaudrait mieux accepter tout de suite.' Il a une barbe d'un noir roux, très parfumée. A chaque mouvement de sa tête, je respirais une bouffée de parfum. Et puis, tout d'un coup, je me réveillai d'un sommeil de six ans. La statue me parut désagréable et stupide et je sentis que je m'ennuyais profondément. Je ne parvenais pas à comprendre pourquoi j'étais en Indochine. Qu'est-ce que je faisais là? Pourquoi parlais-je avec ces gens? Pourquoi étais-je si drôlement habillé? Ma passion était morte. Elle m'avait submergé et roulé pendant des années; à présent, je me sentais vide."

9. See *Morts sans sépulture*, Tableau III, scene 2.

10. *Kean*, Act V, scene 4.

11. *La Nausée*, p. 87.
"Elle verse sans répondre; tout d'un coup il retire prestement le doigt de son nez et pose les deux mains à plat sur la table. Il a rejeté la tête en arrière et ses yeux brillent. Il dit d'une voix froide: 'La pauvre fille.' "

12. *La Mort dans l'âme*, p. 201.
"De petits monstres mous rampent à terre et regardent le gai troupeau de leurs yeux sans prunelles: des masques à gaz."

13. *L'Age de raison*, p. 24.
"Il but. Il pensa: 'Elle est enceinte. C'est marrant: je n'ai pas l'impression que c'est vrai.' "

14. *Le Sursis*, p. 203.
"Des étoffes rouges et roses et mauves, des robes mauves, des robes blanches, des gorges nues, de beaux seins sous des mouchoirs, des flaques de soleil sur les tables, des mains, des liquides poisseux et dorés, encore des mains, des cuisses jaillissant des shorts, des voix gaies, des robes rouges et roses et blanches, des voix gaies qui tournaient dans l'air, des cuisses, la valse de la *Veuve Joyeuse*, l'odeur des pins, du sable chaud, l'odeur vanillée du grand large, toutes les îles du monde invisibles et présentes dans le soleil, l'île sous le Vent, l'île de Pâques, les îles Sandwiches, des boutiques de luxe le long de la mer, l'imperméable de dame à trois mille francs, les clips, les fleurs rouges et roses et blanches, les mains, les cuisses, 'la musique vient par ici,' les voix gaies qui tournaient dans l'air, Suzanne et ton régime? Ah! tant pis, pour une fois. Les voiles sur la mer et les skieurs sautant, bras tendus, de vague en vague, l'odeur des pins, par bouffées, la paix. La paix à Juan-les-Pins."

15. *L'Age de raison*, p. 28.
"Mais il aurait fallu parler: Boris sentait qu'il ne pouvait pas parler. Lola était à côté de lui, lasse et toute chaude et Boris ne pouvait pas s'arracher le moindre mot, sa voix était morte. Je serais comme ça si j'étais muet. C'était voluptueux, sa voix flottait au fond de sa gorge, douce comme du coton et elle ne pouvait plus sortir, elle était morte."

## PART TWO: THINGS

1. *Le Mur*, pp. 26–27.
"Tom aussi était seul, mais pas de la même manière. Il s'était assis à califourchon et il s'était mis à regarder le banc avec une espèce de sourire, il avait l'air étonné. Il avança la main et toucha le bois avec

précaution, comme s'il avait peur de casser quelque chose, ensuite il retira vivement sa main et frissonna. Je ne me serais pas amusé à toucher le banc, si j'avais été Tom; c'était encore de la comédie d'Irlandais, mais je trouvais aussi que les objets avaient un drôle d'air: ils étaient plus effacés, moins denses qu'à l'ordinaire. Il suffisait que je regarde le banc, la lampe, le tas de poussier, pour que je sente que j'allais mourir. Naturellement je ne pouvais pas clairement penser ma mort mais je la voyais partout, sur les choses, dans la façon dont les choses avaient reculé et se tenaient à distance, discrètement, comme des gens qui parlent bas au chevet d'un mourant. C'était *sa* mort que Tom venait de toucher sur le banc."

2. *Théâtre*, pp. 98–99.
"Tu n'es pas chez toi, intrus; tu es dans le monde comme l'écharde dans la chair, comme le braconnier dans la forêt seigneuriale: car le monde est bon; je l'ai créé selon ma volonté et je suis le Bien. Mais toi, tu as fait le mal, et les choses t'accusent de leurs voix pétrifiées: le Bien est partout, c'est la moelle du sureau, la fraîcheur de la source, le grain du silex, la pesanteur de la pierre; tu le retrouveras jusque dans la nature du feu et de la lumière, ton corps même te trahit, car il se conforme à mes prescriptions. Le Bien est en toi, hors de toi: il te pénètre comme une faux, il t'écrase comme une montagne, il te porte et te roule comme une mer; c'est lui qui permit le succès de ta mauvaise entreprise, car il fut la clarté des chandelles, la dureté de ton épée, la force de ton bras. Et ce Mal dont tu es si fier, dont tu te nommes l'auteur, qu'est-il sinon un reflet de l'être, un faux-fuyant, une image trompeuse dont l'existence même est soutenue par le Bien. Rentre en toi-même, Oreste: l'univers te donne tort, et tu es un ciron dans l'univers."

3. *L'Etre et le néant*, p. 226.

## Chapter Four: The Satisfactions of Objects

1. *Théâtre*, p. 24.
"Je savais déjà, moi, à sept ans, que j'étais exilé; les odeurs et les sons, le bruit de la pluie sur les toits, les tremblements de la lumière, je les laissais glisser le long de mon corps et tomber autour de moi; je savais qu'ils appartenaient aux autres, et que je ne pourrais jamais en faire *mes* souvenirs."

2. Ibid., p. 25.
"J'aurais vécu là. . . . Par cette porte, je serais entré et sorti dix mille fois. Enfant, j'aurais joué avec ses battants, je me serais arc-bouté contre eux, ils auraient grincé sans céder, et mes bras auraient appris leur résistance. Plus tard, je les aurais poussés, la nuit, en cachette,

pour aller retrouver des filles. Et plus tard encore, au jour de ma
majorité, les esclaves auraient ouvert la porte toute grande et j'en
aurais franchi le seuil à cheval. Ma vieille porte de bois. Je saurais
trouver, les yeux fermés, ta serrure. Et cette éraflure, là, en bas, c'est
moi peut-être qui te l'aurais faite, par maladresse, le premier jour
qu'on m'aurait confié une lance. *(Il s'écarte.)* Style petit-dorien, pas
vrai? Et que dis-tu des incrustations d'or? J'ai vu les pareilles à
Dodone: c'est du beau travail. Allons, je vais te faire plaisir: ce n'est
pas *mon* palais, ni *ma* porte. Et nous n'avons rien à faire ici."

3. See *L'Etre et le néant*, p. 680 ff.

4. Ibid., p. 681.

5. *Situations II*, pp. 264–65.

6. *Le Mur*, p. 37.
"Mme. Darbédat tenait un rahat-loukoum entre ses doigts. Elle
l'approcha de ses lèvres avec précaution et retint sa respiration de
peur que ne s'envolât à son souffle la fine poussière de sucre dont il
était saupoudré: 'Il est à la rose,' se dit-elle. Elle mordit brusquement dans cette chair vitreuse et un parfum de croupi lui emplit
la bouche. 'C'est curieux comme la maladie affine les sensations.'
Elle se mit à penser à des mosquées, à des Orientaux obséquieux
(elle avait été à Alger pendant son voyage de noces) et ses lèvres
pâles ébauchèrent un sourire: le rahat-loukoum aussi était obséquieux."

7. Ibid., p. 139.
"Et Lucien jouait aussi, mais il finit par ne plus très bien savoir à
quoi. A l'orphelin? Ou à être Lucien? Il regarda la carafe. Il y avait
une petite lumière rouge qui dansait au fond de l'eau et on aurait
juré que la main de papa était dans la carafe, énorme et lumineuse,
avec de petits poils noirs sur les doigts. Lucien eut soudain l'impression que la carafe aussi jouait à être une carafe."

8. *Saint Genet*, p. 244.

9. *Le Mur*, pp. 142–43.
"Il allait s'asseoir au pied du marronnier. Il dit 'marronnier!' et il
attendit. Mais rien ne se produisit . . . 'Marronnier!' C'était cho-
quant: quand Lucien disait à maman: 'ma jolie maman à moi' maman souriait et quand il avait appelé Germaine: arquebuse, Germaine avait pleuré et s'était plainte à maman. Mais quand on disait:
marronnier, il n'arrivait rien du tout. Il marmotta entre ses dents:
'sale arbre' et il n'était pas rassuré mais comme l'arbre ne bougeait
pas, il répéta plus fort: 'sale arbre, sale marronnier! attends voir,
attends un peu!' et il lui donna des coups de pied. Mais l'arbre resta
tranquille, tranquille—comme s'il était en bois."

## Chapter Five: Transformations

1. *Situations I*, pp. 32–33.

2. *Le Sursis*, p. 21.
   "Brunet marchait tout doucement . . . il leva la tête, regarda des lettres d'or noirci accrochées à un balcon; la guerre éclata: elle était là, au fond de cette inconsistance lumineuse, inscrite comme une évidence sur les murs de la belle ville cassable; c'était une explosion fixe qui déchirait en deux la rue Royale; les gens lui passaient au travers sans la voir; Brunet la voyait. Elle avait toujours été là, mais les gens ne le savaient pas encore. Brunet avait pensé: 'Le ciel nous tombera sur la tête.' Et tout s'était mis à tomber, il avait vu les maisons comme elles étaient pour de vrai: des chutes arrêtées. Ce gracieux magasin supportait des tonnes de pierre et chaque pierre, scellée avec les autres, tombait à la même place, obstinément, depuis cinquante ans; quelques kilos de plus et la chute recommencerait; les colonnes s'arrondiraient en flageolant et elles se feraient de sales fractures avec des esquilles; la vitrine éclaterait; des tombereaux de pierre s'effondreraient dans la cave en écrasant les ballots de marchandises. Ils ont des bombes de quatre mille kilos. Brunet eut le coeur serré: tout à l'heure encore sur ces façades bien alignées, il y avait un sourire humain, mélangé à la poudre d'or du soir. Ça s'était éteint: cent mille kilos de pierre; des hommes erraient entre des avalanches stabilisées. Des soldats entre des ruines, il sera tué, peut-être. Il vit des sillons noirâtres sur les joues plâtrées de Zézette. Des murs poussiéreux, des pans de murs avec de grandes ouvertures béantes et des carrés de papier bleus ou jaunes, par endroit, et des plaques de lèpre; des carrelages rouges, parmi les éboulis, des dalles disjointes par la mauvaise herbe. Ensuite des baraques de planche, des campements. Et puis après, on construirait de grandes casernes monotones comme sur les boulevards extérieurs. Le coeur de Brunet se serra: 'J'aime Paris,' pensa-t-il avec angoisse. L'évidence s'éteignit d'un seul coup et la ville se reforma autour de lui."

3. *Esquisse d'une théorie des émotions*, p. 41.

4. *Le Sursis*, p. 21.
   "Brunet s'arrêta; il se sentit sucré par une lâche douceur et pensa: 'S'il n'y avait pas de guerre! S'il pouvait n'y avoir pas de guerre!' Et il regardait avidement les grandes portes cochères, la vitrine étincelante de Driscoll, les tentures bleu roi de la brasserie Weber. Au bout d'un moment, il eut honte; il reprit sa marche, il pensa: 'J'aime trop Paris.' "

5. *Le Sursis*, pp. 274–75.
   "Première nuit de guerre. Non, pas tout à fait. Il restait encore

beaucoup de lumières accrochées au flanc des maisons. Dans un mois, dans quinze jours, la première alerte les soufflerait; pour l'instant ce n'était qu'une répétition générale. Mais Paris avait tout de même perdu son plafond de coton rose. Pour la première fois, Mathieu voyait une grande buée sombre en suspens au-dessus de la ville: le ciel. Celui de Juan-les-Pins, de Toulouse, de Dijon, d'Amiens, un même ciel pour la campagne et pour la ville, pour toute la France. Mathieu s'arrêta, leva la tête et le regarda. Un ciel de n'importe où, sans privilèges. Et moi sous cette grande équivalence: quelconque. Quelconque, n'importe où: c'est la guerre. Il fixait les yeux sur une flaque de lumière, il se répéta, pour voir: 'Paris, boulevard Raspail.' Mais on les avait mobilisés aussi, ces noms de luxe, ils avaient l'air de sortir d'une carte d'état-major ou d'un communiqué. Il ne restait plus rien du boulevard Raspail. Des routes, rien que des routes, qui filaient du sud au nord, de l'ouest à l'est; des routes numérotées. De temps en temps on les pavait sur un kilomètre ou deux, des trottoirs et des maisons surgissaient de terre, ça s'appelait rue, avenue, boulevard. Mais ce n'était jamais qu'un morceau de route; Mathieu marchait, la face tournée vers la frontière belge, sur un tronçon de route départementale issu de la Nationale 14. Il tourna dans la longue voie droite et carrossable qui prolongeait les voies ferrées de la compagnie de l'Ouest, anciennement la rue de Rennes. . . . Au bord du chemin, sous ce ciel indifférencié, les maisons s'étaient réduites à leur fonction la plus fruste: c'étaient des immeubles de rapport. Des dortoirs-réfectoires pour les mobilisables, pour les familles des mobilisés. Déjà l'on pressentait leur destination ultime: elles deviendraient des 'points stratégiques' et, pour finir, des cibles. Après cela, on pouvait bien détruire Paris: il était déjà mort. Un nouveau monde était en train de naître: le monde austère et pratique des ustensiles."

6. *Saint Genet,* pp. 249–50.
"A date fixe la société citadine se décomprime, joue la désintégration; ses membres se transportent dans les campagnes où, sous l'oeil ironique des travailleurs, ils se métamorphosent pour un temps en purs consommateurs. C'est alors que la Nature apparaît. Qu'est-elle? Rien d'autre que le monde extérieur quand nous cessons d'avoir des relations techniques avec les choses . . . la réalité se change en décor; le juste villégiature, il *est là*, simplement là, au milieu des champs et du bétail; réciproquement les champs et le bétail ne lui révèlent que leur simple *être-là*. C'est ce qu'il appelle saisir la vie, la matière dans leur réalité absolue. Pour manifester la Nature au citadin, il suffira d'une route départementale entre deux plants de pommes de terre. Des ingénieurs ont tracé cette route, des paysans cultivent ces plants; mais le citadin ne voit pas la culture, c'est un

genre de travail qui lui reste étranger: il croit surprendre des légumes
à l'état sauvage et du minéral en liberté; qu'un paysan s'amène à
travers champ, on en fera un légume aussi. La Nature paraît donc à
l'horizon des variations saisonnières ou hebdomadaires de nos so-
ciétés; elle reflète aux justes leur désintégration fictive, leur oisiveté
temporaire, bref leurs congés payés. Ils se promènent dans les sous-
bois comme dans l'âme humide et tendre de l'enfant qu'ils ont été;
ils considèrent les peupliers, les platanes qu'on a plantés au bord de
la route, ils ne trouvent rien à en dire puisqu'ils n'en font rien, et
ils s'ébahissent devant la merveilleuse qualité de ce silence: s'ils
cherchent la Nature à l'extérieur, c'est en réalité pour la toucher
au fond d'eux-mêmes: la tranquille croissance des futaies leur renvoie
l'image d'une finalité aveugle et sûre; elle les persuade que la vie
sociale est une agitation de surface: il y a un ordre des instincts qui
ne diffère pas, au fond, de l'ordre du monde et qu'on peut retrouver
en soi lorsqu'on s'abandonne à une douce pâmoison muette en présence des végétaux. Mais l'enfance même est sociale, les puissants
instincts naturels qu'ils cherchent au fond de leur coeur ne sont
que le symbole de la légitimité de leur naissance. L'ordre naturel
qu'ils perçoivent au dehors et en eux-mêmes c'est tout simplement
l'ordre social. La Nature est un mythe social, la jouissance solitaire
de soi-même au sein de la Nature est un moment rituel de la vie en
société; le ciel, l'eau et les plantes ne font que renvoyer au Juste
l'image de sa bonne conscience et de ses préjugés."

7. *La Nausée*, pp. 163–64, 167, 169.
"Ce long serpent mort à mes pieds, ce serpent de bois. Serpent ou
griffe ou racine ou serre de vautour, peu importe . . . cette grosse
patte rugueuse . . . cette peau dure et compacte de phoque . . . une
petite mare noire à mes pieds . . . Il aurait sans doute fallu que je
me la représente comme une griffe vorace, déchirant la terre, lui ar-
rachant sa nourriture."

8. Ibid., p. 164.
"J'avais beau me répéter: 'C'est une racine'—ça ne prenait plus."

9. Ibid., p. 165.
"Louches: voilà ce qu'ils étaient, les sons, les parfums, les goûts.
Quand ils vous filaient rapidement sous le nez, comme des lièvres
débusqués, et qu'on n'y faisait pas trop attention, on pouvait les
croire tout simples et rassurants, on pouvait croire qu'il y avait au
monde du vrai bleu, du vrai rouge, une vraie odeur d'amande ou
de violette. Mais dès qu'on les retenait un instant, ce sentiment de
confort et de sécurité, cédait la place à un profond malaise: les
couleurs, les saveurs, les odeurs n'étaient jamais vraies, jamais tout
bonnement elles-mêmes et rien qu'elles-mêmes. La qualité la plus

simple, la plus indécomposable avait du trop en elle-même, par rapport à elle-même, en son coeur. Ce noir, là, contre mon pied, ça n'avait pas l'air d'être du noir mais plutôt l'effort confus pour imaginer du noir de quelqu'un qui n'en aurait jamais vu et qui n'aurait pas su s'arrêter, qui aurait imaginé un être ambigu, par-delà les couleurs."

10. *L'Etre et le néant*, p. 34.
"L'être est. L'être est en soi. L'être est ce qu'il est."

11. *La Nausée*, p. 162.
"Toutes choses, doucement, tendrement, se laissaient aller à l'existence comme ces femmes lasses qui s'abandonnent au rire et disent: 'C'est bon de rire' d'une voix mouillée; elles s'étalaient, les unes en face des autres, elles se faisaient l'abjecte confidence de leur existence."

12. Ibid., p. 169.
"*Ils n'avaient pas envie* d'exister, seulement ils ne pouvaient pas s'en empêcher; voilà. Alors ils faisaient toutes leurs petites cuisines, doucement, sans entrain; la sève montait lentement dans les vaisseaux, à contrecoeur, et les racines s'enfonçaient lentement dans la terre. Mais ils semblaient à chaque instant sur le point de tout planter là et de s'anéantir. Las et vieux, ils continuaient d'exister, de mauvaise grâce, simplement parce qu'ils étaient trop faibles pour mourir, parce que la mort ne pouvait leur venir que de l'extérieur."

## PART THREE: HUMAN REALITY

### Chapter Six: The Anatomy of Thoughts

1. "Drôle d'Amitié," p. 1036.
"Il y a deux nuits: celle qui s'affale derrière eux, grosse masse coléreuse, déjà hors de combat et l'autre, toute fine, complice, qui commence au-delà de l'enceinte, une lumière noire."

2. *Le Sursis*, p. 22.
"Odette ferma les yeux. Elle gisait sur le sable au fond d'une chaleur sans date, sans âge: la chaleur de son enfance, quand elle fermait les yeux, couchée sur ce même sable et qu'elle jouait à être une salamandre au fond d'une grande flamme rouge et bleue. Même chaleur, même caresse humide du maillot; on croyait le sentir fumer doucement au soleil, même brûlure du sable sous sa nuque, les autres années, elle se fondait avec le ciel, la mer et le sable, elle ne distinguait plus le présent du passé. Elle se redressa, les yeux grand ouverts: aujourd'hui, il y avait un vrai présent; il y avait cette angoisse au creux de son estomac."

3. *La Nausée*, p. 82.

"Je tiens l'enveloppe entre mes doigts, je n'ose pas l'ouvrir; Anny n'a pas changé son papier à lettres, je me demande si elle l'achète toujours dans la petite papeterie de Piccadilly. . . . L'enveloppe est lourde, elle doit contenir au moins six pages. Les pattes de mouches de mon ancienne concierge chevauchent cette belle écriture: 'Hôtel Printania—Bouville.' Ces petites lettres-là ne brillent pas. Quand je décachette la lettre, ma désillusion me rajeunit de six ans: 'Je ne sais comment Anny peut s'y prendre pour gonfler ainsi ses enveloppes: il n'y a jamais rien dedans.' "

4. *La Mort dans l'âme*, p. 254.

"Ils ont écrit à leurs familles et, depuis deux jours, le temps des villes s'est remis à couler. Quand la Kommandantur leur a prescrit de régler leurs montres sur l'heure allemande, ils se sont empressés d'obéir, même ceux qui, depuis le mois de juin, portaient en signe de deuil des montres mortes à leurs poignets: cette durée vague qui croissait en herbe folle s'est militarisée, on leur a prêté du temps allemand, du vrai temps de vainqueur, le même qui coule à Dantzig, à Berlin: du temps sacré."

5. *Le Sursis*, p. 82.

"Il avait dit: nous; il avait accepté la complicité de ce petit métèque. Nous. Nous les Juifs. Mais c'était par charité. Les yeux de Schalom le considéraient avec une insistance respectueuse. Il était maigre et petit, ils l'avaient battu et chassé de Bavière, à présent il était là, il devait coucher dans un hôtel sordide et passer ses journées au café. Et le cousin de Weiss, ils l'ont brûlé avec leurs cigares. M. Birnenschatz regardait Schalom et il se sentit poisseux."

6. See *L'Etre et le néant*, p. 695 ff.

7. *Le Sursis*, p. 285.

"Il y avait ses mains, pourtant, sur la balustrade blanche: quand il les regardait, elles semblaient de bronze. Mais, justement parce qu'il pouvait les regarder, elles n'étaient plus à lui, c'étaient les mains d'un autre, dehors, comme les arbres, comme les reflets qui tremblaient dans la Seine, des mains coupées. Il ferma les yeux et elles redevinrent siennes: il n'y eut plus contre la pierre chaude qu'un petit goût acide et familier, un petit goût de fourmi très négligeable. Mes mains: l'inappréciable distance qui me révèle les choses et m'en sépare pour toujours."

8. *Théâtre*, p. 231.

"Une larme? Je souhaite seulement qu'ils reviennent me chercher et qu'ils me battent pour que je puisse me taire encore et me moquer d'eux et leur faire peur. Tout est fade ici: l'attente, ton amour, le poids de cette tête sur mes genoux. Je voudrais que la douleur me dévore, je voudrais brûler, me taire et voir leurs yeux aux aguets."

9. *Le Sursis*, p. 121–22.

"Il avala péniblement sa salive, elle glissa au fond de sa gorge avec un horrible frôlement soyeux et déjà une eau fade fusait dans sa bouche, fatigant, fatigant, ses idées s'enfuirent, il ne resta plus qu'une grande douceur abandonnée, une envie de monter et de descendre en mesure, de vomir doucement, longuement, de se laisser aller sur l'oreiller, ho hisse, ho hisse, sans pensées, emporté par le grand tangage du monde; il se rattrapa à temps: on n'a le mal de mer que si on veut l'avoir. Il se retrouva tout entier, raide et sec, un lâche, un amant méprisé, un futur mort de la guerre, il retrouva toute sa peur lucide et glacée. . . . Il leva une main et la promena dans les airs avec une douceur vacillante et un peu solennelle. Gestes doux, doux palpitements de mes cils, saveur douce au fond de ma bouche, douce odeur de lavande et de pâte dentifrice, le bateau monte doux, redescend doux; il bâilla et le temps ralentit, devint sirupeux autour de lui; il suffisait de se raidir, de faire trois pas hors de la cabine, à l'air frais. Mais pourquoi faire?"

10. See *L'Etre et le néant*, p. 457.

11. For examples see above, Chap. 3, p. 50, and below, Chap. 6, p. 136.

12. *La Mort dans l'âme*, pp. 184–85.

"Un frein crissa, des portières claquèrent. Mathieu entendit des voix et des pas: il tomba dans un écoeurement qui ressemblait au sommeil: il devait lutter pour tenir les yeux ouverts. . . . Il sombra dans la douceur; il aimait tout le monde, les Français, les Allemands, Hitler. Dans un rêve pâteux, il entendit des cris, suivis d'une violente explosion et d'un fracas de vitres, puis ça se remit à claquer. Il crispa le poing sur son fusil pour l'empêcher de tomber. 'Trop court, la grenade,' dit Clapot entre ses dents."

13. *L'Age de raison*, p. 168.

"Daniel regardait ses épaules et son cou avec avidité. Cette obstination bête l'irritait; il voulait la briser. Il était possédé par un désir énorme et disgracié: violer cette conscience, s'abîmer avec elle dans l'humilité. Mais ça n'était pas du sadisme: c'était plus tâtonnant et plus humide, plus charnel. C'était de la bonté."

14. *La Mort dans l'âme*, p. 108.

" 'Je dis,' cria Mathieu, 'que tu peux boire tant que tu veux: je m'en balance.' Il pensait: 'Je n'ai plus qu'à m'en aller.' Mais il ne pouvait s'y décider. Il se courbait au-dessus d'eux, il respirait la riche odeur sucrée de leur ivresse et de leur malheur; il pensait: 'Où irais-je?' et

il avait le vertige. Ils ne lui faisaient pas horreur, ces vaincus qui
buvaient la défaite jusqu'à la lie."

15. *L'Age de raison*, p. 164.
   "Il se leva, il vint s'asseoir près d'elle et lui prit la main. Une main
   molle et fiévreuse comme une confidence: il la garda dans la sienne
   sans parler."

16. *Théâtre*, p. 34.
   "Son visage semble un champ ravagé par la foudre et la grêle."

17. Ibid., p. 48.
   "Il vous brûle, ce regard invisible et pur, plus inaltérable qu'un sou-
   venir de regard."

18. *L'Age de raison*, p. 254.
   "Il était las et nerveux, il voyait sans cesse une mallette ouverte au
   fond d'une chambre obscure et, dans la mallette, des billets odorants
   et douillets; c'était comme un remords."

19. *La Nausée*, p. 17.
   "Devant moi, posée avec une sorte d'indolence, il y avait une idée
   volumineuse et fade. Je ne sais pas trop ce que c'était, mais je ne
   pouvais pas la regarder tant elle m'écoeurait. Tout cela se confondait
   pour moi avec le parfum de la barbe de Mercier."

20. Ibid., p. 54.
   "Il y a encore cette idée, devant moi, qui attend. Elle s'est mise en
   boule, elle reste là comme un gros chat; elle n'explique rien, elle ne
   bouge pas et se contente de dire non."

21. *L'Age de raison*, p. 70.
   "Ivich ne disait toujours rien. 'Elle me juge,' pensa Mathieu avec
   irritation. Il se pencha; pour la punir, il effleura du bout des lèvres
   une bouche froide et close; il était buté; Ivich se taisait. . . . 'Ça y
   est,' se dit Mathieu, 'c'est irrémédiable.' Il faisait le dos rond, il
   aurait voulu fondre. Un agent leva son bâton, le taxi s'arrêta. Mathieu regardait droit devant lui, mais il ne voyait pas les arbres; il regardait son amour. C'était de l'amour. A présent, c'était de l'amour.
   Mathieu pensa: 'Qu'est-ce que j'ai fait?' Cinq minutes auparavant
   cet amour n'existait pas; il y avait entre eux un sentiment rare et
   précieux, qui n'avait pas de nom, qui ne pouvait pas s'exprimer par
   des gestes. Et, justement, il avait fait un geste, le seul qu'il ne fallait
   pas faire—ça n'était pas exprès d'ailleurs, c'était venu tout seul. Un
   geste et cet amour était apparu devant Mathieu, comme un gros
   objet importun et déjà vulgaire."

22. Ibid., p. 225.
   "Il serra les poings et prononça intérieurement avec une gravité de

grande personne, de bourgeois, de monsieur, de chef de famille: 'Je veux épouser Marcelle.' Pouah! C'étaient des mots, une option enfantine et vaine. 'Ça aussi,' pensa-t-il, 'ça aussi c'est un mensonge: je n'ai pas besoin de volonté pour l'épouser; je n'ai qu'à me laisser aller.' Il referma le Bottin, il regardait, accablé, les débris de sa dignité humaine. Et soudain il lui sembla qu'il voyait sa liberté. Elle était hors d'atteinte, cruelle, jeune et capricieuse comme la grâce: elle lui commandait tout uniment de plaquer Marcelle. Ce ne fut qu'un instant; cette inexplicable liberté, qui prenait les apparences du crime, il ne fit que l'entrevoir: elle lui faisait peur et puis elle était si loin. Il resta buté sur sa volonté trop humaine, sur ces mots trop humains: 'Je l'épouserai.' "

23. Ibid., pp. 193–94.
"Une vie. Il regardait tous ces visages empourprés, ces lunes rousses qui glissaient sur des coussinets de nuages: 'Ils ont des vies. Tous. Chacun la sienne. Elles s'étirent à travers les murs du dancing, à travers les rues de Paris, à travers la France, elles s'entrecroisent, elles se coupent et elles restent toutes aussi rigoureusement personnelles qu'une brosse à dents, qu'un rasoir, que les objets de toilette qui ne se prêtent pas. Je le savais. Je savais qu'ils avaient chacun leur vie. Je ne savais pas que j'en avais une, moi.' "

24. Ibid., p. 216.
"Elle était morte. Sa conscience s'était anéantie. Mais non sa vie. Abandonée par la bête molle et tendre qui l'avait si longtemps habitée, cette vie déserte s'était simplement arrêtée, elle flottait, pleine de cris sans échos et d'espoirs inefficaces, d'éclats sombres, de figures et d'odeurs surannées, elle flottait en marge du monde, entre parenthèses, inoubliable et définitive, plus indestructible qu'un minéral et rien ne pouvait l'empêcher d'avoir été, elle venait de subir son ultime métamorphose: son avenir s'était figé."

25. See *L'Etre et le néant*, p. 626 ff.

26. *Le Sursis*, pp. 52–53.
"Armand Viguier restait bien sagement étendu, tout seul dans sa chambre, ses mains jaunes reposaient sur le drap, il avait renversé sa tête maigre à la dure barbe grise, aux yeux caves, il souriait d'un air distant . . . il était mort. Sur la table de nuit on avait posé son lorgnon et son râtelier dans un verre d'eau. Mort. Et sa vie était là, partout, impalpable, achevée, dure et pleine comme un oeuf, si remplie que toutes les forces du monde n'eussent pas pu y faire entrer un atome, si poreuse que Paris et le monde lui passaient au travers, éparpillée aux quatres coins de la France et condensée tout entière en chaque point de l'espace, une grande foire immobile et criarde; les cris étaient là, les rires, le sifflement des locomotives et

l'éclatement des shrapnells, le 6 mai 1917, ce bourdonnement san-
glant dans sa tête, quand il tombe entre les deux tranchées, les bruits
étaient là, glacés et l'infirmière aux aguets n'entendait qu'un susur-
rement sous ses jupes. Elle se releva, elle ne tira pas la chasse d'eau,
par respect pour la mort, elle revint s'asseoir au chevet d'Armand,
traversant ce grand soleil immobile qui éclaire pour toujours un
visage de femme, à la Grande Jatte, le 20 juillet 1900, dans le canot.
Armand Viguier était mort, sa vie flottait, enfermant des douleurs
immobiles, une grande zébrure qui traverse de part en part le mois
de mars 1922, sa douleur intercostale, d'indestructibles petits joyaux,
l'arc-en-ciel au-dessus du quai de Bercy un samedi soir, il a plu, les
pavés glissent, deux cyclistes passent en riant, le bruit de la pluie sur
le balcon, par une étouffante après-midi de mars, un air de tzigane
qui lui fait venir les larmes aux yeux, des gouttes de rosée brillant
dans l'herbe, un envol de pigeons sur la place Saint-Marc."

27. See *Le Sursis*, p. 41.

28. Ibid., p. 255.

29. Ibid., pp. 257–58.
"Un corps énorme, une planète, dans un espace à cent millions de
dimensions; les êtres à trois dimensions ne pouvaient même pas
l'imaginer. Et pourtant chaque dimension était une conscience au-
tonome. Si on essayait de regarder la planète en face, elle s'effondrait
en miettes, il ne restait plus que des consciences. Cent millions de
consciences libres dont chacune voyait des murs, un bout de cigare
rougeoyant, des visages familiers, et construisait sa destinée sous sa
propre responsabilité. Et pourtant, si l'on était une de ces consciences,
on s'apercevait à d'imperceptibles effleurements, à d'insensibles
changements, qu'on était solidaire d'un gigantesque et invisible poly-
pier. La guerre: chacun est libre et pourtant les jeux sont faits. Elle
est là, elle est partout, c'est la totalité de toutes mes pensées, de
toutes les paroles d'Hitler, de tous les actes de Gomez: mais personne n'est là pour faire le total. Elle n'existe que pour Dieu. Mais
Dieu n'existe pas. Et pourtant la guerre existe."

30. Ibid., p. 285.
"Dehors. Tout est dehors: les arbres sur le quai, les deux maisons du
pont, qui rosissent la nuit, le galop figé d'Henri IV au-dessus de ma
tête: tout ce qui pèse. Au dedans, rien, pas même une fumée, il n'y
a pas de dedans, il n'y a rien. Moi: rien. Je suis libre, se dit-il, la
bouche sèche. Au milieu du Pont-Neuf, il s'arrêta, il se mit à rire:
cette liberté, je l'ai cherchée bien loin; elle était si proche que je ne
pouvais pas la voir, que je ne peux pas la toucher, elle n'était que
moi. Je suis ma liberté."

## Chapter Seven: The Anatomy of Persons

1. *L'Etre et le néant,* p. 412.

2. *La Nausée,* p. 33.
"Ses yeux sont vitreux, je vois rouler, dans sa bouche, une masse sombre et rose."

3. *L'Age de raison,* p. 284.
"La porte de la chambre était entre-bâillée; il la poussa. Ça sentait lourd. Toute la chaleur de la journee s'était déposée au fond de cette pièce, comme une lie. Assise sur le lit, une femme le regardait en souriant, c'était Marcelle."

4. *La Nausée,* p. 33.
"J'entends un souffle court et je vois de temps en temps, du coin de l'oeil, un éclair rougeaud couvert de poils blancs. C'est une main."

5. *L'Age de raison,* p. 20.
"Sa bouche se pinça sur les derniers mots: une bouche vernie avec des reflets mauves, un insecte écarlate, occupé à dévorer ce visage cendreux."

6. *L'Etre et le néant,* pp. 413-14.

7. *La Nausée,* pp. 64-65.
"Sur l'autre trottoir, un monsieur, qui tient sa femme par le bras, vient de lui glisser quelques mots à l'oreille et s'est mis à sourire. Aussitôt, elle dépouille soigneusement de toute expression sa face crémeuse et fait quelques pas en aveugle. Ces signes ne trompent pas: ils vont saluer. En effet, au bout d'un instant, le monsieur jette sa main en l'air. Quand ses doigts sont à proximité de son feutre, ils hésitent une seconde avant de se poser délicatement sur la coiffe. Pendant qu'il soulève doucement son chapeau, en baissant un peu la tête pour aider à l'extraction, sa femme fait un petit saut en inscrivant sur son visage un sourire jeune. Une ombre les dépasse en s'inclinant: mais leurs deux sourires jumeaux ne s'effacent pas sur-le-champ: ils demeurent quelques instants sur leurs lèvres, par une espèce de rémanence. Quand le monsieur et la dame me croisent, ils ont repris leur impassibilité, mais il leur reste encore un air gai autour de la bouche."

8. *Situations II,* p. 95 ff.

9. *La Mort dans l'âme,* p. 106.
"Il vit Ménard, assis, les jambes pendantes, sur le haut d'une petite armoire, qui agitait ses godillots dans la pourpre du couchant. C'était lui qui chantait; ses yeux affolés de gaîté, roulaient au-dessus de sa gueule ouverte; sa voix se tirait de lui toute seule, elle vivait de lui comme un énorme parasite qui lui eût pompé les tripes et le sang

pour les changer en chansons; inerte, bras ballants, il regardait avec stupeur cette vermine qui lui sortait de la bouche."

10. *L'Age de raison,* p. 19.
"Mathieu remarqua que son visage était devenu gris. L'air était rose et sucré, on respirait du rose, on en mangeait: et puis il y avait ce visage gris, il y avait ce regard fixe, on aurait dit qu'elle s'empêchait de tousser."

11. *Le Mur,* pp. 67–68.
" 'Récapitulation.' Pierre avait pris soudain l'air bête et le mot avait coulé hors de sa bouche, long et blanchâtre. Pierre avait regardé devant lui avec étonnement comme s'il voyait le mot et ne le reconnaissait pas; sa bouche était ouverte, molle; quelque chose semblait s'être cassé en lui."

12. *Le Mur,* p. 17.
"Il nous offrit des cigarettes anglaises et des puros, mais nous refusâmes. Je le regardai dans les yeux et il parut gêné. Je lui dis: 'Vous ne venez pas ici par compassion. D'ailleurs je vous connais. Je vous ai vu avec des fascistes dans la cour de la caserne, le jour où on m'a arrêté.' J'allais continuer, mais tout d'un coup il m'arriva quelque chose qui me surprit: la présence de ce médecin cessa brusquement de m'intéresser. D'ordinaire quand je suis sur un homme je ne le lâche pas. Et pourtant l'envie de parler me quitta; je haussai les épaules et je détournai les yeux."

13. See *Esquisse d'une théorie des émotions.*

14. *L'Age de raison,* p. 70.
"Il se rappela le geste d'un type qu'il avait vu, une fois, rue Mouffetard. Un type assez bien mis, au visage tout gris. Le type s'était approché d'une friterie, il avait longuement regardé une tranche de viande froide posée sur une assiette, à l'étalage, puis il avait étendu la main et pris le morceau de viande; il avait l'air de trouver ça tout simple, il avait dû se sentir libre lui aussi. Le patron avait crié, un agent avait emmené le type qui paraissait étonné."

15. *Le Mur,* p. 141.
"M. le curé, qui venait déjeuner à la maison tous les samedis, lui demanda s'il aimait bien sa maman. Lucien adorait sa jolie maman et son papa qui était si fort et si bon. Il répondit 'oui' en regardant M. le curé dans les yeux, d'un petit air crâne, qui fit rire tout le monde. . . . Il dit à Lucien que c'était bien et qu'il fallait toujours bien aimer sa maman; et puis il demanda qui Lucien préférait de sa maman ou du bon Dieu. Lucien ne put deviner sur-le-champ la réponse et il se mit à secouer ses boucles et à donner des coups de pied dans le vide en criant 'Baoum, Tararaboum' et les grandes personnes reprirent leur conversation comme s'il n'existait pas."

16. *Le Sursis*, pp. 163–64.

"—Vous voulez mourir pour les Sudètes? demanda le barbu.

—Ta gueule, dit Maurice.

Le barbu le regarda d'un air mauvais et hésitant, on aurait dit qu'il cherchait à se rappeler quelque chose. Il cria tout d'un coup: —A bas la guerre! . . . A bas la guerre! A bas la guerre! . . . Le barbu continua de crier, d'une voix courtoise et fatiguée—une voix de riche; et Maurice eut tout à coup l'impression déplaisante que la scène était truquée. Il regarda autour de lui et sa joie disparut: c'était la faute aux autres, ils ne faisaient pas ce qu'ils avaient à faire. Dans les meetings, quand un type se met à brailler des conneries, la foule reflue sur lui et l'efface, on voit ses bras en l'air, pendant un instant et puis plus rien du tout. Au lieu de ça, les copains s'étaient reculés, ils avaient fait le vide autour du barbu."

17. *L'Etre et le néant*, pp. 98–99.

"Considérons ce garçon de café. Il a le geste vif et appuyé, un peu trop précis, un peu trop rapide, il vient vers les consommateurs d'un pas un peu trop vif, il s'incline avec un peu trop d'empressement, sa voix, ses yeux expriment un intérêt un peu trop plein de sollicitude pour la commande du client, enfin le voilà qui revient, en essayant d'imiter dans sa démarche la rigueur inflexible d'on ne sait quel automate, tout en portant son plateau avec une sorte de témérité de funambule, en le mettant dans un équilibre perpétuellement instable et perpétuellement rompu, qu'il rétablit perpétuellement d'un mouvement léger du bras et de la main. Toute sa conduite nous semble un jeu. Il s'applique à enchaîner ses mouvements comme s'ils étaient des mécanismes se commandant les uns les autres, sa mimique et sa voix même semblent des mécanismes; il se donne la prestesse et la rapidité des choses. Il joue, il s'amuse. Mais à quoi donc joue-t-il? Il ne faut pas l'observer longtemps pour s'en rendre compte: il joue *à être* garçon de café."

18. See *Réflexions sur la question juive*.

## Conclusions

1. Maurice Blanchot, *La Part du feu* (Paris, Gallimard, 1949), p. 200.

2. See for example *La Nausée*, pp. 75–76, where this experience of simultaneity functions as content *within* the novel.

3. *La Mort dans l'âme*, p. 193.

"Un coup sur tous les types, en bloc, que j'avais envie de détester et que j'ai essayé de comprendre!"

4. See *La Nausée*, p. 22.

5. Roland Barthes, *Le Degré zéro de l'écriture* (Paris, Editions du Seuil, 1953), pp. 58–59.

## AFTERWORD

1. Walter Benjamin, *Passagenwerk* (Frankfurt: Suhckamp, 1983), p. 495: "Der Überbau ist der Ausdruck des Unterbaus."

2. *Fables of Aggression, Wyndham Lewis, The Modernist as Fascist* (Berkeley: University of California Press, 1979); see especially p. 86: "Since there exists no adequate language for 'rendering' the object, all that is left to the writer is to tell us how he would have rendered it had he had such a language in the first place."

3. It will be clear that my reading of Benjamin depends on grasping as a series or theoretical "tryptich" the three central essays of *Illuminations:* "The Storyteller," "On Some Motifs of Baudelaire," and "The Work of Art in the Age of Mechanical Reproduction."

4. Tzvetan Todorov, *Poétique de la prose* (Paris: Seuil, 1971), chapter 6.

5. "Deutscher laid a lot of stress on what he called 'ideological interest.' He meant, for example, that if you've written a lot of books, these can thereafter become your ideological interest. In other words, it is not simply your ideas that are there, but real, material objects, and these are your interest . . ." "A Friend of the People," in *Between Existentialism and Marxism* (New York: Pantheon, 1974), pp. 292–293. Of the more "morbid" features of Sartre's character, as they have become known to us in his last years, and to which allusion is made here and there, Denis Hollier, *Politique de la prose* (Paris: Seuil, 1982), offers an implacable inventory.

6. A fuller discussion of this periodization of the modern will be found in SOCIAL TEXT 9/10, double issue on *The Sixties* (University of Minnesota Press, 1984), in my article, "Periodizing the Sixties."

7. Blanchot made this point long ago, in "Les Romans de Sartre," in *La Part du feu* (Paris: Gallimard, 1949), pp. 195–211.

8. This analysis is pitched on an enormous scale in Sartre's most sustained piece of historical writing, Volume III of *L'Idiot de la famille,* but is also visible in the great journalistic and political essays of the 50s and 60s.

9. For a fuller discussion, see *Marxism and Form* (Princeton: Princeton University Press, 1971), chapter IV.

# Index

Adorno, Theodor, 206
*Age of Reason, The*, 20–21, 35, 41,
    43, 44, 61–62, 137, 139, 141,
    144 ff., 148 ff., 152, 159, 161,
    165, 173, 187, 189 ff., 197, 221
Anecdote, 19, 22 ff., 44 ff.
Aristotle, 207
Assumption, 13–14, 87–88, 109
Astonishment, 167 ff.
Auerbach, Erich, 206

Balzac, Honoré de, 192
Barthes, Roland, 201–202, 206
Baudelaire, Charles, 212
"Beast in the Jungle, The," 213
*Being and Not-Being*, 7, 32, 34, 35,
    67, 72, 76, 107, 116, 157, 162,
    178, 182, 199 ff., 203
Benjamin, Walter, 206–12, 233
Bergson, Henri, 199
Blanchot, Maurice, 185
Brecht, Bertolt, 95

Céline, Louis-Ferdinand, 218
Characters, 191 ff.
"Childhood of a Leader," 82 ff.,
    174–76
*Chips Are Down, The*, 149–50, 203
Cogito, 113 ff.
Coleridge, Samuel Taylor, 221
Collingwood, 207
Contingency, 113 ff.
*Critique of Dialectical Reason*, 225

*Dead without Burial*, 52, 53, 131
*Death in the Soul*, 55, 123–24, 136,
    138, 187
De Man, Paul, 209
Derrida, Jacques, 209

Descartes, René, 90, 115, 183
Description, 76 ff.
*Dirty Hands*, 8 ff., 191
Dos Passos, John, 218
"Douceur," 133 ff.
"Drôle d'amitié," 119 ff., 187
Dumas père, Alexandre, 53

Epic, 118–19
Existential psychoanalysis, 49, 80,
    126–27
Expressionism, 96

Facticity, 4–5, 13–14, 87–88
"Fadeur," 128 ff.
*Family Idiot, The*, 223–27
Faulkner, William, 54
Flaubert, Gustave, 40, 226, 228–31,
    233
*Flies, The*, 7, 70–71, 73 ff., 140–41
Foucault, Michel, 226
Freud, Sigmund, 14, 136

Genet, Jean, 36–37, 47, 83, 174,
    226–27
Gesture, 36 ff.
*Grundrisse*, 209

Hegel, G. W. F., 35, 107, 108
Heidegger, Martin, 113
Husserl, Edmund, 90

*Imagination, The*, 117

James, Henry, 213
Joyce, James, 56, 79, 217

*Kean*, 36, 53

Lacan, Jacques, 223

Lefebvre, Henri, 231
Lewis, Wyndham, 209, 221
Look, 34 ff., 47, 166
*Lucifer and the Lord*, 7, 12

Mallarmé, Stéphane, 196, 224
Malraux, André, 172
Marshall, Paule, 213
Marx, Karl, 38, 183, 209–11
Melodrama, 189–90
"Mitsein," 182

Nabokov, Vladimir, 221
Nature, 101 ff.
*Nausea*, 22 ff., 36, 50, 54, 98,
    104 ff., 123, 143, 158, 160, 162–
    63, 184 ff., 188, 194, 208, 218
*No Exit*, 3 ff., 13, 149–50

"On a Fundamental Idea of Hus-
    serl's Phenomenology," 90–91
Original choice, 46 ff.
*Outline of a Theory of the Emotions*, 94

Port-Royal, 207
Proust, Marcel, 25, 202

Psychoanalysis, *See* Existential

*Reflections on the Jewish Question*, 178
*Reprieve, The*, 59 ff., 92 ff., 98 ff.,
    122, 126, 128 ff., 132 ff., 150 ff.,
    154 ff., 164 ff., 176 ff., 187 ff.,
    194, 197
Richard, Jean-Pierre, 205
"Room, The," 81 ff., 168–69, 171,
    193

*Saint Genet*, 36–37, 101 ff.
Sapir-Whorf hypothesis, 207–8
Simile, 140 ff.
Simultaneity, 188, 203
*Situations*, 206
Spitzer, Leo, 206
Style, vii ff., 202 ff.

Thingification, 117
Todorov, Tzvetan, 213
Twelve-tone system, 196

"Wall, The," 68–69, 109, 170
*What is Literature?*, 77, 219, 233
*Words, The*, 224